Scarcity

Scarcity

Why Having Too Little Means So Much

SENDHIL MULLAINATHAN

ELDAR SHAFIR

TIMES BOOKS   HENRY HOLT AND COMPANY   NEW YORK

Times Books
Henry Holt and Company, LLC
Publishers since 1866
175 Fifth Avenue
New York, New York 10010

Henry Holt® is a registered trademark of
Henry Holt and Company, LLC.

Library of Congress Cataloging-in-Publication Data

Mullainathan, Sendhil.
    Scarcity : why having too little means so much / Sendhil Mullainathan and Eldar Shafir.
        pages cm
    Includes bibliographical references and index.
    ISBN 978-0-8050-9264-6
    1. Supply and demand.   2. Scarcity.   3. Decision making.   I. Shafir, Eldar.   II. Title.
    HB801.M83 2013
    338.5'21—dc23   2013004167

Henry Holt books are available for special promotions and premiums.
For details contact: Director, Special Markets.

First Edition 2013

Designed by Kelly S. Too

Printed in the United States of America
10   9   8   7   6   5   4   3   2   1

For Amma, Appa, and e3,
for and with unconditional love

SM

For Anastasia, Sophie, and Mia—loves of my life

ES

CONTENTS

Scarcity

INTRODUCTION

If ants are such busy workers, how come they find time to go to all the picnics?

—MARIE DRESSLER,
ACADEMY AWARD–WINNING ACTRESS

We wrote this book because we were too busy not to.

Sendhil was grumbling to Eldar. He had more to-dos than time to do them in. Deadlines had matured from "overdue" to "alarmingly late." Meetings had been sheepishly rescheduled. His in-box was swelling with messages that needed his attention. He could picture his mother's hurt face at not getting even an occasional call. His car registration had expired. And things were getting worse. That conference one connecting flight away seemed like a good idea six months ago. Not so much now. Falling behind had turned into a vicious cycle. Re-registering the car was now one more thing to do. A project had taken a wrong direction because of a tardy e-mail response; getting it back on track meant yet more work. The past-due pile of life was growing dangerously close to toppling.

The irony of spending time lamenting the lack of time was not lost on Eldar. It was only partly lost on Sendhil who, undeterred, described his plan for getting out.

He would first stem the tide. Old obligations would need to be fulfilled, but new ones could be avoided. He would say no to every new request. He would prevent further delays on old projects by working meticulously to finish them. Eventually, this austerity would pay off. The to-do pile would shrink to a manageable level. Only then would he even think about new projects. And of course he would be more prudent going forward. "Yes" would be rare and uttered only after careful scrutiny. It would not be easy, but it was necessary.

Having made the plan felt good. Of course it did. As Voltaire noted long ago, "Illusion is the first of all pleasures."

A week later, another call from Sendhil: Two colleagues were putting together a book on the lives of low-income Americans. "This is a great opportunity. We should write a chapter," he said. His voice, Eldar recalls, lacked even a trace of irony.

Predictably, the chapter was "too good to pass up," and we agreed to do it. Just as predictably, it was a mistake, written in a rush and behind schedule. Unpredictably, it was a worthwhile mistake, creating an unexpected connection that eventually led to this book.

Here is an excerpt from our background notes for that chapter:

Shawn, an office manager in Cleveland, was struggling to make ends meet. He was late on a bunch of bills. His credit cards were maxed out. His paycheck ran out quickly. As he said, "There is always more month than money." The other day, he accidentally bounced a check after overestimating the money in his account; he had forgotten a $22 purchase. Every phone call made him tense: another creditor calling to "remind" him? Being out of money was also affecting his personal life. Sometimes at dinner he would put in less than his fair share because he was short. His friends understood, but it didn't feel good.

And there was no end in sight. He had bought a Blu-ray player on credit, with no payments for the first six months. That was five months ago. How would he pay this extra bill next month? Already, more and more money went to paying off old debts. The bounced check had a hefty overdraft charge. The late bills meant late fees. His finances were a mess. He was in the deep end of the debt pool and barely staying afloat.

Shawn, like many people in his situation, got financial advice from many sources, all of it pretty similar:

Don't sink any deeper. Stop borrowing. Cut your spending to the minimum. Some expenses may be tough to cut, but you'll have to learn how. Pay off your old debts as quickly as possible. Eventually, with no new debts, your payments will become manageable. After this, remain vigilant so as not to fall back in. Spend and borrow wisely. Avoid unaffordable luxuries. If you must borrow, be clear about what it takes to pay it back.

This advice worked better in theory than in practice for Shawn. Resisting temptation is hard. Resisting all temptations was even harder. A leather jacket he had coveted went on sale at a great price. Skimping on his daughter's birthday gift felt less sensible as the day got closer. There were too many ways to spend more than he planned. Shawn eventually sank back into the debt pool.

It did not take long for us to notice the resemblance between Sendhil's and Shawn's behavior. Missed deadlines are a lot like overdue bills. Double-booked meetings (committing time you do not have) are a lot like bounced checks (spending money you do not have). The busier you are, the greater the need to say no. The more indebted you are, the greater the need to not buy. Plans to escape sound reasonable but prove hard to implement. They require constant vigilance—about what to buy or what to agree to do. When vigilance flags—the slightest temptation in time or in money—you sink deeper. Shawn ended up stuck with accumulating debt. Sendhil ended up stuck under mounting commitments.

This resemblance is striking because the circumstances are so different. We normally think of time management and money management as distinct problems. The consequences of failing are different: bad time management leads to embarrassment or poor job performance; bad money management leads to fees or eviction. The cultural contexts are different: falling behind and missing a deadline means one thing to a busy professional; falling behind and missing a debt payment means something else to an urban low-wage worker. The surroundings differ. The education levels differ. Even aspirations can differ. Yet despite these differences, the end behavior is remarkably similar.

Sendhil and Shawn did have one thing in common: each of them was feeling the effects of scarcity. By scarcity, we mean *having less than you feel you need*. Sendhil felt harried; he felt he had too little time to do all the things he needed to do. Shawn felt cash strapped, with too little money for all the bills he needed to pay. Could this common connection explain their behavior? Could it be that scarcity itself led Sendhil and Shawn to behave in such similar ways?

Uncovering a common logic to scarcity would have big implications. Scarcity is a broad concept that extends well beyond these personal anecdotes. The problem of unemployment, for example, is also the problem of financial scarcity. The loss of a job makes a household's budget suddenly tight—too little income to cover the mortgage, car payments, and day-to-day expenses. The problem of increasing social isolation—"bowling alone"—is a form of social scarcity, of people having too few social bonds. The problem of obesity is also, perhaps counterintuitively, a problem of scarcity. Sticking to a diet requires coping with the challenge of having less to eat than you feel accustomed to—a tight calorie budget or calorie scarcity. The problem of global poverty—the tragedy of multitudes of people around the world making do with a dollar or two a day—is another kind of financial scarcity. Unlike the sudden and possibly fleeting tightening of one's budget due to job loss, poverty means a perpetually tight budget.

Scarcity connects more than just Sendhil's and Shawn's problems: it forms a common chord across so many of society's problems.

These problems occur in different cultures, economic conditions, and political systems, but they all feature scarcity. Could there be a common logic to scarcity, one that operates across these diverse backdrops?

We had to answer this question. We were too busy not to.

SCARCITY CAPTURES THE MIND

Our interest in scarcity led us to a remarkable study from more than a half century ago. The authors of that study did not think of themselves as studying scarcity, but to our eyes they were studying an extreme form of it—starvation. It was toward the end of World War II, and the Allies realized they had a problem. As they advanced into German-occupied territories, they would encounter great numbers of people on the edge of starvation. The problem was not food; the Americans and British had enough to feed the prisoners and the civilians they were liberating. Their problem was more technical. How do you begin feeding people who have been on the edge of starvation for so long? Should they be given full meals? Should they be allowed to eat as much as they want? Or should you start by underfeeding them and slowly increase their intake? What was the safest way to bring people back from the edge of starvation?

The experts at the time had few answers. So a team at the University of Minnesota conducted an experiment to find out. Understanding how to feed people, though, requires first starving them. The experiment started with healthy male volunteers in a controlled environment where their calories were reduced until they were subsisting on just enough food so as not to permanently harm themselves. After a few months of this, the real experiment began: finding out how their bodies responded to different feeding regimens. Not an easy experiment to be a subject in, but this was "the Good War," and conscientious objectors who did not go to the front were willing to do their part.

The thirty-six subjects in the study were housed in a dormitory and were carefully monitored, with every behavior observed and noted. Though the researchers cared most about the feeding part of the study, they also measured the impact of starvation. Much of what happens to starving bodies is quite graphic. Subjects lost so much fat on their butts that sitting became painful; the men had to use pillows. Actual weight loss was complicated by edema—the men accumulated as much as fourteen pounds of extra fluid due to starvation. Their metabolism slowed down by 40 percent. They lost strength and endurance. As one subject put it, "I notice the weakness in my arms when I wash my hair in the shower; they become completely fatigued in the course of this simple operation."

Not only did their bodies weaken; their minds changed as well. Sharman Apt Russell describes a lunch scene in her book *Hunger*:

> The men became impatient waiting in line if the service was slow. They were possessive about their food. Some hunched over their trays using their arms to protect their meal. Mostly they were silent, with the concentration that eating deserved. . . . Dislikes for certain foods, such as rutabagas, disappeared. All food was eaten to the last bite. Then they licked their plates.

This is largely what you might expect of people who are starving. But some mental changes they showed were more unexpected:

> Obsessions developed around cookbooks and menus from local restaurants. Some men could spend hours comparing the prices of fruits and vegetables from one newspaper to the next. Some planned now to go into agriculture. They dreamed of new careers as restaurant owners. . . . They lost their will for academic problems and became far more interested in cookbooks. . . . When they went to the movies, only the scenes with food held their interest.

They were focused on food. Of course if you are starving, getting more food should be a priority. But their minds focused in a way that transcended practical benefits. The delusions of starting a restaurant, comparing food prices, and researching cookbooks will not alleviate hunger. If anything, all this thinking about food—almost a fixation—surely heightened the pain of hunger. They did not choose this. Here is how one participant in the Minnesota study recalled the frustration of constantly thinking about food:

> I don't know many other things in my life that I looked forward to being over with any more than this experiment. And it wasn't so much . . . because of the physical discomfort, but because it made food the most important thing in one's life . . . food became the one central and only thing really in one's life. And life is pretty dull if that's the only thing. I mean, if you went to a movie, you weren't particularly interested in the love scenes, but you noticed every time they ate and what they ate.

The hungry men did not choose to ignore the plot in favor of the food. They did not choose to put food at the top of their mind. Instead, hunger captured their thinking and their attention. These behaviors were only a footnote in the Minnesota study, not at all what the researchers were interested in. To us, they illustrate how scarcity changes us.

Scarcity captures the mind. Just as the starving subjects had food on their mind, when we experience scarcity of any kind, we become absorbed by it. The mind orients automatically, powerfully, toward unfulfilled needs. For the hungry, that need is food. For the busy it might be a project that needs to be finished. For the cash-strapped it might be this month's rent payment; for the lonely, a lack of companionship. Scarcity is more than just the displeasure of having very little. It changes how we think. It imposes itself on our minds.

This is a lot to infer from just one study. Starvation is an extreme case: it involves scarcity but it also involves many other physiological changes. The study had only thirty-six subjects. The evidence we cite consists largely of the mutterings of hungry men, not hard numbers.

But many other, more precise studies have shown the same results. Not only that, they give a window into exactly how scarcity captures the mind.

One recent study asked subjects to come to a lab around lunch-time, not having eaten for three to four hours. Half of these hungry subjects were sent out to grab lunch, the others weren't. So half were hungry and half were sated. Their task in the study was simple: Watch a screen. A word will flash. Identify the word you just saw. So, for example, *TAKE* might flash and the subjects would have to decide whether they just saw *TAKE* or *RAKE*. This seems a trivial task and it would have been except that everything happened quickly. Very quickly. The word itself flashes for 33 milliseconds—that is, 1/30 of a second.

Now you might think that the hungry subjects might do worse, being tired and unfocused from their hunger. But on this particular task, they did as well as the sated subjects. Except in one case. The hungry did much *better* on food-related words. They were much more likely to accurately detect the word *CAKE*. Tasks such as these are designed to tell us what is at the top of someone's mind. When a concept occupies our thoughts, we see words related to it more quickly. So when the hungry recognize *CAKE* more quickly, we see directly that food is at the top of their minds. Here we do not rely on odd behaviors such as leafing through cookbooks or making plans to be a restaurateur to infer their fixation. The speed and accuracy of their responses directly show us that scarcity has captured the hungry subjects' minds.

And it does so on a subconscious level. The tiny time scales in this task—outcomes measured in milliseconds—were devised to observe fast processes, fast enough to remain beyond conscious control. We now know enough about the brain to know what these time scales mean. Complex higher-order calculations require more than 300 milliseconds. Faster responses rely on more automatic subconscious processes. So when the hungry recognize *CAKE* more quickly, it is not because they *choose* to focus more on this word. It happens faster than they could choose to do anything. This is why we use the word *capture* when describing how scarcity focuses the mind.

This phenomenon is not specific to hunger. One study finds that when subjects are thirsty, they are much quicker (again at the level of tens of milliseconds) to recognize the word *WATER*. In all these cases, scarcity operates unconsciously. It captures attention whether the mind's owner wishes it or not.

Now, both thirst and hunger are physical cravings. Other, less visceral forms of scarcity also capture the mind. In one study, children were asked to estimate from memory, by adjusting a physical device, the size of regular U.S. coins—from a penny to a half-dollar. The coins "looked" largest to the poorer children, who significantly overestimated the size of the coins. The most valuable coins—the quarter and half-dollar—were the most distorted. Just as food captures the focus of the hungry, the coins captured the focus of poor children. The increased focus made these coins "look" bigger. Now, it's possible that poor children are simply unskilled at remembering size. So the researchers had the kids estimate sizes with the coins in front of them, an even simpler task. In fact, the poor children made even *bigger* errors with the coins in front of them. The real coins drew even more focus than did the abstract ones in memory. (And with no coins around, the kids were highly accurate at estimating similarly sized cardboard disks.)

The capture of attention can alter experience. During brief and highly focused events, such as car accidents and robberies, for example, the increased engagement of attention brings about what researchers call the "subjective expansion of time," a feeling that such events last longer, precisely because of the greater amount of information that is processed. Similarly, scarcity's capture of attention affects not only what we see or how fast we see it but also how we interpret the world. One study of the lonely flashed pictures of faces for one second and asked subjects to describe which emotion was being expressed. Were the faces conveying anger, fear, happiness, or sadness? This simple task measures a key social skill: the ability to understand what others are feeling. Remarkably, the lonely do *better* at this task. You might have thought they would do worse—after all, their loneliness might imply social ineptitude or inexperience. But this superior performance makes sense when you consider the psychology of scarcity. It is just what you would predict if the lonely focus on their own form of scarcity, on managing social contacts. They ought to be particularly attuned to reading emotions.

This implies that the lonely should also show greater recall for social information. One study asked people to read from someone's diary and to form an impression of the writer. Later they were asked to recall details from the diary entries. The lonely did about as well as the nonlonely. Except in one case: they were much better at remembering the entries that involved social content, such as interactions with others.

The authors of this study relay an anecdote that nicely summarizes how loneliness changes focus: Bradley Smith, unlucky in love and lacking close friends, finds his perception changes after a divorce.

> *Suddenly, Bradley cannot escape noticing connections between people—couples and families—in exquisite and painful detail. At one time or another, Bradley's plight may have befallen most of us. Perhaps, similar to Bradley, a romantic relationship ends, and you find yourself noticing lovers holding hands in the park. Or your first days in a new school or job place you in a world of strangers, in which each smile, scowl, or glance in your direction assumes added significance.*

Bradley, you might say, is the social equivalent of the starving men, leafing through his own cookbooks.

THE ORIGINAL SCIENCE OF SCARCITY

When we told an economist colleague that we were studying scarcity, he remarked, "There is already a science of scarcity. You might have heard of it. It's called economics." He was right, of course. Economics is the study of how we use our limited means to achieve our unlimited desires; how people and societies manage physical scarcity. If you spend money on a new coat, you have less money for a dinner out. If the government spends money on an experimental procedure for prostate cancer, there is less money for highway safety. It is remarkable how frequently otherwise clever discussions tend to overlook trade-offs (an oversight that our theory helps explain). Other economic insights come from the recognition that physical scarcity responds to prices, sometimes in unexpected ways. European paleontologists in nineteenth-century China learned this the hard way. Seeking to acquire scarce dinosaur bones, they paid villagers for bone fragments. The result? Supply responded. More bone fragments. When peasants found bones, they would smash them to increase the number of pieces they could sell. Not quite what the paleontologists were hoping for.

Our approach to scarcity is different. In economics, scarcity is ubiquitous. All of us have a limited amount of money; even the richest people cannot buy everything. But we suggest that while physical scarcity is ubiquitous, the feeling of scarcity is not. Imagine a day at work where your calendar is sprinkled with a few meetings and your to-do list is manageable. You spend the unscheduled time by lingering at lunch or at a meeting or calling a colleague to catch up. Now, imagine another day at work where your calendar is chock-full of meetings. What little free time you have must be sunk into a project that is overdue. In both cases time was physically scarce. You had the same number of hours at work and you had more than enough activities to fill them. Yet in one case you were acutely aware of scarcity, of the finiteness of time; in the other it was a distant reality, if you felt it at all. The feeling of scarcity is distinct from its physical reality.

Where does the feeling of scarcity come from? Physical limits, of course, play a role—the money in our savings account, the debts we owe, the tasks we must complete. But so does our subjective perception of what matters: how much do we need to accomplish? How important is that purchase? Such desires are shaped by culture, upbringing, even genetics. We may deeply desire something because of our physiology or because our neighbor has it. Just as how cold we feel depends not only on absolute temperature but also on our own private metabolism, so the feeling of scarcity depends on both what is available and on our own tastes. Many scholars—sociologists, psychologists, anthropologists, neuroscientists, psychiatrists, and even marketers—have tried to decipher what accounts for these tastes. In this book, we largely avoid that discussion. We let preferences be what they are and focus instead on the logic and the consequences of scarcity: What happens to our minds when we feel we have too little, and how does that shape our choices and our behaviors?

As a blunt approximation, most disciplines, including economics, say the same thing about this question. The consequence of having less than we want is simple: we are unhappy. The poorer we are, the fewer nice things we can afford—be it a house in a good school district or as little as salt and sugar to flavor our food. The busier we are, the less leisure time we can enjoy—be it watching television or spending time with our families. The fewer calories we can afford, the fewer foods we can savor. And so on. Having less is unpleasant. And it can have repercussions, for example, on health, safety, or education. Scarcity leads to dissatisfaction and struggle.

While certainly true, we think this misses something critical. Scarcity is not just a physical constraint. It is also a mindset. When scarcity captures our attention, it changes how we think—whether it is at the level of milliseconds, hours, or days and weeks. By staying top of mind, it affects what we notice, how we weigh our choices, how we deliberate, and ultimately what we decide and how we behave. When we function under scarcity, we represent, manage, and deal with problems differently. Some fields have studied mindsets created by particular instances of scarcity: how dieting affects mood, or how a particular cultural context might affect the attitudes of the local poor. We are proposing something much more universal: Scarcity, in every form, creates a similar mindset. And this mindset can help explain many of the behaviors and the consequences of scarcity.

When scarcity captures the mind, we become more attentive and efficient. There are many situations in our lives where maintaining focus can be challenging. We procrastinate at work because we keep getting distracted. We buy overpriced items at the grocery store because our minds are elsewhere. A tight deadline or a shortage of cash focuses us on the task at hand. With our minds riveted, we are less prone to careless error. This makes perfect sense: scarcity captures us because it is important, worthy of our attention.

But we cannot fully choose when our minds will be riveted. We think about that impending project not only when we sit down to work on it but also when we are at home trying to help our child with her homework. The same automatic capture that helps us focus becomes a burden in the rest of life. Because we are preoccupied by scarcity, because our minds constantly return to it, we have less mind to give to the rest of life. This is more than a metaphor. We can directly measure mental capacity or, as we call it, *bandwidth*. We can measure fluid intelligence, a key resource that affects how we process information and make decisions. We can measure executive control, a key resource that affects how impulsively we behave. And we find that scarcity reduces all these components of bandwidth—it makes us less insightful, less forward-thinking, less controlled. And the effects are large. Being poor, for example, reduces a person's cognitive capacity more than going one full night without sleep. It is not that the poor have less bandwidth as individuals. Rather, it is that the experience of poverty reduces anyone's bandwidth.

When we think of the poor, we naturally think of a shortage of money. When we think of the busy, or the lonely, we think of a shortage of time, or of friends. But our results suggest that scarcity of all varieties also leads to a shortage of bandwidth. And because bandwidth affects all aspects of behavior, this shortage has consequences. We saw this with Sendhil and Shawn. The challenges of sticking to a plan, the inability to resist a new leather jacket or a new project, the forgetfulness (the car registration, making a phone call, paying a bill) and the cognitive slips (the misestimated bank account balance, the mishandled invitation) all happen because of a shortage of bandwidth. There is one particularly important consequence: it further perpetuates scarcity. It was not a coincidence that Sendhil and Shawn fell into a trap and stayed there. Scarcity creates its own trap.

This provides a very different explanation for why the poor stay poor, why the busy stay busy, why the lonely stay lonely, and why diets often fail. To understand these problems, existing theories turn to culture, personality, preferences, or institutions. What attitudes do the indebted have toward money and credit? What are the work habits of the overly busy? What cultural norms and constructed preferences guide the food choices of the obese? Our results suggest something much more fundamental: many of these problems can be understood through the mindset of scarcity. This is not to say that culture, economic forces, and personality do not matter. They surely do. But scarcity has its own logic, one that operates on top of these other forces.

Analyzing these scarcity traps together does not imply that all forms of scarcity have consequences of the same magnitude. The scarcity mindset can operate with far greater import in one context than in another. The structure of human memory, for example, can be used to understand everything from the trivial (why we forget our keys) to the important (the credibility of eyewitnesses) to the tragic (the onset of Alzheimer's). Likewise, though the logic of scarcity can be similar across different domains, its impact can be quite different. This will be particularly true when we analyze the case of poverty. The circumstances of poverty can be far more extreme, often associated with contexts that are more challenging and less forgiving. The bandwidth tax, for example, is likely to be larger for the poor than for the busy or for dieters. For this reason, we will later pay special attention to the poor.

In a way, our argument in this book is quite simple. Scarcity captures our attention, and this provides a narrow benefit: we do a better job of managing pressing needs. But more broadly, it costs us: we neglect other concerns, and we become less effective in the rest of life. This argument not only helps explain how scarcity shapes our behavior; it also produces some surprising results and sheds new light on how we might go about managing our scarcity.

AN INVITATION

This book describes a "science in the making," an attempt to unravel the psychological underpinnings of scarcity and to use that knowledge to understand a large variety of social and behavioral phenomena. Much of the book draws on original research conducted in settings ranging from university laboratories, shopping malls, and train stations, to soup kitchens in New Jersey and sugar cane fields in India. We also revisit older studies (such as the hunger study) through the lens of our new hypothesis, reinterpreting them in ways that the original authors probably did not anticipate. We use this evidence to build our case, to put forward a new perspective.

One advantage of working on something so new is that it can be presented to experts and nonexperts alike. Because our argument relies on a variety of fields, from cognitive science to development economics, few people will be experts in all these areas, and most will be novices for at least some of the material we present. To accommodate this, we have worked hard to make the whole book, even the technical parts, easily accessible to a wide audience. We also use anecdotes and vignettes extensively. Of course, these never serve as substitutes for careful evidence, but they are used to make concepts intuitive, to bring ideas to life. Ultimately, the strength of our argument will naturally rely on the evidence we present. For the readers who would like greater technical detail, we have included extensive endnotes. More than merely providing references, these discuss details of studies presented, mention other studies that seemed too tangential to include but still relevant, and generally allow you to go even deeper should you find something of particular interest.

This book is not meant to be the final word. It raises a new perspective on an age-old problem, one that ought to be seriously entertained. Anytime there is a new way of thinking, there are also new implications to be derived, new magnitudes to be deciphered, and new consequences to be understood. There is much more to be done, and in that sense our book is an invitation—a front-row seat to a process of discovery.

PART ONE

The Scarcity Mindset

1

FOCUSING AND TUNNELING

One evening not long ago we went to a vegetarian restaurant called Dirt Candy, its name coming from the owner-chef Amanda Cohen's belief that vegetables are "candy" from the earth. The restaurant was known for a particular dish—the crispy tofu with broccoli served with an orange sauce—that all the reviewers raved about. They were right to rave. It was delicious, the table favorite.

Our visit was well timed. We learned the next day that Amanda Cohen was to appear on *Iron Chef*, a popular TV show in which chefs compete by preparing a three-course meal under great time pressure. At the beginning of the show, they learn the surprise ingredient that must be used in every course and have a few hours to design and cook the dishes. The show is extremely popular with aspiring cooks, food connoisseurs, and people who just like looking at food.

Watching the show, we thought Cohen had gotten fantastically lucky. Her surprise ingredient was broccoli, and she of course prepared her signature dish, the one we had just eaten, and the judges loved it. But Cohen did not get lucky in the way we thought. The surprise ingredient, the broccoli, did not allow her to showcase a dish already in her repertoire. Quite the opposite. Episodes are filmed a year in advance. Instead, as she puts it, "The Crispy Tofu that's on the menu now was created for *Iron Chef*." She created her signature dish that night. This kind of "luck," if one can call it that, is even more remarkable. Here was an expert who had spent years perfecting her craft, yet one of her best dishes was created under intense pressure, in a couple of hours.

Of course, this dish was not created from scratch. Creative bursts like this build on months and years of prior experience and hard work. The time pressure focuses the mind, forcing us to condense previous efforts into immediate output. Imagine working on a presentation that you need to deliver at a meeting. In the days leading up to the meeting, you work hard but you vacillate. The ideas may be there, but tough choices need to be made on how to pull it all together. Once the deadline closes in, though, there is no more time for dawdling. Scarcity forces all the choices. Abstractions become concrete. Without the last push, you may be creative without producing a final product. Going into her appearance on *Iron Chef*, Cohen had several secret ingredients of her own, ideas she had been playing with for months or even years. Scarcity did not create them. Rather, it pushed her to bring them together into one terrific dish.

We often associate scarcity with its most dire consequences. This was how we had initially conceived of this book—the poor mired in debt; the busy perpetually behind on their work. Amanda Cohen's experience illustrates another side of scarcity, a side that can easily go undetected: scarcity can make us more effective. We all have had experiences where we did remarkable things when we had less, when we felt constrained. Because she was keenly aware of the lack of time, Amanda Cohen focused on pulling everything from her bag of tricks into one great dish. In our theory, when scarcity captures the mind, it focuses our attention on using what we have most effectively. While this can have negative repercussions, it means scarcity also has benefits. This chapter starts by describing these benefits and then shows the price we pay for them, foreshadowing how scarcity eventually ends in failure.

GETTING THE MOST OUT OF WHAT YOU HAVE

Some of us hate meetings. Connie Gersick, a leading scholar of organizational behavior, has made a living out of studying them. She has conducted numerous detailed qualitative studies to understand how meetings unfold, and how the pattern of work and conversation changes over the course of a meeting. She has studied many kinds of meetings—meetings between students and meetings between managers, meetings intended to weigh options to produce a decision and meetings intended to brainstorm to produce something more tangible like a sales pitch. These meetings could not be more distinct. But in one way they are all the same. They all begin unfocused, the discussions abstract or tangential, the conversations meandering and often far off topic. Simple points are made in lengthy ways. Disagreements are aired but without resolution. Time is spent on irrelevant details.

But then, halfway through the meeting, things change. There is, as Gersick calls it, a *midcourse correction*. The group realizes that time is running out and becomes serious. As she puts it, "The midpoint of their task was the start of a 'major jump in progress' when the [group] became concerned about the deadline and their progress so far. [At this point] they settled into a . . . phase of working together [with] a sudden increase of energy to complete their task." They hammer out their disagreements, concentrate on the essential details, and leave the rest aside. The second half of the meeting nearly always produces more tangible progress.

The midcourse correction illustrates a consequence of scarcity capturing the mind. Once the lack of time becomes apparent, we focus. This happens even when we are working alone. Picture yourself writing a book. Imagine that the chapter you are working on is due in several weeks. You sit down to write. After a few sentences, you remember an e-mail that needs attention. When you open your in-box, you see other e-mails that require a response. Before you know it, half an hour has passed and you're still on e-mail. Knowing you need to write, you return to your few meager sentences. And then, while "writing," you catch your mind wandering: How long have you been contemplating whether to have pizza for lunch, when your last cholesterol check was, and whether you updated your life insurance policy to your new address? How long have you been drifting from thought to vaguely related thought? Luckily, it is almost time for lunch and you decide to pack up a bit early. As you finish lunch with the friend you haven't seen in a while, you linger over coffee— after all, you have a couple of weeks for that chapter. And so the day continues; you manage to get in a little bit of writing, but far less than you had hoped.

Now imagine the same situation a month later. The chapter is due in a couple of days, not in several weeks. This time when you sit down to write, you do so with a sense of urgency. When your colleague's e-mail comes to mind, you press on rather than get distracted. And best of all, you may be so focused that the e-mail may not even register. Your mind does not wander to lunch, cholesterol checks, or life insurance policies. While at lunch with your friend (assuming you didn't postpone it), you do not linger for coffee—the chapter and the deadline are right there with you at the restaurant. By day's end this focus pays off: you manage to write a significant chunk of the chapter.

Psychologists have studied the benefits of deadlines in more controlled experiments. In one study, undergraduates were paid to proofread three essays and were given a long deadline: they had three weeks to complete the task. Their pay depended on how many errors they found and on finishing on time; they had to turn in all the essays by the third week. In a nice twist, the researchers created a second group with more scarcity—tighter deadlines. They had to turn in one proofread essay every week, for the same three weeks. The result? Just as in the thought experiment above, the group with tighter deadlines was more productive. They were late less often (although they had more deadlines to miss), they found more typos, and they earned more money.

Deadlines do not just increase productivity. Second-semester college seniors, for example, also face a deadline. They have limited time to enjoy the remaining days of college life. A study by the psychologist Jaime Kurtz looked at how seniors managed this deadline. She started the study six weeks from graduation. Six weeks is far enough away that the end of college may not yet have fully registered, yet it is short enough that it can be made to feel quite close. For half the students, Kurtz framed the deadline as imminent (only so many hours left) and for the others she framed it as far off (a portion of the year left). The change in perceived scarcity changed how students managed their time. When they felt they had little time left, they tried to get more out of every day. They spent more time engaging in activities, soaking in the last of their college years. They also reported being happier—presumably enjoying more of what college had to offer.

This impact of time scarcity has been observed in many disparate fields. In large-scale marketing experiments, some customers are mailed a coupon with an expiration date, while others are mailed a similar coupon that does not expire. Despite being valid for a longer period of time, the coupons with no expiration date are less likely to be used. Without the scarcity of time, the coupon does not draw focus and may even be forgotten. In another domain, organizational researchers find that salespeople work hardest in the last weeks (or days) of a sales cycle. In one study we ran, we found that data-entry workers worked harder as payday got closer.

The British journalist Max Hastings, in his book on Churchill, notes, "An Englishman's mind works best when it is almost too late." Everyone who has ever worked on a deadline may feel like an Englishman. Deadlines are effective precisely because they create scarcity and focus the mind. Just as hunger led food to be top of mind for the men in the World War II starvation study, a deadline leads the current task to be top of mind. Whether it is the few minutes left in a meeting or a few weeks left in college, the deadline looms large. We put more time into the task. Distractions are less tempting. You do not linger at lunch when the chapter is due soon, you do not waste time on tangents when the meeting is about to end, and you focus on getting the most out of college just before graduating. When time is short, you get more out of it, be it work or pleasure. We call this the *focus dividend*—the positive outcome of scarcity capturing the mind.

THE FOCUS DIVIDEND

Scarcity of any kind, not just time, should yield a focus dividend. We see this anecdotally. We are less liberal with the toothpaste as the tube starts to run empty. In a box of expensive chocolates, we savor (and hoard) the last ones. We run around on the last days of a vacation to see every sight. We write more carefully, and to our surprise often better, when we have a tight word limit.

Working with the psychologist Anuj Shah, we had an insight about how to take advantage of the breadth of these implications to test our theory. If our theory applies to all kinds of scarcity—not just money or time—it should also apply to scarcity produced artificially. Does scarcity created in the lab also produce a focus dividend? The lab allows us to study how people behave under conditions that are more controlled than the world typically allows, revealing mechanisms of thought and action. This follows a long tradition in psychological research of using the lab to study important social issues—conformity, obedience, strategic interaction, helping behavior, and even crime.

To do this, we created a video game based on Angry Birds for our research. In this variant, which we called Angry Blueberries, players shoot blueberries at waffles using a virtual slingshot, deciding how far back to pull the sling and at what angle. The blueberries fly across the screen, caroming off objects and "destroying" all the waffles they hit. It is a game of aim, precision, and physics. You must guess the trajectories and estimate how the blueberries will bounce.

In the study, subjects played twenty rounds, earning points that translated to prizes. In each new round they received another set of blueberries. They could shoot all the blueberries they had or they could bank some for use in future rounds. If they ended the twenty rounds with blueberries saved up, they could play more rounds and continue accumulating points as long as they had blueberries left. In this game, blueberries determined one's wealth. More blueberries meant more shots, which meant more points and a better prize. The next step was to create blueberry scarcity. We made some subjects blueberry rich (they were given six blueberries per round) and others blueberry poor (given only three per round).

So how did they do? Of course, the rich scored more points because they had more blueberries to shoot with. But looked at another way, the poor did better: they were more accurate with their shots. This was not because of some magical improvement in visual acuity. The poor took more time on each shot. (There was no limit on how long they could take.) They aimed more carefully. They had fewer shots, so they were more judicious. The rich, on the other hand, just let the blueberries fly. It is not that the rich, simply because they had more rounds, got bored and decided to spend less time on the task. Nor is it that they became fatigued. Even on the first shots they were already less focused and less careful than the poor. This matches our prediction. Having fewer blueberries, the blueberry poor enjoyed a focus dividend.

In a way it is surprising that blueberry scarcity had effects similar to those observed with deadlines—time scarcity. Having few blueberries in a video game bears little resemblance to having only a few minutes left in a meeting or only a few hours to finish a project. Focusing on each shot, how far back to pull the sling, and when to release bears little resemblance to the complex choices that determine conversation and pace at work. We had stripped the world of all its complexity, all except for scarcity, and yet the same behavior emerged. These initial blueberry results illustrate how—whatever else may happen in the world—scarcity by itself can create a focus dividend.

The observed effects of scarcity in controlled conditions show one more thing. In the real world, the poor and the rich differ in so many ways. Their diverse backgrounds and experiences lead them to have different personalities, abilities, health, education, and preferences. Those who find themselves working at the last minute under deadline may simply be different people. When they are seen to behave differently, scarcity may be one reason, but any of several other differences may be playing a role as well. In Angry Blueberries, a coin flip determined who was "rich" (in blueberries) and who was "poor." Now, if these individuals are seen to behave differently, it cannot be attributed to any systematic inherent personal differences; it must be due to the one thing that distinguishes between them: their blueberry scarcity. By creating scarcity in the lab in this way, we can untangle scarcity from the knots that usually surround it. We know that scarcity itself must be the reason.

The focus dividend—heightened productivity when facing a deadline or the accuracy advantage of the blueberry poor—comes from our core mechanism: scarcity captures the mind. The word *capture* here is essential: this happens unavoidably and beyond our control. Scarcity allows us to do something we could not do easily on our own.

Here, again, the game provides a suggestive glimpse. In theory, the rich in Angry Blueberries could have employed a strategy that simulated being poor. They could have used only three shots each round (like the poor) and saved the rest. This would have led them to play twice as many rounds as the "truly" poor and thus allowed them to earn twice as many points. In actuality, the blueberry rich did not earn anywhere near twice as much in the course of each game. Of course, the players may not have realized this strategy. But even if they had, they would not have been able to do much about it.

It is very hard to fake scarcity. The scarcity dividend happens because scarcity imposes itself on us, capturing our attention against all else. We saw that this happened in a way that is beyond conscious control—happening in milliseconds. It is why an impending deadline lets us avoid distractions and temptations so readily—it actively pushes them away. Just as we cannot effectively tickle ourselves, it is exceedingly difficult to fool ourselves into working harder by faking a deadline. An imaginary deadline will be just that: imagined. It will never capture our mind the way an actual deadline does.

These data show how scarcity captures attention at many time scales. We saw in the introduction that scarcity captures attention at the level of milliseconds—the time it took the hungry to recognize the word *CAKE*. We see it at the scale of minutes (aiming blueberries) and of days and weeks (college seniors getting the most out of their time before graduation). The pull of scarcity, which begins at milliseconds, cumulates into behaviors that stretch over much longer time scales. Altogether, this illustrates how scarcity captures the mind, both subconsciously and when we act more deliberately. As the psychologist Daniel Kahneman would say, scarcity captures the mind both when thinking fast and when thinking slow.

TUNNELING

At 10 p.m. on April 23, 2005, Brian Hunton of the Amarillo Fire Department received what was to be his last call.

Some calls turn out to be false alarms. Some—like this burning house on South Polk Street—turn out to be all too real. Not knowing which is which, firefighters take each one seriously. Each alarm creates a literal fire drill: firefighters must go from a relaxed evening at the firehouse to being at the fire scene, ready to face the flames. Not only must they get there quickly, but they must arrive in full gear and fully prepared. They rehearse and optimize each step. They even train getting dressed quickly. All this pays off. Within sixty seconds of the call, Hunton and the rest of the crew were fully loaded on the truck, their pants, jackets, hoods, gloves, helmets, and boots already on.

Those outside the firefighting community are surprised by how Hunton died. He did not die because of burns from the fire. Nor did he die from smoke inhalation or from building collapse. In fact, Hunton never made it to the fire. As the fire truck raced to South Polk Street, it took a sharp turn. As it turned the corner at full speed, the left rear door swung open. Hunton came tumbling out and his head struck the pavement. The massive force of the strike caused serious trauma to his head, from which he died two days later.

Hunton's death is tragic because it could have been prevented. If he had been wearing a seat belt when the door accidentally swung open, he might have been rattled but he would have been safe.

Hunton's death is particularly tragic because it is not unique. Some estimates place vehicle accidents as the second leading cause of firefighter deaths, after heart attacks. Between 1984 and 2000, motor vehicle collisions accounted for between 20 and 25 percent of firefighter fatalities. In 79 percent of these cases the firefighters were not wearing a seat belt. Though one cannot know for sure, it stands to reason that simply buckling up could have saved many of these lives.

Firefighters know these statistics. They learn them in safety classes. Hunton, for one, had graduated from a safety class the year before. "I don't know of a firefighter who doesn't wear his or her seat belt when driving a personal vehicle," wrote Charlie Dickinson, the deputy administrator of the U.S. Fire Administration, in 2007. "I don't know of a firefighter who doesn't also insist family members buckle up as well. Why is it then that firefighters lose their lives being thrown from fire apparatus?"

Rushing to a call, firefighters confront time scarcity. Not only must they get on the truck and to the fire quickly, but a lot of preparation also needs to take place by the time they arrive at the fire. They strategize en route. They use an onboard computer display to study the structure and layout of the burning building. They decide on their entry and exit strategies. They calculate the amount of hose they will need. All this must be done in the brief time it takes to get to the fire. And firefighters are terrific at managing this scarcity. They get to distant fires in minutes. They reap a big focus dividend. But this dividend comes at a cost.

Focusing on one thing means neglecting other things. We've all had the experience of being so engrossed in a book or a TV show that we failed to register a question from a friend sitting next to us. The power of focus is also the power to shut things out. Instead of saying that scarcity "focuses," we could just as easily say that scarcity causes us to *tunnel*: to focus single-mindedly on managing the scarcity at hand.

The term *tunneling* is meant to evoke tunnel vision, the narrowing of the visual field in which objects inside the tunnel come into sharper focus while rendering us blind to everything peripheral, outside the tunnel. In writing about photography, Susan Sontag famously remarked, "To photograph is to frame, and to frame is to exclude." By *tunneling*, we mean the cognitive equivalent of this experience.

Firefighters, it turns out, do not merely focus on getting to the fire prepared and on time; they tunnel on it. Unrelated considerations—in this case the seat belt—get neglected. Of course, there is nothing unique to firefighters when it comes to tunneling, and there may be other reasons firefighters do not wear seat belts. But a seat belt that never crosses your mind cannot be buckled.

Focus is a positive: scarcity focuses us on what seems, at that moment, to matter most. *Tunneling* is not: scarcity leads us to tunnel and neglect other, possibly more important, things.

THE PROCESS OF NEGLECT

Tunneling changes the way we choose. Imagine that one morning you skip your regular gym session in order to get some work done. You are facing a tight deadline and that is your priority. How did this choice come about? It is possible that you made a reasoned trade-off. You calculated how often you've been to the gym recently. You weighed the benefits of one more visit against the immediate needs of your project and decided to skip. The few extra hours of work that morning were more important to you than exercise. In this scenario, if you were free of the mental influence of scarcity, you still would have agreed that skipping the gym that day was the best choice.

When we tunnel, in contrast, we choose differently. The deadline creates its own narrow focus. You wake up with your mind focused on—buzzing with—your most immediate needs. The gym may never even cross your mind, never enter your already full tunnel. You skip the gym without even considering it. And even if you do consider it, its costs and benefits are viewed differently. The tunnel magnifies the costs—less time for your project now—and minimizes the benefits—those distant long-term health benefits appear much less urgent. You skip the gym whether or not it is the right choice, whether or not a neutral cost-benefit calculation would have led you to the same conclusion. For the very same reason that we are more productive under the deadline—fewer distracting thoughts intrude—we also choose differently.

Tunneling operates by changing what comes to mind. To get a feel for this process, try this simple task: list as many white things as you can. Go ahead and give it a try. To make things easier, we will give you a couple of obvious ones to start you off. Take a minute and see what other white things you can name.

Snow	Milk			

How many could you name? Was the task harder than you thought it would be?

Research shows that there is one way to make this task easier for you—and that is *not* to give you "milk" and "snow." In experiments, people given these "helpers" name fewer total items, even counting the freebies.

This perverse outcome is a consequence of what psychologists call *inhibition*. Once the link between "white" and "milk" is activated in your mind, each time you think, "things that are white," that activated link draws you right back to "milk" (and activates it further). As a consequence, all other things white are inhibited, made harder to reach. You draw a blank. Even thinking of examples for this paragraph proved hard. "Milk" is such a canonically white object that, once activated, it crowds out any others. This is a basic feature of the mind: focusing on one thing inhibits competing concepts. Inhibition is what happens when you are angry with someone, and it is harder to remember their good traits: the focus on the annoying traits inhibits positive memories.

The mind does not inhibit just words or memories. In one study, subjects were asked to write down a personal goal, an attribute that describes a trait (e.g., "popular" or "successful") that they would like to attain. One half were asked to list a personally important goal. The other half were asked to list just any goal. Following this, as in the milk experiment above, both groups were asked to list as many goals (important or not) as they could. Starting off with an important goal led to 30 percent fewer goals being named. Just as "milk" tends to shut out other white objects, activating an important goal shuts off competing goals. Focusing on something that matters to you makes you less able to think about other things you care about. Psychologists call this *goal inhibition*.

Goal inhibition is the mechanism underlying tunneling. Scarcity creates a powerful goal—dealing with pressing needs—that inhibits other goals and considerations. The fireman has one goal: to get to the fire quickly. This goal inhibits other thoughts from intruding. This can be a good thing; his mind is free from thoughts about dinner or retirement savings, focusing instead on the upcoming fire. But it can also be bad. Things unrelated to the immediate goal (such as the seat belt) will not cross his mind; and even if they do, more urgent concerns drown them out. It is in this sense that the seat belt and the risk of an accident get neglected.

Inhibition is the reason for both the benefits of scarcity (the focus dividend) and the costs of scarcity. Inhibiting distractions allows you to focus. In our earlier example, why were we so productive working under a deadline? Because we were less distracted. The colleague's e-mail does not come to mind, and if it does it is easily dismissed. And goal inhibition is why we were less distracted. The primary goal—to finish writing the chapter—captured our mind. It inhibited all those distractions that create procrastination, like e-mail, a video game, or a light snack. But it also inhibited things we ought to have attended to, such as the gym or an important phone call.

We focus and tunnel, attend and neglect for the same reason: things outside the tunnel get inhibited. When we work on a deadline, skipping the gym may or may not make sense. We just don't think (or think enough) about it that way when we decide to forgo the gym for the deadline. Our mind is not on that subtle cost-benefit problem; it is on the deadline. Considerations that fall within the tunnel get careful scrutiny. Considerations that fall outside the tunnel are neglected, for better or worse. Think of an air traffic controller who manages several planes in the air. When a large passenger plane reports engine problems, she focuses on it. During that time, she neglects not only her lunch plans but also the other planes under her control, including ones that might suddenly find themselves on a collision course.

We saw the focus dividend in the Angry Blueberries experiment. And in the lab we can also see the negative consequences of tunneling. If scarcity-induced neglect is insensitive to the weighing of costs and benefits, we ought to see scarcity creating neglect even when it is detrimental to the person's outcomes. To test for this, we ran another study with Anuj Shah, in which we gave participants simple memory tasks, each containing four items, such as this one:

Subjects memorized these pictures and were later asked to reconstruct them. They were given one of the four items and asked to recall the other three. For example, after seeing the picture above, they might be asked:

Reconstruct the scene that contained:

Click here if you want to move on to a new round.

Subjects had to retrieve from memory which of the other objects—a food, a vehicle, and a monument—went along with the spider in the original picture. They got points for correct responses, and they could take as long as they wanted. There was no time scarcity. But there was guess scarcity. They only had a fixed number of guesses they were allowed to make. As before, we created the guess poor and the guess rich.

To measure the cost of tunneling, we added a wrinkle. We had participants play two such games side by side. They were given two pictures to memorize and to reconstruct. And we made them poor (few guesses) in one game and rich (many guesses) in the other. So they experienced scarcity in trying to reconstruct one picture but not the other. Their total earnings depended on their performance on both games: they had to maximize total points earned. Think of it as having two projects, one with a deadline tomorrow and the other a week later. If people were to tunnel, then what they gain in one picture would be offset by worse performance on the other.

Consistent with the focus dividend, people were more effective guessers on the picture they were poor on. But they also tunneled: they neglected the other picture. And this was not efficient. They performed so much worse on the neglected picture that they earned, overall, fewer points than subjects who were poor on *both pictures*. They earned less even though they had more total guesses. A scarcity of guesses in both games meant they could not neglect either one, whereas abundance in one game led them to neglect that game in favor of the one they felt poor on. And they overfocused. Had the shift in focus to the poor game been deliberate, they would not have taken it to such an extreme. Clearly they did not gauge the costs and benefits of tunneling. They simply tunneled, and in this environment it hurt them.

We will call these negative consequences the *tunneling tax*. Naturally, whether this tax dominates the focus dividend is a matter of context and of payoffs. Change the game a bit and the dividend wins out. The point of the study was not to show that the costs of tunneling always dominate the benefits of focusing. Rather, what the study shows is that cost-benefit considerations do not determine whether we tunnel. Scarcity captures our minds automatically. And when it does, we do not make trade-offs using a careful cost-benefit calculus. We tunnel on managing scarcity both to our benefit and to our detriment.

THE TUNNELING TAX

> *I took a speed-reading course and read* War and Peace *in twenty minutes. It involved Russia.*
>
> —WOODY ALLEN

Since the examples above are abstract, we close with a few intuitive vignettes of how the tunneling tax can play out in daily life. These illustrate not necessarily how people might be mistaken but how tunneling can lead us to overlook certain considerations. First, some advice from the *Wall Street Journal* on how to save money.

> *OK. So you want to save an extra $10,000 by next Thanksgiving. How can you do it? You've heard the usual finger-wagging frugality lessons over and over. And you already do the obvious things, like cutting back on lattes, **raising your insurance deductibles** [emphasis added] and steering clear of expensive stores.*

Is raising deductibles a good idea? For someone on a tight budget this is a hard question to answer. Yes, it saves money, but it comes at a cost. You may save money up front, but you run the risk of having to pay more of the cost in case of an accident. A reasoned choice about the deductible would trade off such considerations. But within the tunnel, one consideration looms large: the need to save money right now. Raising deductibles—like cutting back on lattes or on movies—saves money now and is firmly in the tunnel. The other concern—how to pay for repairs in case the car breaks down—falls outside the tunnel.

This can lead people not just to raise deductibles but to forgo insurance altogether. Researchers in poor countries have found it hard to get poor farmers to take up many kinds of insurance, from health insurance to crop insurance. Rainfall insurance, for example, would protect these farmers from the havoc that low (or very heavy) rainfall could do to their livelihood. Even with extremely large subsidies, most (in some cases more than 90 percent of farmers) do not insure. The same is true of health insurance. When asked why they are uninsured, the poor often explain they cannot afford insurance. This is ironic since you might think the exact opposite: that they cannot afford *not* to be insured. Here, insurance is a casualty of tunneling. To a farmer who is struggling to find enough money for food and vital expenses this week, the threat of low rainfall or medical expenses next season seems abstract. And it falls clearly outside the tunnel. Insurance does not deal with any of the needs—food, rent, school fees—that are pressing against the mind right now. Instead, it exacerbates them—one more strain on an already strained budget.

Another manifestation of tunneling is the decision to multitask. We may check e-mail while "listening in" on a conference call, or squeeze in a bit more e-mail on the cell phone over dinner. This has the benefit of saving time, but it comes at a cost: missing something on the call or at dinner or writing a sloppy e-mail. These costs are notorious when we drive. When you think about the multitasking driver, you think of the driver who is talking on a cell phone. Indeed, studies have shown that talking on a (non-handheld) cell phone while you drive can be worse than driving at above legal alcohol levels. But you might also want to think about that driver eating a sandwich. Studies show that eating while driving can be as big a danger. And it is a very common practice: one study found that 41 percent of Americans have eaten a full meal—breakfast, lunch, or dinner—while driving. Eating while driving saves you a bit of time, but you run the risk of staining your upholstery, having an accident, and increasing the chances of a different kind of spare tire: people consume more calories when they are distracted. Tunneling promotes multitasking because the time saving it allows is within the tunnel whereas the problems it creates often fall outside.

Sometimes when we tunnel, we neglect other things completely. When we are busy with a pressing project, we skimp on time with our family, put off getting our finances in order, or defer a regular medical checkup. When you are extremely rushed for time, it is easier to say, "I can spend time with the kids next week," rather than, "Actually, the kids really need me. When exactly will I really have time next?" Things outside the tunnel are harder to see clearly, easier to undervalue, and more likely to get left out.

Companies are not immune to the psychology of scarcity. For example, during lean times, many firms slash their marketing budgets. Some experts believe that this is not a sound business decision. In fact, it looks a lot like tunneling. As one adviser for small businesses puts it:

> In lean times, many small businesses make the mistake of cutting their marketing budget to the bone or even eliminating it entirely. But lean times are exactly the times your small business most needs marketing. Consumers are restless and looking to make changes in their buying decisions. You need to help them find your products and services and choose them rather than others by getting your name out there. So don't quit marketing. In fact, if possible, step up your marketing efforts.

Settling this debate—whether cutting marketing expenses during recessions is efficient—would require a great deal of empirical work. What we can say is that the benefits of marketing look a lot like the kind of thing you would neglect in the tunnel, when you are focused on trimming your budget this quarter. Marketing—like the insurance policy—has a cost that falls inside the tunnel while its benefits fall outside.

In many of these examples, one can fairly question whether the choices made are bad. How do we know that the time saved eating while driving is not worth the increased accident risk? It is always a challenge to decide whether a particular choice was wrong. If by focusing on a deadline you neglect your kids, was that a bad choice? Who is to say? It depends on the consequences of performing poorly at work, the impact of your absence on your children, and even what you want out of life. An outside observer would need to struggle to untangle these considerations. But by exposing *how* tunneling operates, how some considerations are often ignored, the scarcity mindset can shed light on the issue even without settling these debates.

It tells us, for example, that we should be cautious about inferring preferences from behavior. We might see the busy person neglect his children and conclude that he does not care as much about his kids as he does about his work. But that may be wrong, much as it would be wrong to conclude that the uninsured farmer does not particularly care about the loss of his crop to the rains. The busy person may be tunneling. He may value his time with his children greatly, but the project he is rushing to finish pushes all that outside the tunnel. He may look back later in life and report a great deal of anguish about not having spent more time with his children. This is genuine anguish and not merely compliance with a social norm. It is the predictable disappointment of anyone who tunnels. Projects must be finished now; the children will be there tomorrow. Looking back at how our time or money was spent during moments of scarcity, we are bound to be disappointed. Immediate scarcity looms large, and important things unrelated to it will be neglected. When we experience scarcity again and again, these omissions can add up. This should not be confused with a lack of interest; after all, the person himself regrets it.

We started this chapter by showing how scarcity captures our attention. We see now that this primitive mechanism compounds into something much larger. Scarcity alters how we look at things; it makes us choose differently. This creates benefits: we are more effective in the moment. But it also comes at a cost: our single-mindedness leads us to neglect things we actually value.

2

Here are three vignettes about scarcity that illustrate a different consequence of focusing:

> One of your biggest clients has informed you that it will be taking its business elsewhere. You convince the account manager to listen to one last pitch. She agrees but says it must take place tomorrow. You cancel all your meetings and put off all your other tasks. You pour all your time into the pitch. One appointment, though, cannot be avoided. Your daughter has her city championship softball game tonight. For a moment you even consider skipping that, but your better side (barely) wins out: surely her pitches feel as important to her as your sales pitch feels to you. On the way to the game, your daughter realizes she forgot her lucky charm. You snap at her before turning around to pick it up. By the time you have regained your composure, it's too late. She was already nervous for the game and now you've made her more nervous. Something fun has become tension filled. At the game, you can't enjoy yourself. Your mind keeps

turning to that presentation. Not that you can work on it now—you just can't focus on the game. You're distracted, and when your daughter occasionally catches a glimpse of you, you know she knows it. Lucky for you, her team wins and the jubilation helps cover your mistakes. But certainly your performance that evening would not put you in any parenting Hall of Fame.

John has an exam tomorrow. He is putting himself through college. Though his parents saved for all their kids' education, they did not save enough. They never dreamed that tuition would rise so much. John is the youngest of four kids, and by the time his turn came around, the college fund was meager and tuition was even higher. Still, he chose to go to a more prestigious but more expensive college. If he was going to invest in a college degree, he reasoned, he might as well invest in the one that would be worth the most. He patched together student loans, the college's financial aid, and scholarships. It was messy, but somehow he made it work. It always seemed like a good choice. Until now. Two scholarships that were to be automatically renewed have suddenly evaporated; the foundations that award them were hit hard by the recession and were forced to cut back. How would he make tuition for next semester? The payment was due in less than a month. Would the bank give him another student loan? Could he afford it? He could borrow from his aunt and uncle; his father would hate it but did he have a choice? Should he just transfer to the local college? John just can't focus. He keeps thinking about what to do. Preoccupied, he misses a study group meeting that he wanted—needed—to attend. This is no time to take the exam, but he has no choice. When the day arrives, he tries to focus, but his mind keeps going elsewhere. He misses some easy questions and is doubly upset at the end of the day. Not only is he struggling with tuition; he is annoyed at his abysmal performance on the exam.

A manager of a fast-food burger shop laments his trouble with his (low-wage) employees. "They are just so unreliable," he says. He complains that most of his time is spent cajoling them into behaving better with the customers. "Customer service means just that," he tells them. "Put on a smile. Be friendly. When the customer talks to you, make small talk. When the customer is a jerk, don't get snippy. It's your job to be polite." The rest of his time is spent dealing with careless mistakes. "When someone says they want medium fries, how hard is it to press the button that says 'fries'?" he asks incredulously. He is clearly frustrated with his workers. "Maybe it's that they just don't care. Maybe it's the education in this country. Maybe it's the way they were raised," he says.

These vignettes illustrate different consequences of scarcity capturing attention. In the previous chapter, we saw how tunneling distorts the trade-offs we make. Trying to focus on making ends meet right now, we fail to consider the impact in the future of raising the insurance deductible. In the vignettes above, in contrast, we catch people as they are trying to focus on something unrelated to their immediate scarcity. We catch the harried executive not when she is putting together her sales pitch but when she is a parent. We catch the student not when he is dealing with making ends meet but when he is trying to focus on his exam. We catch the low-income worker not when she is at home managing her finances but when she is at work serving food.

These anecdotes illustrate a central hypothesis: because the focus on scarcity is involuntary, and because it captures our attention, it impedes our ability to focus on other things. The executive is trying to focus on her daughter's baseball game, but scarcity keeps pulling her mind away. Even when we try to do something else, the tunnel of scarcity keeps drawing us in. Scarcity in one walk of life means we have less attention, less mind, in the rest of life.

The concept of *less mind* is well studied by psychologists. Though careful research in psychology employs several fine distinctions to capture this idea, we will use the single umbrella term *bandwidth* to cover them all. Bandwidth measures our computational capacity, our ability to pay attention, to make good decisions, to stick with our plans, and to resist temptations. Bandwidth correlates with everything from intelligence and SAT performance to impulse control and success on diets. This chapter makes a bold claim. By constantly drawing us back into the tunnel, scarcity taxes our bandwidth and, as a result, inhibits our most fundamental capacities.

IT'S LOUD IN HERE

Imagine sitting in an office located near the railroad tracks. Trains rattle by several times an hour. They are not deafening. They do not disrupt conversation. In principle they are not loud enough to prevent you from working. But, of course, they do. As you try to concentrate, the rattle of each train pulls you away from what you were doing. The interruption itself is brief, but its effect lasts longer. You need time to refocus, to collect your thoughts. Worse, just when you have settled back in, another train rattles by.

This description mirrors the conditions of a school in New Haven that was located next to a noisy railroad line. To measure the impact of this noise on academic performance, two researchers noted that only one side of the school faced the tracks, so the students in classrooms on that side were particularly exposed to the noise but were otherwise similar to their fellow students. They found a striking difference between the two sides of the school. Sixth graders on the train side were a full year behind their counterparts on the quieter side. Further evidence came when the city, prompted by this study, installed noise pads. The researchers found that this erased the difference: now students on both sides of the building performed at the same level. A whole host of subsequent studies have shown that noise can hurt concentration and performance. Even if the impact of noise does not surprise you, the size of the impact (a full school year level at sixth grade) should. In fact, these results mirror many laboratory studies that have documented the powerful effects of even slight distraction.

Now picture yourself working in a pleasant, quiet office: no disruptions, no trains. Instead, you are struggling with your mortgage and the fact that freelance work is hard to come by. Your spouse and you are living a two-earner life with only one and a quarter earners. You sit down to focus on your work. Soon your mind is wandering. *Should we sell the second car? Should we take another loan?* Suddenly, that quiet office is not so quiet anymore. These noisy trains of thought are every bit as hard to ignore. They arrive at even greater regularity and are every bit as uninvited. But these trains pull you on board. *Should we sell the second car?* leads to *That would raise some money, but it would make the logistics so much harder, just when I need to be working as hard as I can. We don't want to risk the one steady job we do have.* You can ride these trains of thought for some time before you break free and return to focusing on your task. Though this room seems quiet, it is full of disruptions—disruptions that come from within.

This is how scarcity taxes bandwidth. The things that distract us, that occupy our mind, need not come from outside us. We often generate them for ourselves, and these distractions can disrupt our attention more than a physical train. These trains of thought rumble with personal relevance. The mortgage distraction lingers because it matters. It is not a passing nuisance but an intensely personal concern. It is a distraction precisely because it causes us to tunnel. The persistent concern pulls at the mind, drawing us in. Just like an external noise that distracts us from thinking clearly, scarcity generates *internal* disruption.

The notion of an "internal disruption" is commonplace in the cognitive sciences and in neuroscience. A great many studies have documented the profound impact of internal thoughts—even something as trivial as rehearsing a sequence of numbers in your head—on general cognitive function. And years of lab studies compounded by fMRI evidence have taught us about the way the brain focuses and is disrupted. One common distinction is between "top-down" processing, where the mind is directed by our conscious choice of what to focus on, and "bottom-up" processing, where attention is captured by one stimulus or another in ways that we find hard to control.

We saw this in the introduction, when food-related words captured the attention of the hungry. You know the feeling well, from any time a quick movement or sound captured your attention away from what you were doing. A particularly noteworthy form of distraction, one that requires no external distractors at all, is mind wandering. Without our realizing it, the brain's resting state—the default network—tends to pull us away from what we are doing. True to its name, this happens without our conscious input, when our mind "wanders." So while we are often able to direct our brain's activity, at other times we lose that control. For the kids in the school near the trains, the ability to remain focused in the presence of bottom-up distractors depends also on how much work the brain is doing, on how "loaded" it is. Behavioral and neuroimaging studies have shown that distraction along with brain activity related to the presence of distractors increase when the load is high. Top-down attention cannot prevent bottom-up intrusions. When someone says your name across the room at a party, your attention shifts no matter how intently you are trying to focus on something else.

Scarcity itself also captures attention via a bottom-up process. This is what we mean when we say it is involuntary, happening below conscious control. As a result, scarcity, too—like trains or sudden noises—can pull us away even when we are trying to focus elsewhere.

An early study tested this idea by giving subjects a simple enough task: push a button when you see a red dot on the screen. Sometimes, just before the dot appeared, another picture would flash on the screen. For nondieters, this picture had no effect on whether people saw the dot. For dieters, in contrast, something interesting happened. They were less likely to see the red dot if they had just seen a picture of food. Flashing a picture of a cake, for example, reduced dieters' chance of seeing the red dot immediately afterward: it was as if the cake had blinded them. This happened only with pictures of food; nonfood pictures had no effect. Of course the dieters were not physically blinded; they were just mentally distracted. Psychologists call this an *attentional blink*. The food picture, now gone, had made them mentally blink. When the dot appeared, their minds were elsewhere, still thinking about the food. All of this happened in a fraction of a second, too quick to control. Too quick to even be aware of. The title of the study says it best: "All I Saw Was the Cake."

The attentional blink occurs briefly. The distracting effects of scarcity, we conjectured, would last significantly longer. To test this, we ran a study with the psychologist Chris Bryan, in which we gave subjects word searches such as this one:

WORD SEARCH

D	N	O	V	I	G	Z	**STREET**
I	T	J	M	S	F	U	TREE
Q	L	E	W	O	X	N	PICTURE
							CLOUD
K	W	C	E	P	B	X	CARPET
H	R	E	B	R	X	J	LAMP
							DAYTIME
W	P	D	S	W	T	A	RAIN
N	U	X	K	R	Z	S	VACUUM
							DOOR

Subjects searched for the highlighted word (*STREET* in this case). When they found and clicked it, a new grid appeared and they would look for the next word. A second group of subjects was given the same task but with slightly different words. For example:

WORD SEARCH

O	Q	M	V	T	W	A	**CAKE**
J	O	R	G	T	M	G	TREE
							DONUT
R	M	X	H	T	D	K	CLOUD
N	A	R	E	E	E	C	SWEETS
							LAMP
T	O	E	K	F	P	Z	INDULGE
Q	X	G	T	P	I	V	RAIN
J	C	A	K	E	Q	P	DESSERT
							DOOR

The even-numbered words were the same for both groups. The odd-numbered words were neutral words for the first group but tempting ones for the second: STREET became CAKE, PICTURE became DONUT, and so on. We then looked at how long it took participants to find the same words, those they had in common, the even-numbered neutral ones.

For most subjects, changing the odd-numbered words had no effect. Not so for dieters. Dieters took 30 percent longer to find CLOUD after they had just searched for DONUT. Dieters were not slow overall—they found CLOUD just as quickly as nondieters when it was preceded by PICTURE. The DONUT was the problem. What is happening here is clear. It is a version of what psychologists call *proactive interference*. The mention of a donut brings it top of mind. The nondieter searches for it, finds it, and moves on. The dieter, in contrast, finds it hard to move on. Even while searching for the next word, for CLOUD, that donut, every bit as disruptive as a passing train, is still there, drawing attention. And it is hard to find CLOUD when your mind is elsewhere.

Surely you've experienced something similar. If not with food, then perhaps with time. You are against a tight project deadline but must attend an unrelated meeting. How much of this meeting will you process? Sitting at the meeting you try to focus, but despite your best efforts, your mind keeps wandering back to that deadline. Your body is at the meeting, but your mind is elsewhere. Like the word DONUT for the dieter, the deadline keeps pulling you away.

Imagine that you are surfing the web on your laptop. On a reasonably fast computer, you easily go from page to page. But imagine now that there are many other programs open in the background. You have some music playing, files downloading, and a bunch of browser windows open. Suddenly, you are crawling, not surfing, the web. These background programs are eating up processor cycles. Your browser is limping along because it has less computing power to work with.

Scarcity does something similar to our mental processor. By constantly loading the mind with other processes, it leaves less "mind" for the task at hand. This leads us to the central hypothesis of this chapter: *scarcity directly reduces bandwidth*—not a person's inherent capacity but how much of that capacity is currently available for use.

To test this hypothesis, we need to refine our definition of *bandwidth*. We are using the term as a placeholder for several more nuanced and carefully researched psychological constructs. In effect, we are walking a fine line. As psychologists, we care about the distinctions, functional and otherwise, between the various constructs and their corresponding brain function. And *bandwidth* is a generic term that obscures those distinctions. But as social scientists interested in the effects of scarcity, we are willing to leave the fine distinctions alone, much as one might refer to *democracy* or *subatomic particles* while avoiding the many finer distinctions that these afford. By way of compromise, we will continue to use the blanket term *bandwidth* to refer to two broad and related components of mental function, which we will now explain in greater depth.

The first might be broadly referred to as *cognitive capacity*, the psychological mechanisms that underlie our ability to solve problems, retain information, engage in logical reasoning, and so on. Perhaps the most prominent in this category is fluid intelligence, the ability to think and reason abstractly and solve problems independent of any specific learning or experience. The second is *executive control,* which underlies our ability to manage our cognitive activities, including planning, attention, initiating and inhibiting actions, and controlling impulses. Much like a central processor, executive control is essential to our ability to function well. It determines our ability to focus, to shift attention, to retain things in memory, to multitask, to self-monitor. Cognitive capacity and executive control are multifaceted and rich in nuance. And scarcity affects both.

COGNITIVE CAPACITY

A central feature of cognitive capacity is fluid intelligence. To test for the impact of scarcity on people's cognitive capacity, we use the most prominent and universally accepted measure of fluid intelligence, the Raven's Progressive Matrices test, named after the British psychologist John Raven, who developed the test in the 1930s. For an example, look at the following, which is similar to a typical Raven's test item, and ask yourself which of options 1–8 fits in the missing space:

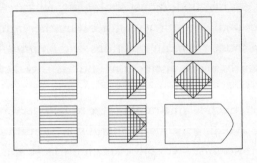

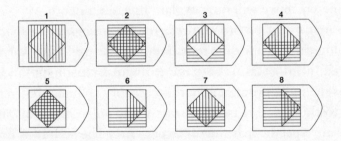

You may recognize this test from your school days. It is a common component of IQ tests. While IQ tests are complex and variegated, most agree that the Raven's Progressive Matrices test is one of the most important and reliable components. Raven's requires no knowledge of world events and little formal study. It is the most common way that psychologists, educators, the military, and others measure what is called fluid intelligence, the capacity to think logically, analyze and solve novel problems, independent of background knowledge. A mechanic reasoning about why an engine won't start uses both background automotive knowledge and reasoning skills. The same mechanic looking at a Raven's Matrix is applying his reasoning skills in a context in which he has no expertise—he's on par with a farmer in India. This has made Raven's particularly useful as a measure of general intelligence, one that supposedly transcends specific culture. Still, there are skeptics. Those who have familiarity with tests and test taking will surely perform better. Those who have taken geometry might do better. In fact, it is known that there are benefits to schooling—children with more years of school do better than those of equal age with fewer years. The debates about what IQ really measures persist even for fluid intelligence. Fortunately, these debates do not matter for our purposes. We will not be comparing fluid intelligence between one person and another or from one culture to the next. We are interested in how scarcity affects the same person's cognitive capacity. It may strike you as odd that a person's "capacity" can be so easily affected, but that is precisely the point—we are used to thinking of cognitive capacity as fixed, when in fact it might change with circumstances.

To see the effect of scarcity on fluid intelligence, we ran some studies with our graduate student, Jiaying Zhao, in which we gave people in a New Jersey mall the Raven's Progressive Matrices test. First, half the subjects were presented with simple hypothetical scenarios, such as this one:

> *Imagine that your car has some trouble, which requires a $300 service. Your auto insurance will cover half the cost. You need to decide whether to go ahead and get the car fixed, or take a chance and hope that it lasts for a while longer. How would you go about making such a decision? Financially, would it be an easy or a difficult decision for you to make?*

We then followed this question with a series of Raven's Matrices problems. Using self-reported household income, we divided subjects, by median split, into rich and poor. In this setup we found no statistically significant difference between the rich and poor mall-goers. Of course, there may have been some difference, but it was not big enough for us to detect in this sample. The rich and the poor looked equally smart.

For the remaining subjects, we ran the same study but with a slight twist. They were given this question instead (with the change shown in bold):

> *Imagine that your car has some trouble, which requires an **expensive $3,000 service**. Your auto insurance will cover half the cost. You need to decide whether to go ahead and get the car fixed, or take a chance and hope that it lasts for a while longer. How would you go about making such a decision? Financially, would it be an easy or a difficult decision for you to make?*

All we have done here is replace the $300 with $3,000. Remarkably, this change affected the two groups differently. Coming up with half of $300 or $3,000 was easy for those who were well off. They could just pay out of savings or put it on a credit card. For the less well off, finding $150 for an important need was not too hard either. Not enough to make them think too much about scarcity and their own finances.

Not so for the $3,000 car expense: finding $1,500 was going to be hard for those with low incomes. A 2011 study found that close to half of all Americans reported that they would be unable to come up with $2,000 in thirty days even if they really needed it. Of course the question we gave the mall respondents was hypothetical. But it was realistic, and it likely got them thinking about their own money concerns. They may not have a broken car, but experiencing money scarcity would mean they had monetary issues close to top of mind. Once we tickled that part of the brain, the all-too-real nonhypothetical thinking about scarcity would come spilling out. *Coming up with $1,500 would be hard. My credit cards are maxed out. Already the minimum payment due is so large. How will I make the minimum payment this month? Can I afford to miss another payment? Should I take a payday loan this time instead?* A little tickle could raise a racket in the brain.

And this racket affected performance. The well-off subjects, with no racket, did just as well here as if they had seen the easy scenario.

The poorer subjects, on the other hand, did significantly worse. A small tickle of scarcity and all of a sudden they looked significantly less intelligent. Preoccupied by scarcity, they had lower fluid intelligence scores.

We have run these studies numerous times, always with the same results. This is not merely an artifact of the $3,000 being *mathematically* more challenging. When we ran nonfinancial problems, we found absolutely no effect of giving similarly small versus large numbers. The effect is specific to hard problems that are financial in nature (for those who are short on money). It is also not the result of a lack of motivation. In one replication of the study, we paid people for every correct answer on the Raven's test. Presumably the low-income participants have a *greater* incentive to do better: after all, the money matters to them more. But they did not do any better; in fact, they did just a tiny bit worse than before. Low-income participants who presumably could have used the extra pay left the mall with less money after having contemplated the harder scenarios, an effect that was absent for those financially more comfortable.

In all the replications, the effects were equally big. To understand how big these effects are, here is a benchmark from a study on sleep. In this study, one group of subjects was put in bed at a normal time. Another group was forced to stay awake all night. Pulling an all-nighter like this is terribly debilitating. Imagine yourself after one night without any sleep. The next morning, the sleeping group was awakened, and both groups were given a Raven's test. Not surprisingly, the sleep deprived did much worse.

In comparison, how big was our effect at the mall? It was even bigger. How smart do you feel after a night of no sleep? How sharp would you be the next morning? Our study revealed that simply raising monetary concerns for the poor erodes cognitive performance even more than being seriously sleep deprived.

There is another way to understand the size of our findings. Because the Raven's test is used to measure fluid intelligence, it has a direct analogue with IQ. Typical studies of IQ assume a normal distribution of IQ scores, with a mean of 100 and a standard deviation of 15. (Standard deviation is a measure of the dispersion of scores around their mean. In a normal distribution, almost 70 percent of scores fall within one standard deviation of the mean.) One can calibrate the impact of an intervention by looking at how its effect compares to the standard deviation. For example, if an intervention has an effect equivalent to one-third of a standard deviation, then that effect corresponds to about five IQ points.

By that measure our effects correspond to between 13 and 14 IQ points. By most commonly used descriptive classifications of IQ, 13 points can move you from the category of "average" to one labeled "superior" intelligence. Or, if you move in the other direction, losing 13 points can take you from "average" to a category labeled "borderline deficient." Remember: these differences are not between poor people and rich people. Rather, we are comparing how the same person performs under different circumstances. The same person has fewer IQ points when she is preoccupied by scarcity than when she is not. This is key to our story. The poor responded just like the rich when the car cost little to fix, when scarcity had not been rendered salient. Clearly, this is not about inherent cognitive capacity. Just like the processor that is slowed down by too many applications, the poor here *appear* worse because some of their bandwidth is being used elsewhere.

EXECUTIVE CONTROL

The second component of bandwidth is executive control. As discussed above, executive control is multifaceted, so we begin by considering one of the many important functions to which it contributes, namely, self-control. In the late 1960s Walter Mischel and his colleagues performed one of the most interesting (at the very least, the cutest) psychology experiments on impulsivity. Mischel's research staff would seat a four- or five-year-old in a room and put a marshmallow in front of him. Some children would stare entranced at it, some would fidget with excitement; all of them wanted it. And the child could have it. But, before he could eat it, he was told there was a catch. More of an opportunity, really. The researcher was going to leave the room. If the child hadn't eaten the marshmallow before the researcher returned, he would get a second marshmallow. The children were faced with one of the oldest problems known to man, what the social scientist Thomas Schelling calls "the intimate contest for self-command," the problem of self-control.

Self-control remains one of the more difficult parts of the study of psychology. We know many ingredients go into the manufacturing of self-control. It depends on how we weigh the future. And we appear to do it inconsistently. Immediate rewards (a marshmallow now) are salient and receive a heavy weight. Rewards in the distant future (two marshmallows later) are less salient and thus receive lower weight. So when we think about one versus two marshmallows in the abstract future, two is better than one. But when one marshmallow is right in front of us now, it suddenly beats two. Self-control also depends on willpower, a resource whose functioning we do not fully understand, but which is affected, among other things, by personality, fatigue, and attention.

Self-control relies heavily on executive control. We use executive control to direct attention, initiate an action, inhibit an intuitive response, or resist an impulse. In fact, a less publicized but often replicated part of Mischel's study is highly instructive here. The children who were most successful in resisting the marshmallow temptation did so by focusing their attention elsewhere. Instead of looking at and thinking about the marshmallow, they thought about other things. Instead of having to resist the desire, they simply arranged not to notice it. As Mischel put it, "Once you realize that willpower is just a matter of learning how to control your attention and thoughts, you can really begin to increase it."

This provides a telling link between executive control and self-control. Since executive control helps direct attention and control impulses, reduced executive function will hamper self-control. A number of experiments have vividly illustrated this connection. One experiment gave subjects a memory task. Some were asked to remember a two-digit number; some were given a seven-digit number. The subjects were then led to a lobby where they would await further testing. In front of them in the waiting area were slices of cake and fruit. The real test was what they would choose while they waited, while rehearsing those numbers in their heads. Those whose minds were not terribly occupied by the two-digit number chose the fruit most of the time. Those whose minds were busy rehearsing the seven-digit number chose the cake 50 percent more often. The cake is the impulsive choice. It requires conscious action to prevent the automatic choice. When our mental bandwidth is used on something else, like rehearsing digits, we have less capacity to prevent ourselves from eating cake.

In another study, white Australian students were served food, but in this case it was something they found revolting: a chicken foot cooked in a Chinese style that preserved the entire foot intact, claws included. The challenge for the subjects was that this was served by a Chinese experimenter, creating some pressure to act civilized. As in the cake study, some subjects' minds were loaded: they were asked to remember an eight-digit number. Those whose minds were not loaded managed to maintain composure, keeping their thoughts to themselves. Not so with the cognitively loaded subjects. They would blurt out rude comments, such as "This is bloody revolting," despite their best intentions.

Whether it is eating cake we would rather resist or saying things we do not mean to say, a tax on bandwidth makes it harder for us to control our impulses. And because scarcity taxes bandwidth, this suggests that scarcity not only can lower fluid intelligence but can also reduce self-control. Hence, the Australian student snaps at the Chinese experimenter, the executive consumed by the impending presentation snaps at her daughter, and the employee thinking about his unpaid bills snaps at a rude customer.

To explore whether scarcity reduces executive control, we gave subjects at the New Jersey mall a test that is frequently used to measure executive control, one that directly tested their ability to inhibit automatic responses. First, the subjects were presented with the hypothetical financial scenarios, either easy or hard, as before. They would then see pictures such as these:

or

in rapid succession on a computer screen. They placed the fingers of both hands on the keyboard, and their task was to press the same side as the heart and the *opposite* side of the flower. So if the heart appears on the right, you press right. And if the flower appears on the right, you press left.

The flower creates an automatic impulse that needs to be resisted: hitting the same side as the heart comes easy; hitting the opposite side of the flower is hard. Doing well requires overriding your impulse to quickly hit the same side. The more executive control you have, the better you will do. This test measures how capable you are at inhibiting your first impulse in favor of a different response, be it resisting a cake, biting your tongue, or, in this case, resisting the flower.

Though this task tests executive control, quite different from fluid intelligence, the results were the same. After the financially easy questions, the poor and the well off looked similar. They were able to control their impulses to the same degree, and they made about the same number of errors. But the financially hard questions changed things dramatically for the poor. The well-off subjects continued to do just as well as if they had seen the easy scenario. They exhibited the same level of executive control. The poorer subjects, on the other hand, now did significantly worse. They were more impulsive, mistakenly hitting the same side as the flower more often. While they had hit the correct key 83 percent of the time in the context of the financially easy scenarios, correct key presses went down to 63 percent in the context of scenarios that were financially more challenging. A small tickle of scarcity and they were suddenly more impulsive. Beyond fluid intelligence, scarcity appears to reduce executive control.

HARVESTS

These experiments at the mall test our hypothesis. But in a way, they are artificial. They show how people respond when we trigger in them thoughts about scarcity, which we induce through hypothetical questions about financial hardship. Our interest, though, is in people's everyday lives outside the confines of an experiment. Does scarcity tax people's cognitive resources even when there are no experimenters lurking at the mall to get them to think about it?

Showing this is essential to our argument. But it is hard. We cannot simply look at how poor people compare to rich people in cognitive capacity or self-control. Too many other things—health, friends, education—differ between the rich and the poor for us to be able to attribute any observed differences to scarcity. Such comparisons have been attempted endlessly with no obvious solution to the statistical problems that are inherent to such comparisons. How could we see the effect of scarcity free from all these intricacies?

It was around this time that we were doing fieldwork on farming in India with the economist Anandi Mani, when we noticed something interesting. Farmers get their income in a big lump, all at once at harvest time. This means the farmer has a very different financial life from most workers, who get paid regularly (daily, weekly, or monthly). Instead, a farmer might get paid twice a year or sometimes even once a year. Now picture a farmer who gets paid in June. The next few months are quite good: he's got cash. But even if he's prudent and tries hard to smooth his spending over this period, by the time next April or May rolls around, he will be tight on cash. So the *same farmer* is rich in the months after harvest and poor in the months before harvest.

This was quite close to what we needed: we could examine the same farmer's bandwidth in the months before harvest and in the months after harvest. Instead of comparing rich and poor people, we'd be seeing how the same person behaves differently when tight for cash and when flush with cash. But there was one wrinkle. Might not harvest months impose different obligations from ordinary months? For example, festivals and weddings are common during harvest months—exactly because people are cash rich. So instead of seeing the effects of scarcity, we might just see the effects of celebrations.

To get around this, we used sugar cane farming, which has a peculiar feature. Sugar cane requires an enormous factory to crush the cane and extract the juice (which, once evaporated, forms sugar). The factories can only process so much and the crop can't sit after harvesting for long. So sugar cane is harvested during a four-to-five-month window. In some areas it is harvested throughout the year. Neighboring plots are often on very different harvest cycles. One farmer may be harvesting while his neighbor to one side harvested several months ago and his other neighbor has months to go before harvesting. This rather obscure fact gave us the break we needed. We could now study the same farmers when they're poor and rich *and* know that there's nothing specific about the preharvest and postharvest calendar months. After all, the same month was preharvest for one farmer and postharvest for his neighbor.

As we expected, the data showed that the farmers were more strapped for cash preharvest. Seventy-eight percent of them had pawned something in the month before harvest (and 99 percent took some sort of loan), but only 4 percent pawned something in the month after harvest (and only 13 percent took any kind of loan). Before harvest, they were also more likely to report having trouble coping with ordinary bills.

As at the mall, we again measured executive control and fluid intelligence. We gave the farmers a Raven's Matrices task, but we could not do the heart–flower task because it was difficult to administer it in the field. So for an executive control task, we chose a close cousin, something called the Stroop task. In this task, subjects see strings of items, such as *F F F F*, and have to quickly say how many items are in the string. (In this case, the answer is four.) When you see 2 2 2 2, quickly saying "four" is quite hard. It is hard for the same reason that it is hard to quickly hit the opposite side each time you see the flower.

Using these tasks, we found that farmers performed much worse before harvest than after harvest. The same farmer fared worse on fluid intelligence and executive control when he was poor (preharvest) than when he was rich (postharvest). Much like the subjects at the mall, the same person looked less intelligent and more impulsive when he was poor. Yet in this case it was not us who triggered scarcity-related thoughts or even tried to bring them to the surface. These thoughts were there naturally when the farmers were poor (the harvest money dissipated to a small amount) but not when they were rich (still flush with cash from the harvest).

And again the magnitudes were large. The postharvest farmers got about 25 percent more items correct on Raven's. Put in IQ terms, as in the earlier mall study, this would correspond to about 9 or 10 IQ points. Not as big a gap as at the mall, but that is to be expected. After all, here we hadn't induced them to think about money. We simply measured their mental state at an arbitrarily selected point in time, their *latent* tendency to have their bandwidth taxed by scarcity. On the executive control task, they were 11 percent slower in responding and made 15 percent more errors while poor, quite comparable to the mall study. Had we met a farmer when he was poor, we would have been tempted to attribute his limited capacity to a personal trait. But we know from our study that his limitation has little to do with his genuine capacity as a person. The very state of having less money in the months before harvest had made him perform less intelligently and show less cognitive control.

Before notching this as a victory for our theory, however, a few doors must be shut. We know that scarcity (poverty) changes before and after harvest. But are there other things that change with it? And if so, might these be the drivers of the psychic changes? Three alternatives stand out.

First, if the farmers are poorer preharvest, might they also be eating less? If so, would it be such a surprise then to find that their cognitive function was also lower? Worse nutrition and simple hunger could leave anyone's brain in a weakened state. For our farmers, though, this was not the case. These farmers are not so poor when they are short on cash that they are forced to cut back on food. If anything, they spent slightly less money on food postharvest. Although we find that they spend less preharvest, they do not spend less on food. Instead, they spend less on other things that matter. For example, they might give a cousin a smaller gift for his wedding. In a culture like India's, where gift giving is not simply a bonus but an obligation (a repayment of past gifts), such cutbacks can be painful.

Second, might they not be working harder preharvest? Preparing for harvest is hard work and might leave farmers tired. Physical exhaustion could easily bring mental exhaustion. In fact, our surveys sufficiently preceded the actual harvest date (four weeks is a long time in agriculture) that preparation for harvest had not started in any serious way. Farmers were not working any more or harder in the preharvest week than in the postharvest week.

Finally, harvest time is not only when you get your money; it's also when you find out how much you got. Farming is notoriously variable. Some harvests are bountiful, others meager. Could the simple anxiety of not knowing what he will earn affect the farmer's mental state? For some crops, such as rice, this is a serious concern. But not so with sugar cane. By surveying his land, a farmer can readily estimate his income. Almost all the crop growth has happened several months before harvest. The last months are just to increase the sugar content of the crop, not its volume. But this is the mill's problem: the farmers get paid solely on volume, not on sugar content. The only reason farmers do not harvest earlier is that the sugar mill does not allow it. In short, several months ahead of time farmers have an accurate understanding of how much they will get paid. They know as much before as they do after the harvest.

There are other minor quibbles we could discuss. But the bottom line is clear. Poverty *itself* taxes the mind. Even without an experimenter around to remind us of scarcity, poverty reduces fluid intelligence and executive control. Returning to where we started, this suggests a major twist in the debate over the cognitive capacity of the poor. We would argue that the poor do have lower *effective* capacity than those who are well off. This is not because they are less capable, but rather because part of their mind is captured by scarcity.

OTHER FORMS OF SCARCITY

> About that time, it occurred to me that I was
> succeeding in the world with only part of my brain
> engaged. While a tenth of it was devoted to school,
> a tenth devoted to my daughter, and perhaps
> another tenth devoted to family crises and
> illnesses, the other 70 percent of my mind was
> constantly focused on food—the calorie count of
> a grape, the filling bulk of popcorn, the clever use
> of water as a placebo. "How much farther," I
> thought, "can I go in the world if I use that 70
> percent more wisely?"
>
> —NATALIE KUSZ, "THE FAT LADY SINGS"

We all understand that dieting can be hard: resisting tasty foods can be difficult for all of us. The bandwidth tax, however, suggests that dieting is more than hard. It is mentally taxing. Dieters, when doing anything, should find they have fewer mental resources because they are partly preoccupied with food. In fact, this is what a few studies have shown. They have compared dieters to nondieters on various cognitive measures, the kind that psychologists use to gauge effective cognitive capacity. Sometimes they compare restrained eaters to nonrestrained eaters. Sometimes they compare the same person over time, during periods when he is dieting compared to periods when he is not. However they do it, they find the same effect. Across a variety of cognitive tests, they find that people simply perform worse when they are dieting. And when psychologists interview the respondents, they find a common pattern: concerns related to dieting are top of mind for these dieters and interfere with their performance.

These results do not appear to come from a simple lack of calories. Not surprisingly (since many of those who attempt to diet fail), the effects appear even in cases where there is no weight loss. Furthermore, direct physiological measures show that nutritional deficiencies do not cause these cognitive impairments. Think of it this way—while losing weight you are preoccupied and face a bandwidth tax. But if you are able to settle into a new equilibrium and find yourself no longer needing to restrain eating, then the bandwidth tax disappears. Of course, one can poke holes in these data: dieters and nondieters may differ for other reasons. More research will be needed to quantify the size of the bandwidth tax for dieters, but it is striking that the results around calorie scarcity mirror what we have found in studying income scarcity.

Something similar happens with the lonely. One study gave lonely and nonlonely subjects a different kind of bandwidth measure, a rather elegant procedure called a *dichotic listening task*. Subjects are asked to listen to two different sounds, one in each ear. They might hear a woman's voice in one ear and a man's voice in the other. The test measures how well people can track one ear and shut out the distraction coming in from the other. This test relies on an interesting fact about the brain: brain lateralization. Most people are right-ear dominant for language, which means that verbal information presented to the right ear is easier for them to attend to. When given no instructions, they tend to focus on the voice presented to the right ear. In fact, when asked to track what was said in the right ear, the lonely and the nonlonely did equally well. In contrast, focusing on the nondominant ear—the left ear—requires bandwidth. It requires executive control to override the natural proclivity to focus on the right and instead to attend to the left. And now the lonely did significantly less well. They were less effective at overriding their natural urge, less effective at tuning out the right ear and listening to the left. The lonely in other words showed impaired bandwidth—in this case, lesser executive control.

In other studies, researchers did something similar to what we did at the mall. They had subjects fill out what they thought were personality tests, and then, by random assignment, they gave these subjects feedback leading them to believe the tests clearly indicated they were going to be either socially well adjusted or else very lonely. They randomly, and instantaneously, created perceived scarcity by leading their subjects to anticipate loneliness. After the information had sunk in, they gave the subjects a Raven's test and found that those who anticipated being lonely did much worse. In fact, when they placed subjects in the scanner, they saw that making people think they would be lonely reduced activation of the executive control areas of the brain. Finally, in a study looking at impulse control, when subjects who anticipated being lonely were given the opportunity to taste chocolate-chip cookies, they ate roughly twice as many. Consistent with this, research on the diets of older adults has found that those who feel lonely in their daily lives have a substantially higher consumption of fatty foods.

Finally, we see similar effects even for artificial scarcity. Recall the Angry Blueberries study from chapter 1. We have found in similar games that the "poor" subjects (those given fewer resources in the game) do worse on the heart–flower task after having played the game. Even though (being poor) they play far shorter games, they are so focused that they have less bandwidth at the end. Like the dieters, the money poor, and the lonely, these blueberry-poor subjects are taxed by scarcity.

SCARCITY AND WORRY

Of course, scarcity is not the only thing that can tax bandwidth. Imagine you had a fight with your spouse one morning. You might not be very productive at work. You might look and act "dumber" that day. You might not hold your tongue when you should. Part of your bandwidth is being used up fussing, fretting, and maybe fuming over the fight. You, too, would have less brain left for everything else. Under this view, everyone has concerns and needs that can tax the mind.

What, then, is so special about scarcity?

Scarcity, by its nature, is a clustering of several important concerns. Unlike a marital spat that can happen anywhere and to anyone, preoccupations with money and with time cluster around the poor and the busy, and they rarely let go. The poor must contend with persistent monetary concerns. The busy must contend with persistent time concerns. Scarcity predictably creates an additional load on top of all their other concerns. It consistently and predictably taxes bandwidth. Everyone can be preoccupied: rich and poor people fight with their spouses; rich and poor people can be flustered by their bosses. But whereas only some people who experience abundance will be preoccupied, everyone experiencing scarcity will be preoccupied.

This discussion raises another important question. In all this talk about scarcity, are we just referring to stress in a roundabout way? In everyday life, *stress* is used liberally, to mean many things. Scientifically, however, there has been considerable progress in the understanding of stress. We now have a firmer grasp of the biochemistry of the generalized stress response. We can even identify several of the molecules involved—glucocorticoids (such as cortisol), norepinephrine, and serotonin—as well as some of their function. This knowledge allows us to more carefully consider whether stress is the biological mechanism by which scarcity affects the mind.

There is, even in our data, some reason to think that stress plays some role. Predictably, experiencing scarcity can be stressful. In the harvest study, for example, we found that postharvest farmers were less stressed than they were before harvest. We also found sizable reductions in heart rate variability, a frequently used measure of stress.

At the same time, stress is unlikely to be the primary driver of many of the effects we have observed. Some of the most important effects had to do with scarcity taxing what we have come to call bandwidth. Stress, in contrast, does not have these predictable effects. Some studies find that stress *heightens* working memory. Still other studies have found mixed evidence, including some indication that executive control might improve during periods of stress. Of course, the chronic effects of stress are still different, but the effects of scarcity that we have studied are immediate: in the mall study, simply reminding people about their money had an almost instantaneous effect on their mental capacity. In addition, we have shown a particular pattern of improved performance (the focus dividend) and diminished performance (the bandwidth tax), a pattern that anxiety and stress alone cannot explain.

Finally, to think of all of this as stress and worry misses a deeper point. The bandwidth tax is not a finding in isolation. It emerges from the same core mechanism as the focus dividend or the way tunneling shapes our choices. A focus on stress alone would miss these deeper connections and ultimately limit our understanding of the scarcity mindset.

WHAT THE BANDWIDTH TAX MEANS

The vignettes with which we opened this chapter may seem obvious in light of the bandwidth tax. You wouldn't be surprised if the cashier hadn't heard the order of fries just when a train passed by. So you (and her manager) shouldn't be surprised if, lost in thought about how to make rent this month, she overlooks the order of fries. She is not being careless. She is preoccupied. Thoughts such as, Should I risk being late again on my credit card? can be every bit as loud as a passing train. The manager with the impending sales pitch tries to focus on her daughter's game. Yet before she knows it, she finds herself ruminating on the sales pitch. The student tries to focus on the exam at hand but is constantly interrupted by thoughts of the looming tuition bill. Even smiling and being pleasant is hard when your mind is taxed. The employee snaps at rude customers more often than she intends. The parent snaps at the child. A taxed bandwidth leads to carelessness. The student forgets his study group meeting. The server rings up the wrong item.

The bandwidth tax changes us in surprising and powerful ways. It is not merely its presence but also its magnitude that is surprising. Psychologists have spent decades documenting the impact of cognitive load on many aspects of behavior. Some of the most important are the behaviors captured in these vignettes: from distraction and forgetfulness to impulse control. The size of these effects suggests a substantial influence of the bandwidth tax on a full array of behaviors, even those like patience, tolerance, attention, and dedication that usually fall under the umbrella of "personality" or "talent." So much of what we attribute to talent or personality is predicated on cognitive capacity and executive control. The restaurant manager looks to all the usual places to explain his employees' behavior—lack of skill, no motivation, or insufficient education. And a taxed bandwidth can look like any of these. The harried sales manager, when she snaps at her daughter, looks like a bad parent. The financially strapped student who misses some easy questions looks incapable or lazy. But these people are not unskilled or uncaring, just heavily taxed. The problem is not the person but the context of scarcity.

Recall the metaphor of the computer slowed down by programs open in the background. Imagine you are sitting at that computer unaware of these other programs. As your browser crawls from page to page, you might draw the wrong conclusion. What a slow computer, you might think, confusing the processor loaded down by other tasks for one that is inherently slow. Similarly, it is easy to confuse a mind loaded by scarcity for one that is inherently less capable. This, after all, is the attribution that the fast-food restaurant manager makes of his employees. Unlike the manager, we are emphatically not saying that poor people have less bandwidth. Quite the opposite. We are saying that all people, if they were poor, would have less effective bandwidth.

All this suggests that we ought to broaden our notion of scarcity. When we think of having very little (time, money, calories), we focus on the physical implications of scarcity: less time for fun, less money to spend. The bandwidth tax suggests there is another, perhaps more important, shortfall. We must now get by with fewer mental resources. Scarcity doesn't just lead us to overborrow or to fail to invest. It leaves us handicapped in other aspects of our lives. It makes us dumber. It makes us more impulsive. We must get by with less mind available, with less fluid intelligence and with diminished executive control—making life that much harder.

PART TWO

Scarcity Creates Scarcity

3

PACKING AND SLACK

You are about to leave on a business trip.

Imagine how you might pack a suitably large suitcase. You might start by putting in all the essentials—toiletries, business clothes, electronics. With room left over, you might add a few less essential items. You pack an umbrella in case it rains. You take a sweater in case it is cold. You pack your gym clothes and running shoes. (Perhaps this time you'll actually get in a workout.) Satisfied, you close the suitcase with some room to spare. There are other things you could take, but you feel fine with what you have.

Now imagine instead packing a small suitcase for the same trip. As before, you might start by casually tossing in the bare essentials. But these already quickly fill the suitcase. You take everything out and pack again, this time more methodically. You carefully stack and arrange. You become creative in making room. You stuff socks and a phone charger inside your shoes and uncoil your belt and slide it along the suitcase edge. This leaves a bit of room to spare. Should you take the sweater? The (optimistic) gym clothes? The umbrella? Is it better to risk the rain and give yourself at least a chance to start getting in shape? Packing the small suitcase forces trade-offs. After some deliberation, you choose the sweater and squeeze the suitcase shut.

Both the large and small suitcase impose limits: no matter the size of the suitcase, you obviously cannot fit every possibly useful item. Both suitcases require a choice of what to pack and what to leave out. Yet psychologically only the small suitcase really feels like a problem. The large suitcase is packed casually. The small suitcase is packed carefully and intently.

This is a metaphor for many other problems in life. We have a time suitcase that must fit our work, leisure, and family time. We have a money suitcase into which we must fit our housing, clothing, and all our expenses. Some of us even have a self-imposed calorie suitcase into which we must fit all our meals.

As this metaphor illustrates, when scarcity focuses us, it also changes how we pack. It changes how we manage each dollar, each hour, or each calorie. It also leaves us with differently packed suitcases. The big suitcase is packed carelessly, with room to spare. The small suitcase is packed carefully and tightly.

Understanding these differences in how we pack is crucial for understanding how scarcity creates more scarcity.

TRADE-OFF THINKING

> The cost of one modern heavy bomber is this: a modern brick school in more than thirty cities. It is two electric power plants each serving a town of 60,000 people. It is two fine, fully equipped hospitals. It is some fifty miles of concrete highway. We pay for a single fighter with a half million bushels of wheat. We pay for a single destroyer with new homes that could have housed more than 8,000 people.
>
> —DWIGHT EISENHOWER, 1953

You are at a restaurant, having dinner with friends. The waiter describes the specials and then asks if you'd like to have a drink. You don't typically order a cocktail but something on the menu catches your eye. How do you decide whether to order it? You may calculate how long before you'll need to drive. You may wait to see if any of your friends order drinks. You may even wonder whether you'll be splitting the bill. Or you may consider whether $10 is a reasonable price. What's notable, though, is the dog that didn't bark. There is one question you don't ask yourself: "If I buy this drink, what will I not buy instead?" You do not ask this question because it almost seems silly. It *feels* as if you can buy this cocktail without giving up any other purchase. It feels as if there is no trade-off.

Think about how remarkable this is. As a matter of basic accounting, of course there is a trade-off. No matter how rich you may be, you have a finite amount of money. If you spend $10 on anything, it is $10 less left for something else (even if that something else is the inheritance you leave your children). Those $10 must come from somewhere. But it often does not feel that way. Many of us make $10 purchases as if there are no trade-offs. We do not have to sacrifice some other purchase just to make this one. Taken to the extreme, it feels as if there is an endless supply of $10 bills in our budget. If pushed, we know at some level that there isn't, but we do not act that way.

Sometimes, though, we do recognize trade-offs. Picture yourself on a diet and contemplating the same cocktail. Even though the $10 price tag may not lead you to consider trade-offs, the "calorie price tag" might. Suddenly, those extra three hundred calories must be accounted for. Drink that cocktail and something else must be given up. Is it worth forgoing dessert? Or the bagel tomorrow morning? Diets make us calorie accountants. The books must balance. We recognize that having one thing means not having something else. We engage in what we call *trade-off thinking*.

Of course, for those on a tight money budget, the $10 is just like the dieter's three hundred calories: the money spent must be accounted for. In the packing metaphor, a small suitcase forces us to recognize that putting in one item means some other item must come out. The packer of a big suitcase who contemplates adding a pair of sneakers simply thinks about whether he wants them. The packer of a small suitcase thinks about what he must take out to make room.

Scarcity forces trade-off thinking. All those unmet needs capture our attention and become top of mind. When we are tight on cash, we are highly attentive to all the bills that must be paid. So when we consider buying something else, all the bills are there, making the trade-off apparent. When we are working on a tight deadline, all the things we must get done are foremost on our mind. So when we think about spending an hour on anything else, the trade-offs again are salient. When time or money is not so tight, we are not as focused and the trade-off is less apparent. By this account, trade-off thinking is an inherent consequence of scarcity.

To test this more rigorously, we did a survey of commuters in a train station in Boston. We asked them to list everything they think about when contemplating buying a TV. All the obvious candidates—the size of the TV, the screen resolution, and the fairness of the price—showed up. When we then divided our sample into lower- and higher-income groups, a pattern emerged. Only some people also reported trade-off thinking, volunteering such thoughts as, "What do I have to give up to buy it?" The people who asked themselves these questions were disproportionately poor. The poor reported trade-off thinking almost twice as often as the better off (75 percent vs. 40 percent). This was a striking difference, especially since the income cutoff we used was at best a crude proxy for scarcity. Some of those whom we classified as well off might well have been experiencing scarcity—for example, some were surely burdened by mortgage payments, credit card debt, college loans, or large families.

The same study produced a noteworthy wrinkle when we conducted it in India. We saw how scarcity is determined by an interaction of one's budget and the size of items. As before, when asked to think about buying a blender, richer subjects mentioned tradeoffs less than 30 percent of the time while the poorer ones mentioned them over 65 percent of the time. But when we asked about a more expensive item—a television—both the rich and the poor reported trade-offs. Whether or not we think about trade-offs depends on the size of the item relative to our budget. The blender was a significant fraction of the budget for the poor but not for the rich. The TV, in contrast, was a significant expense even for the richer households in India. Put differently, the blender evoked scarcity for some, but the TV—because it would have been big relative to everyone's budget—evoked scarcity for all, much as contemplating a car would most likely have generated trade-off thinking in most American households.

SLACK

The packing metaphor illustrates why scarcity creates trade-off thinking. We pack big suitcases loosely. Not every nook and cranny is filled. There is space left unused here and there. We call this space *slack*—the part of our budget that is left untapped because of the way we pack. It is typical of large suitcases. Slack is a consequence of not having the scarcity mindset when we pack with room to spare, of a particular approach to managing resources when we experience abundance. The concept of slack can explain our tendency to consider (or fail to consider) trade-offs and to attend to (or fail to notice) prices.

Imagine that after having packed a large suitcase, you want to add an item. You can just throw it in. No item needs to come out. You do not need to rearrange the contents because the suitcase had extra room to begin with—it had slack. But with a smaller suitcase, adding something necessitates taking something out. Slack is what allows us to feel there is no trade-off. Where does the money for the $10 cocktail come from? If you are well off, the cocktail will feel like it comes at the expense of nothing because in a way it does. Slack picks up the tab. Slack frees us from making trade-offs.

We all have experienced slack in time. On a not-too-busy week, we leave holes in our schedule. You leave a fifteen-minute window between meetings, where in busier times you would have squeezed in a quick phone call. This time is just there, like loose change lying around the house. You feel no compulsion to use it. You do not work hard to keep things tight. When a colleague says she'll call you some-time between ten and eleven, you don't bother to pin her down; you just allocate the whole hour for a thirty-minute call.

Many people enjoy slack in money as well. One study showed that high-income shoppers are twice as likely to report that they do not track their spending because they "don't have to; [they] make enough money." A Dutch study found that wealthier people don't practice mental budgeting at all. And financial planners often assume slack. They meticulously account for the big items but then often leave the remainder to be spent as you want. Richard Jenkins on MSN, for example, suggests leaving 10 percent aside as "fun money"—the slack in the budget, literally play money.

Of course, it can be very sensible deliberately and carefully not to spend everything you can. Leaving room for unanticipated expenses can be a conscious, deliberate, and smart strategy, an insurance pol-icy of sorts against life's vagaries. Even if it takes only twenty-five minutes to get to the airport, you give yourself forty-five minutes, just in case. We, however, do not use *slack* to refer to the sort of room deliberately created to deal with the unexpected, the kind that's actually carefully budgeted. You might leave room in the suit-case for later eventualities, say, for shopping while in Rome. But notice, that's intended slack, the kind you allocate carefully, as you would for any other item.

Slack the way we use it is not space deliberately left unused but, rather, the by-product of packing under abundance. During good times, we don't meticulously account for every dollar. We generally choose a house and a car that leave us a comfortable amount of room for everything else. We have a rough sense of what kind of restaurants we ought to patronize and how often, so we can stay broadly within our budget. We choose a vacation that is broadly of the kind we can afford instead of calculating what we have in the bank account and choosing one that exactly brings us to the edge of our budget. This mindset is a feature of abundance, and slack is the result.

Why do the poor end up with less slack and the rich with more? A metaphor from nature illustrates our answer.

POOR BEES AND RICH WASPS

No man-made structure is built with the care of a single honeycomb. Young worker bees gorge on honey and excrete tiny specks of wax. The exchange rate is steep: each pound of wax requires eight pounds of honey, which requires more than ninety thousand individual bee trips to collect nectar from flowers. The wax is collected in small clumps while the bees cluster together and use their body heat to warm it so they can mold it. Bit by bit the bees put these pieces into place to create the tile work that makes the honeycomb. The work is piecemeal and local, with no boss to oversee it all. Imagine building a sand castle grain by grain, never stopping to survey where you are and with no one to give you directions. Now imagine doing that with hundreds of your friends, in total darkness. Yet it works. The bees create walls that meet at a remarkably precise 120 degrees, forming hexagons that are perfect to the eye. Each wall is less than 0.1 mm thick, with deviations of only +/− 0.002 mm. That's a 2 percent tolerance—not a bad building standard. By way of comparison, the National Institute of Standards and Technology allows a 10 percent tolerance in the width of manufactured plyboards used in construction.

Like the bees, mud dauber wasps are also nest builders, but they build their nests out of mud. They then sting spiders and cram as many as two dozen carcasses into the nest, lay their eggs, and seal it. The hatched larvae feed on the stung prey, surviving the winter inside the sealed nest. Unlike honeybees, the wasps are not elegant builders. The cells are roughly cylindrical, but they are plastered together erratically, with none of the precision of the hive.

Why do bees create such precise structures and the wasps such messy ones? Scarcity. The wasps build with material that is abundant: mud. The bees build with material that is scarce: wax. The bees' wax—like space in a tight suitcase or dollars during hard times—must be conserved. Building badly means wasting wax, which is an incentive to be efficient, to pack well. The wasps, on the other hand, have abundant material, plenty of mud to waste. Wasps can afford slack—to build sloppily—because their building material is cheap. The bees cannot because theirs is expensive.

Something similar happens for the poor and the rich. Imagine that before packing a suitcase, you lay on the bed the items you want to take with you, with the most valuable items on the left and the least valuable ones on the right. For a three-day trip, the first pair of underwear would be on the far left; a fifth pair would be on the far right. You start putting the items in your suitcase starting with the most valuable, from left to right. You can pack quite a few items before your suitcase is full, by which point you'd be packing things you do not care much about, like the fifth pair of underwear. Unused room in the suitcases of the rich comes at the expense of items of little consequence. The suitcases of the poor get full while they are still packing items they very much need. Space is at a premium in the small suitcase, whereas its limits matter less when suitcases are big. Economists call this diminishing marginal utility: the more you have, the less each additional item is worth to you.

There is an almost economic logic to all this: the poor have less slack because they can afford less of it. Packing material—space in the suitcase—is cheap for the rich, like mud, but it is expensive for the poor, like wax. So the rich pack like wasps, casually, inefficiently, and with slack. And the poor pack like bees, carefully, and with no slack.

There is also a deep psychological dynamic at work. When the poor and the rich take a pause from packing, they each have items left outside their suitcase. Because those items that don't fit have a great deal of value for the poor, the items capture their anxious attention. The poor tunnel on those items and cannot help but wonder, *Can I not rearrange and fit these in, too?* Packing captures their attention because the items in danger of being left behind matter. When the rich take a pause, the items left out by now are of low value. They could be added, but they could just as well be left out. The rich leave slack because they are less engaged in packing.

WHAT WE BUY WITH SLACK

A house is just a pile of stuff with a cover on it.
—GEORGE CARLIN

Where does all the slack go? If you are like many people, you can see for yourself. Just go to your kitchen and look in your pantry. It is probably full of items bought in the distant past. In this you are not alone. Kitchen cabinets across the United States are full of soups, jams, and canned food that have not been used for ages. So common is this phenomenon that food researchers have a name for it: they call these items *cabinet castaways*. Some estimates suggest that one in ten items bought in the grocery store is destined to become a cabinet castaway.

In fact, many of our houses are castaway museums. Think of the last time you moved or cleaned out a closet and thought to yourself, "I don't remember owning this!" These closet castaways are so common that space, not money, becomes the scarce commodity. People need to rent out self-storage facilities to house all their stuff. Some estimate that over $12 billion is spent annually on self-storage, three times as much as is spent on music purchases. In fact, the United States has more than two billion square feet allocated to self-storage space. The Self Storage Association notes that "every

American could stand—all at the same time—under the total canopy of self-storage roofing."

Not surprisingly, the fortunes of the self-storage industry are closely dependent on the slack that comes from abundance. As one writer described in the *New York Times Magazine*:

> *"Human laziness has always been a big friend of self-storage opera-*
> *tors," Derek Naylor, president of the consultant group Storage Mar-*
> *keting Solutions, told me. "Because once they're in, nobody likes to*
> *spend all day moving their stuff out of storage. As long as they can*
> *afford it, and feel psychologically that they can afford it, they'll leave*
> *that stuff in there forever." Now [during the Great Recession that*
> *started in 2008], though, "there are people who are watching their*
> *credit-card bills closer than before," he said. "They're really paying*
> *attention to the stuff they're storing and realizing that it's probably*
> *not worth $100 a month to keep. So they just get rid of it."*

Slack frees us to indulge in castaways. It allows us to buy an exotic canned soup or a remote-controlled model airplane on a whim. With slack, we do not feel compelled to question how really useful an item will be. We do not ask, "Will I end up using that juicer enough to make it worthwhile?" or "Will I really ever wear that bold pair of shoes to warrant buying them instead of a pair of pants?" Because there is no trade-off, we simply think, "Why not?" Since slack frees us from trade-offs, it licenses us to buy items that on their own, devoid of any other considerations, have some appeal.

The result, of course, is inefficiency and waste. When we have plenty of time, we loll around, and time evaporates. Minutes here and there add up to hours frittered away. We end up getting six hours of good use out of a sixteen-hour day. We take a week to finish a job we know could have been done in two days. And again, we are not referring here to hours you thoughtfully allocated to "having nothing important to do." We mean those that were never allocated at all. When we have free time, we fritter and waste the hours in an offhand way. And when we have easy money, we buy things we'll cast away and forget. We end up with hours we are not sure what we did with, cabinets full of soups we don't eat, and storage units full of items we forgot we own.

But slack is more than just inefficiency. Consider the following hypothetical decision we presented to a group of university students:

> *You plan to spend the evening in the library working on a short paper due the following day. As you walk across campus, you discover that an author you have always admired is about to give a public lecture. Do you proceed to the library anyway or go to the lecture instead?*

Another group was presented with the same problem with an option added (shown in bold), which provided further enticement to skip out on the library.

> *You plan to spend the evening in the library working on a short paper due the following day. As you walk across campus, you discover that an author you have always admired is about to give a public lecture **and that—in another hall—they are about to screen a foreign movie that you have been wanting to see.** Do you proceed to the library anyway or go to the lecture or to the movie instead?*

Given only one appealing alternative, the lecture, 60 percent stuck with the library. But given two appealing alternatives, even *more* people (80 percent) chose the library. This looks like a peculiar outcome: people are given more attractive options, yet, they are less likely to choose any of them. It happens because choice is hard. When the choice is between the lecture and the library, you can decide which is more important that day—studying or leisure. But when there are two leisure activities, you have one more choice: which is the leisure activity that's right for you? Faced with this additional choice, people simply say, "Forget it. I'll just stick with the library." They avoid the burden of choosing by sticking with the original plan, in effect choosing not to choose.

Slack provides an easy way to avoid the burden of choosing. The only reason you must choose between the lecture and the movie is that your time budget is tight. If you had slack, you could do both. When you're shopping for clothes and see two things you like, a tight budget forces you to choose. If you see two flavors of ice cream you like, a diet forces you to pick the one you prefer. Slack—in money, time, or calories—allows you the luxury of not choosing. It allows you to say, "I'll take both." Contrary to Milton Friedman's ideal of "free to choose," slack leaves us free *not* to choose.

ROOM TO FAIL

Slack provides one other important benefit, captured in the following vignette:

> *Alex and Ben walk by a clothing store. Each sees a leather jacket. Neither owns one but both have always wanted one. This one is perfect. It just costs too much, $200, and it's not terribly practical. The right thing to do is to walk away, but long-standing desires are hard to resist. Each says, "Why not?" gives in, and makes an ill-advised purchase.*
>
> *Alex is financially comfortable at the time. He goes home and thinks, "What a bad purchase!"*
>
> *Ben is tight for cash. He goes home and thinks, "What a bad purchase!" Followed by, "Now I won't have the money to repair my car. That might make me late for work, which might lead to . . ."*

Ben faces a more challenging world than Alex. By their own admission, both Alex and Ben gave in to a $200 temptation and made a foolish purchase. Both are out the same price of the leather jacket. Alex can brush off the mistake. Ben cannot. Same mistake, different consequences. Ben's world is not more challenging because he faces pushier salesmen or higher interest rates. It is more challenging because he lacks slack.

How will the $200 temptation be financed? For well-off Alex, his slack pays for it. Even before the ill-advised purchase, he was not spending up to his full budget. The $200 will come from that leftover space. The financially tight Ben, on the other hand, has no slack. His $200 must come at the expense of something he had planned on, something he thought was essential. His mistake costs him something real. Slack not only absolves you of the need to make trade-offs. It means mistakes do not entail real sacrifice.

Consider a similar example with time. In one study, psychologists asked college seniors to estimate the time required to finish their senior theses. The average estimate was thirty-four days. When probed for the possibility of good and bad turns of events, they agreed it could range from twenty-seven days (if everything went really well) to forty-eight days (if things went badly). In reality, it took them fifty-five days on average. This is not just the folly of inexperienced undergraduates. Everyone from managers to movie producers suffers from the planning fallacy: we are all much too optimistic with our future plans. Even top-notch chess players can allocate too much time to earlier rounds and end up in "time trouble," with too little time on the clock later in the game.

Though the planning fallacy is common to many people, not everybody experiences the same consequences from it. Suppose you have a project due at the end of the month. In reality the project requires forty hours of work, but you mistakenly think it will take only thirty, and you plan accordingly. As the deadline approaches, your error becomes clear. You are ten hours short. How do you make up the shortfall?

Suppose you are not terribly busy. The shortfall is nothing more than an annoyance. You look at your schedule and find ways to create time. There are a few commitments that can be easily moved around, a few to-dos that can be put off and, most important, you have empty spaces here and there in your calendar already. With a little jiggling, you're set; you've found the ten hours you need.

Suppose, instead, that you are already heavily committed this week. Now this is more than annoying. You look at your schedule and you are overwhelmed. It's really bad. Like a wobbly Jenga tower, if you delay or move any one thing around, the whole structure will collapse. Having no alternative, you reluctantly make some hard choices. You put off another (only slightly less urgent) project, rightly fearing—but not thinking about—the consequences this will have. You have borrowed, and there will be a price to pay; the following week will be yet a bigger nightmare.

For the less busy person, slack absorbs the error, thus minimizing the consequences. The busy person, on the other hand, cannot shrug it off so easily. Each added hour must come at the expense of something else. The *same* mistake has bigger consequences. We just saw how slack can be inefficient. We buy items destined to become cabinet castaways, and we use time and money inefficiently. Here we see that slack provides a hidden efficiency. It gives us room to maneuver, to reshuffle when we err. Slack gives us room to fail.

Slack also insulates us in another way. Alex and Ben paid the same dollar amount for that jacket. Yet, in some sense, it cost Ben more. That $200 expense is a small fraction of Alex's income, a small fraction of his slack, but a large fraction of Ben's. The same dollar mistake is *proportionally* more expensive for Ben. As the economist Abhijit Banerjee describes it, the *temptation tax* is regressive; it is levied more heavily on those who have less.

An economics graduate student, Dan Bjorkegren, tested this notion using a large survey of people's consumption patterns in Indonesia. He classified some of their expenditures as *temptation goods*. This classification is surely subjective and open to dispute; future research would ask people to classify their temptation goods on their own. But for a first pass, this was a worthwhile exercise, and the list was eminently sensible: cigarettes, alcohol, other addictive substances, and so on. By looking at the proportion of spending that

went to purchasing these goods, Bjorkegren quantified the temptation tax. What he found was that for the poorest group the temptation tax was as high as 10 percent of their total consumption. And as
people got richer their tax got lower; it got to be as low as 1 percent
of their consumption. Of course, the wealthy were spending a lot
more money on these temptations but proportionally less.

If errors are more costly and there are more chances to fail, might
scarcity not make us more careful? This is easier said than done.
Effort often is not sufficient to reduce error. Many of these mistakes
do not stem from carelessness but are deeply rooted in our mental
processes. Effort and attentiveness alone cannot rid us of the planning fallacy, remind us of things that are out of mind, or provide us
with an iron will to resist all temptation. Our biases, a direct outcome of the workings of the brain, are not always responsive to the
consequences. We may give in to momentary temptation and have
a snack when we are healthy; we may also give in when we are dia-
betic. We may get distracted when playing a silly video game; we
may get distracted when driving a car on a highway. Psychological
biases often persist despite more extreme consequences.

If anything, scarcity will lead us to greater errors. The bandwidth
tax places us in a position where we are prone to make mistakes. The
busy person is likely to commit an even bigger planning error; after
all, he is likely still needing to attend to his *last* project and is more
distracted and overwhelmed—a surefire way to misplan. With compromised bandwidth, we are more likely to give in to our impulses,
more likely to cave in to temptations. With little slack, we have less
room to fail. With compromised bandwidth, we are more likely to fail.

This allows a look at the conditions of scarcity through a new
lens. Late fees are a penalty for misplanning or forgetting, yet they
create an even more hostile environment for those living with scarcity. Readily available junk food may cause obesity in the poor and
the busy, who are, in turn, more exposed and less attentive; it is less
of a threat for the rich and the relaxed. The hard-to-read disclosures
on low-cost mortgage forms will be particularly misunderstood (and

carry bigger consequences) for those living with financial scarcity. Environments that create room for errors, which are then penalized, are a challenge for us all. But they are particularly challenging for those in contexts of scarcity.

Scarcity does not just mean less room to fail. It also means a greater opportunity to fail. In our earlier story of Alex and Ben, the leather jacket was a temptation—buying it was a mistake for both men. But imagine we had written the story as follows:

Alex and Ben walk by a clothing store. Each sees a leather jacket. Neither owns one but both have always wanted one. This one is perfect. It just costs too much, $200, and it's not terribly practical. Alex, who is flush with cash, decides, "Why not?" It's not as if he has obviously better uses for his money. Ben, who is tight on cash, realizes it is an ill-advised purchase. He must resist.

Here, buying the leather jacket is a mistake for Ben but not for Alex. This, after all, is what abundance affords us. It allows us to buy more things. Wealth transforms temptations into affordable luxuries. The same good can be a temptation when you have little but a mere frivolity when you have plenty. The dieter must avoid the same cookie that the nondieter eats thoughtlessly. The busy must avoid distractions—having a drink with friends or watching mindless TV—that the nonbusy enjoy without thinking.

Scarcity not only raises the costs of error; it also provides more opportunity to err, to make misguided choices. It is harder to do things right, because many items—time commitments for the busy, expenses for the poor—must be carefully made to fit into a constrained budget. To see this, think again about packing. Imagine that the two of us—Sendhil and Eldar—are invited to a picnic. Sendhil has to bring fruit for a fruit salad, and Eldar's job is to bring the jellybeans. Sendhil must carefully consider how best to pack: one watermelon and much of the space in his bag is taken. And even the pineapple makes it hard to fit much else. Maybe he can align some bananas around the edges or fit a few grapes or strawberries in between the apples and the pears. There are nontrivial logistics to his packing problem: finding the best arrangement is a challenge. Contrast this with Eldar's much simpler task. He simply pours in some watermelon-flavored jellybeans and some orange. He shakes his bag to let the pile settle, then pours in a few other flavors. Eldar may also have to make some trade-offs; he may not be able to fit all the flavors he wants. But once he has made his choices, his packing is inherently easier. No ingenuity is required to pack the jellybeans. What distinguishes the two tasks is granularity. The fruit are bulky items, whereas the jellybeans are small, almost like grains of sand. The complexity of packing gets easier as the items get more granular.

In life, do you pack grains or bulky items? It depends on your budget. On a small budget, that iPod feels bulky, taking up a large fraction of what you will spend this month. As your budget grows, the iPod takes up less and less room. It becomes a smaller and smaller fraction of your disposable income—it gets more and more granular. A bigger budget does not just make decisions less consequential; it reduces the complexity of packing. Small budgets make for bulky items and for complex packing; large budgets make for granular items and for easier packing.

Of course, even with a big budget, large enough items still create complexity. Serving as a juror on a major (and long!) criminal trial will produce complexity even for someone with lots of free time; the decision to buy an elegant summer house will require attention even from the person who is well off. But with abundance, your choices on average get more and more granular. They stop straining your budget or your planning.

All this suggests an additional layer. While our focus here is on the psychology that comes from scarcity, the effect of scarcity may be more than psychological; it can be a mathematical fact. Scarcity may create a logistically *harder* packing problem. The mind, challenged by the psychology that emerges from scarcity, may find itself needing to navigate a world that is computationally more complex.

SCARCITY AND SLACK

We opened this book with a definition of scarcity: a subjective sense of having more needs than resources. This is above and beyond actual physical limits—only so much money, time, and so forth—that all of us necessarily face. The concept of packing brings this distinction into sharp focus. Physical limits and trade-offs are always there: suitcases, no matter how large, are of a fixed size. But we do not experience them that way. A small suitcase makes us feel scarcity. We notice trade-offs; we feel we have too little space. A small suitcase can also make scarcity objectively more complicated to manage. A big suitcase does not just permit more room; it removes the feeling of scarcity. We not only feel we have enough space; we do not even notice trade-offs. While actual limits and trade-offs are universal, the experience is not.

In this sense, the concept of slack cuts to the core of the psychology of scarcity. Having slack allows us the feeling of abundance. Slack is not just inefficiency; it is a mental luxury. Abundance does not just allow us to buy more goods. It affords us the luxury of packing poorly, the luxury of not having to think, as well as the luxury of not minding mistakes. As Henry David Thoreau observed, "A man is rich in proportion to the number of things he can afford to let alone."

4

A few years ago, Sendhil and a PhD student (call him Alex) were on the outskirts of the city of Chennai in India, looking for an auto rickshaw to take to their next meeting. It was a location where rickshaws were rare, and the wait could be long. And painful: the day was humid and sticky, the air filled with dirt and grit; the thermometer reading of 98 degrees did not fully capture the misery. (South Indian summers need their own temperature corrections, the heat equivalent of the northern "wind chill.") Ten gritty minutes later a rickshaw stopped, and Sendhil was relieved, prematurely, it would turn out.

Everything in Chennai requires bargaining. Their ride normally would have cost 40 rupees (80 cents), but with Alex there the driver saw a chance to charge a foreigner a higher fee. He started at 100, but with some haggling, he inched down to 60, from which he would not budge. Sendhil was about to hop in; the heat was oppressive and they had a meeting to get to.

Alex was adamant, however, that he would not pay 60 rupees,

and he told Sendhil that he wouldn't take this ride. "Another auto will come by. Let's wait," he said. Sendhil cursed himself for bargaining in English rather than Tamil, but he was too depleted to argue, so they let the auto go. Ten grueling minutes passed before another one stopped. Luckily for them, this driver agreed to 40 rupees, and Alex got in. Sendhil got in behind him, pledging to work in the future with more sensible PhD students.

Why did Alex not take the initial offer? His refusal was partly driven by fairness: no one wants to be overcharged. But Alex had been in India for a while, enough time to adjust to the reality that being overcharged was nothing personal, merely a fact of life. He viewed these transactions in purely monetary terms. "I am happy to pay more," Alex said, "but not 50 percent more!" Alex had made a clear choice: he decided he would suffer through ten or more minutes of heat and dirt in order to avoid paying a 50 percent surcharge.

Now, suppose in another context, Sendhil had proposed, "Alex, I want you to spend ten minutes in a sauna with your clothes on, with the sound of car horns blaring in your ears. Oh, I'll also occasionally throw some dirt in your face. But to make it worth your while, here's fifty cents." Alex would likely not have accepted; more likely he would have looked for a new faculty adviser. Yet this was the trade-off he accepted in Chennai. He didn't just accept it; he insisted on it. Why?

On a separate occasion, Sendhil found himself bargaining with another rickshaw driver over a few rupees on behalf of a foreigner. This time the driver switched from English to Tamil. "Why are you bargaining for this amount?" he asked. "This amount of money means nothing to him!" In a way, of course, the driver was right: such small amounts *shouldn't* mean much to well-off people. In a way, though, he was wrong. People act—at least at times—as if these small amounts mean a lot.

To psychologists who study judgment and decision making, Alex's behavior is highly predictable and, of course, you don't have to go to India to see it. It fits in with some of the oldest and most persistent findings on how people make choices. Take this example, of subjects who are presented with one of two scenarios:

Imagine you have spent the day shopping. One item you have been shopping for is a DVD player. At the end of the day, you find yourself at a store that has the brand and model you want for $100. This is a good price but not the best you have seen today. One store—a thirty-minute detour on your way home—has it for $65. Do you buy the $100 DVD player and go home, or do you instead decide to take the detour to buy it for $65 at the other store? Think about what you would do.

Imagine you have spent the day shopping. One item you have been shopping for is a laptop. At the end of the day, you find yourself at a store that has the brand and model you want for $1,000. This is a good price but not the best you have seen today. One store—a thirty-minute detour on your way home—has it for $965. Do you buy the $1,000 laptop and go home, or do you instead decide to take the detour to buy it for $965 at the other store? Think about what you would do.

Both scenarios offer a chance to travel a half hour in order to save $35. And what you find is that most people choose to take the detour for the DVD player but not for the laptop. This contradicts the standard economic model: the exchange rate between time and money ought to be constant. Yet here it varies dramatically. To make this precise, one can ask people to explicitly state what savings they would need in order to make the detour; one can calculate the value people are (implicitly) placing on their time. The results are striking. By varying the price, one can change the value of an hour from $5.64 (for those considering a $3 pen) to $1,364 (for those considering a $30,000 car). This means our frugality has a perverse consequence. We pinch pennies on small items, yet we blow dollars on big ones. Our frugality is thereby largely wasted. We spend hours surfing the web to save $50 on a $150 pair of shoes. Yet we forgo a few hours' search to save a couple of hundred dollars on a $20,000 car.

These findings are important because they demonstrate how people routinely violate economists' standard "rational" models of human behavior. If the value that a person attaches to a dollar changes so easily, traditional analyses of economic behavior are severely stretched. These and related findings have fueled the rise of "behavioral economics," the attempt to incorporate psychology into economic models. Their impact has been large because the results are broadly applicable. They describe not only Alex's curious behavior in India but also the behavior of college students, MBAs, professional gamblers, and executives of all stripes. We had always presumed this basic finding was a fact about everyone's behavior.

THE EFFECT OF SCARCITY

Along with a PhD student, Crystal Hall, we ran a version of the laptop/DVD question:

> Imagine that a friend goes to buy an appliance priced at $100. Although the store's prices are good, the clerk informs your friend that a store forty-five minutes away offers the same item on sale for $50 less. Would you advise your friend to travel to the other store to save $50 on the $100 expense?

As with the laptop/DVD question we manipulated what people saw. For some, the appliance was priced at $100; for others, it was $500, and for others still, it was $1,000. The savings was always the same ($50). We began by testing a sample of relatively well-off people. When we ran this study among commuters at the Princeton, New Jersey, train station, we found what many others before us had found: 54 percent of people would recommend going to the other store when the appliance cost $100; 39 percent when it cost $500, and only 17 percent when it cost $1,000. The $50 savings looked smaller and smaller as the background price got bigger and bigger; for a big-ticket item, it seemed hardly worth the effort.

But then we ran the exact same study twelve miles away, in a soup kitchen in Trenton, New Jersey. As with most American soup kitchens, the visitors to this soup kitchen varied greatly in age, gender, and race, but they shared one trait: for them money was very tight. This led us to predict that they would be more willing to travel to save money. In fact, that's what we found. For the $100 item, 76 percent now thought one should travel to save $50. Now, this is not 100 percent and could be so for a variety of reasons. Perhaps time was also tight, or there were other things to take care of, or perhaps travel is unappealing, since many of the poor do not have cars. Perhaps the people at the soup kitchen—like anyone else—put some value on their time.

What made the study remarkable, though, is what happened when we raised the background price. When the appliance cost $500, the percentage willing to travel barely changed; it was 73 percent. And when it rose to $1,000, the percentage willing to travel actually went up slightly, to 87 percent. The slight increase may be due to the feeling that one really must try to save when spending so much.

For most people, a $35 savings looks large for the $100 DVD player (35 percent off!), but small for the $1,000 laptop (a mere 3.5 percent savings). Yet those at the Trenton soup kitchen seemed unmoved by all this; their responses barely changed. How did scarcity—in this case in money—upend this traditional finding?

To understand how, we need to take a detour into the psychophysics of perception.

A LITTLE ABOUT PERCEPTION

A German physician by the name of Ernst Weber, considered one of the founders of experimental psychology, discovered an important fact about how our senses operate. In one of his pioneering experiments, a blindfolded subject held in one hand a plate with weights on it and was asked to signal when he noticed a change in weight, as metallic filings were silently added. How much additional weight was needed for a person to detect it? What was the "just noticeable difference"? Weber found that the just noticeable difference is a constant fraction of the background amount. For weight, the constant is roughly one-thirtieth. So if you are holding a three-pound weight, at least one-tenth of a pound needs to be added for you to detect a difference. But if you were to hold a thirty-pound weight, a full pound would have to be added before you noticed.

Weber showed that perception was highly relative. For example, the eye is not a light meter. It judges luminosity relative to the background. When you stand in a dark cave, a struck match can produce a bright flare of light, powerful enough to illuminate your surroundings. That same match struck at an outdoor cafe on a sunny afternoon would be barely detectable. Similar effects in the perception of relative size, for example, often show up in our daily lives. Makers of laundry detergent realized long ago that people use more detergent when the cap is larger. Filling almost to the top is satisfying in a small cap. With a bigger cap, the fill line accounts for only a fraction of the available space, and because we are moved by relative rather than absolute amounts, that looks like very little. So people fill a little more, and more detergent is sold. Money, at least to some extent, is also judged relative to background. That's why we care more about saving 40 percent on a $20 book than about saving 1 percent on a $1,000 refrigerator. In Chennai, Alex simply saw money a little bit the way his eyes would see a match: relative to the background. Sixty rupees looked like too much when the fair price was forty.

While relative perception is inherently part of how the mind processes information, experience and expertise allow us to transcend it. A study conducted by the psychologists Simon Grondin and Peter Killeen asked two groups—one of nonmusicians and the other of musicians who had received between eleven and twenty-three years of musical training—to replicate intervals of six, twelve, eighteen, and twenty-four seconds. Nonmusicians behaved as expected. They committed errors proportionate to the length of the interval: the longer the tone, the greater the variance. They were approximating length in relative terms. In contrast, subjects who had received extensive training in music exhibited decreasing relative variability with interval length; for longer tones these musicians committed less-than-proportional errors. They appeared to be judging closer to an absolute scale.

What this tells us is that expertise, a deeper understanding of the units, can alter perception. Musicians who are expert in time intervals have an *internal* metric—they do not rely on intuitive heuristic estimates of time lengths. Studies have shown that more experienced bartenders are better at pouring and are less likely to be affected by bottle height when asked to pour a certain amount.

Scarcity also makes us experts—expert packers. Without the luxury of slack, we come to understand the value of each inch of space in our suitcases. The poor ought to know the value of a dollar, the busy the value of an hour, and dieters the value of a calorie.

Marketing researchers have studied this expertise in a very specific way. They stop shoppers exiting a supermarket for a quick survey. They take the shoppers' receipts and ask questions like, "How much was the Crest toothpaste you just bought?" Affluent shoppers do not do well on this quiz. "The price of the Crest toothpaste? Something like three dollars? Maybe five?" Most don't even know how much they spent in total, the size of the bill they had just paid minutes before. But the lower-income shoppers do. They are more accurate in knowing both how much they spent and the prices of the items they bought. We found this in a study of our own, which we devised carefully so as to separate knowledge from frequency of experience. We asked commuters in Boston the fare at which the taximeter starts. The rich gave the correct answer only 12 percent of the time; the less affluent were correct three times as often. This despite the fact that the rich take taxis much more frequently.

Knowing prices often involves more than just reading the label. It requires vigilance since what you see is often not what you pay. Cigarette taxes, for example, come in two varieties. The excise tax shows up in the posted price, but the sales tax does not; it is added at the register. If you look at just the posted price, you will miss the sales tax. When excise taxes—the visible price—change, rich and poor smokers respond. Both smoke less. Not so for a change in the sales tax—the hidden price. Only low-income consumers respond to that. Only the low-income weigh sales and excise taxes equally (as they ought to). They not only notice prices; they are better at deciphering that the total price is more than the one posted.

Low-income consumers are savvier in other ways as well. When you shop at a supermarket—say for a bag of chips or a can of tuna—you naturally assume that buying the bigger package must be cheaper per unit and thus will save you money. As it turns out, you often would be wrong. The bigger package can cost you more per unit; there might be a "quantity surcharge." One survey found that 25 percent of brands that offered more than one size imposed some form of quantity surcharge. These surcharges are not errors. *Consumer Reports* has called them a "sneaky consumer product trick." The trick works best on consumers who don't pay much attention to prices, who just assume the bigger package will be the better deal. (How often have you done this?) One study examined which supermarkets practice this "trick" and found just what our discussion so far would have predicted: supermarkets in low-income neighborhoods are the least likely to have quantity surcharges. It is harder to trick someone into paying more when she is careful to squeeze the most out of every dollar spent.

The poor, in short, are expert in the value of a dollar. They have their own internal metric by which to assess a dollar's worth. They do not rely on the environment to get a sense of how much to pay. The pressing needs that are top of mind help generate their own internal scale. Having this internal metric means that the background affects them less, like the precise beats of expert musicians. The participants in the soup kitchen did not show the same bias as Alex in Chennai, or countless other higher-income subjects, because they were less prone to using arbitrary features of the context to value money.

Think of how striking this is. The poor in these studies behave more "rationally." They are closer in this case to the rational economic ideal, closer to *homo economicus*. This not only tells us something about poverty; it also tells us something about behavioral economics. That money is valued in relative terms is considered a classic finding in behavioral economics: presumably something that characterizes everyone's thinking. Yet here we see that scarcity overturns—or at the very least waters down—this classic finding. In fact, scarcity alters many other findings as well.

WHAT IS THIS REALLY COSTING ME?

One day when Sendhil was an undergraduate he was contemplating buying a Walkman. (For those of you who don't know what that is, it is like an iPod, but for cassettes. For those of you who don't know what cassettes are, well, never mind.) The Walkman cost $70. Was the Walkman *worth* $70? Should he buy it? Certainly the price was fair: he had looked and it wasn't available for less elsewhere. But what would he prefer to have—$70 in cash or the Walkman? What was $70, really? It's hard to make sense of what a dollar is truly worth. Sendhil had developed a technique for decisions such as this. At the time, his primary food (really his only food) was bean burritos at Taco Bell. Though he did not understand dollars very well, he understood burritos. So he decided to put everything on a bean burrito scale. Instead of asking whether he would rather have the Walkman or $70, he could ask himself whether he wanted the Walkman or seventy-eight bean burritos. The burritos seemed more tangible, more real than dollars.

Why is there the need to construct a benchmark, some way to make sense of $70? Because of slack. Abundance means freedom from trade-offs. When we buy something under abundance, we do not feel we have to give anything up. Psychologically, this is pleasing. But it can be a hindrance when making decisions. If you do not know what you are giving up, it is hard to figure out what something costs and whether it's worth it. Slack, and the absence of trade-offs, means we have no intuitive, easy way of valuing things.

Of course, the burrito metric was not a raging success for Sendhil. But it is not too far from what some experts suggest. One psychologist who studies decision making has suggested an iPhone app that would do something similar: "You would say, 'I like vacations in the Bahamas, shoes, lattes, and books.' And now, when you are tempted to buy something, that thing translates in terms of the things you are interested in. So, it [asks you], 'Hey, this particular item is like half a day in the Bahamas, two [pairs of] shoes, and one latte.'" Other experts have suggested using a "time price." Assume you earn $20 an hour where you work (net: after deducting travel costs, taxes, and so on). When you buy an $80 ice-cream maker, you've just committed to four hours of work; and when you opt for a monthly cable package that's $60 pricier, you've just committed to three more hours of work every single month henceforth. (A daily tall skinny latte would require another roughly fifty work hours a year.)

While deliberating about the Walkman, Sendhil realized how misleading this reasoning was. He was already eating all the burritos he wanted. Suppose he chose not to buy the Walkman. He would not go out and eat seventy-eight *more* burritos. He was not trading off the Walkman against seventy-eight burritos. For this thinking to work, he needed to know where the money saved would be spent. It certainly would not have gone to bean burritos, any more than refraining from buying something would send you on vacation to the Bahamas. Making the trade-off concrete requires tracing the money that was saved and understanding how it would be spent. This was true of the other suggestions as well: how should we pick the items to compare in a way that makes tangible sense?

Instead, people tend to look for comparisons to similarly priced items. And that can be terribly misleading. Many such items may not be things that you would buy in any case. Similarly, the time price ("this is like four hours of work") is misleading because in many cases you wouldn't be able to opt for fewer work hours if you refrained from buying an item, nor would you work more hours if you were to buy it. Looking at the best use of the money is equally misleading. If I spend $40 on an amazing dinner, it is unfair to say that every $40 I spend should provide the same pleasure. Even if I spend correctly, very few $40 expenditures will match this terrific buy. But how many terrific dinners a day can I have? The principle of diminishing returns says that the last $40 I spend—the one I am deliberating about, the one I am making trade-offs on—will not produce anywhere near that pleasure.

The problem with all these benchmarks is that they are not real. Thinking trade-offs under slack is like trying to have your cake and eat it, too. Since we do not actually make many trade-offs, they remain largely an invention. Without such trade-offs, the value of small amounts is not something you ever really need to bother yourself with. If you had $20 more, what would you buy that you haven't bought thus far? If you are financially well off, that is a question you never really need to answer—or even think of asking. If you wanted that small something, you would have bought it.

These problems arise because we do not, under abundance, have a sense of what $10 is worth. And this ambiguity can leave us open to manipulation. Purchases can be made to look more or less attractive through judicious comparisons. Upgrading to a better room on your vacation is a pittance if you think of it as a fraction of what you pay in rent. But it can seem a fortune if you think of it in terms of the terrific desserts you could eat instead. Marketing agencies—and nonprofits—use this strategy. Supporting a child in Africa or buying a vacuum cleaner only costs you pennies a day. With slack, of course, those pennies feel like they come from nowhere.

We have some well-off friends who are frugal. Often, when we tell them about our work, they nod along and say, "That's the way I am: very focused on money." But frugality does not capture the experience of scarcity. The frugal have a principled conscientious-ness about money. The poor must be vigilant about trade-offs. When making a purchase, the frugal consider whether the price is "good." The poor, in contrast, must ask themselves what they must give up to afford that price. Without engaging in real trade-offs, the frugal, like all those who live with abundance, have a hard time making sense of a dollar. So they rely on context. Such was the case with Alex and the rickshaw. He sold his time so cheaply (and inconsistently) because he used his context to determine the "reasonable" price for a rick-shaw ride. Alex was frugal but not poor.

A friend of ours, also a behavioral researcher, recently purchased a cognac truffle for $3. When later asked if it was worth it, he con-sidered what else he could have purchased: "six Snickers bars, a copy of *The Sporting News*, or a finer glass of wine with dinner." Or he could have saved the money—it's not much, but if he made other sacrifices, maybe he could get a bigger apartment next year. He also recalled that satellite TV costs $49 a month and that he'd hardly been watching any TV lately. With the $49 he'd save, he could have all the truffles he wants. He finally admitted, "I don't know." Abun-dance leaves us less able to know the value of a dollar.

Many biases and inconsistencies uncovered by behavioral eco-nomics are really about people struggling to make sense of a dollar. Without a clear sense of how to value a $50 savings, people in our study with Hall used the base price as background against which to value the $50. The poor, in contrast, because they *do* face $50 trade-offs, have an expert's internal metric (possibly a rough one) for what $50 is worth. Consequently, they are less prone to inconsistency. Under this interpretation, there ought to be situations where scarcity gives the poor a sense of the value of things that those who live with abundance will lack. And when lacking a clear value leads to predictable errors, in those cases the poor will avoid the errors that those with abundance commit.

CONSTRUAL

Research on perception gives us another clue into how people might go about making sense of an uncertain value. In perception the brain uses plenty of contextual cues to interpret visual data. And once you understand the cues that the brain uses, you can manipulate them a little, which sometimes leads to perverse outcomes. The checkershadow illusion, by Ted Adelson of MIT, is one of our favorite visual illustrations that take advantage of this knowledge:

In this remarkable illusion, square A clearly looks darker than B. What makes it an illusion is that A and B are the exact same shade of gray. You probably don't believe this; even we occasionally feel compelled to check again, because it seems so wrong. If you don't want to take our word for it, take a sheet of paper and cut a couple of holes in it that show just squares A and B. You will see that the two squares are identical in color. Why are our eyes fooled so badly?

Here the visual system uses background cues in the image to make sense of things. Background cues affect how items in the foreground are seen. Square B has a different background from square A. Not only is it surrounded by darker squares; it also sits in the cylinder's apparent shadow. Because things in shadows look darker, the eye will correct for the shadow, making the item appear lighter. Perceived color, much like perceived distance, depends on surrounding cues. And as it turns out, so does perceived value.

A classic experiment once reported by the economist Richard Thaler does the equivalent of this optical illusion for money. We re-created this experiment along with Anuj Shah. We had subjects consider two scenarios that differ only in the bracketed words—a grocery store in one case, a fancy resort in the other:

> *Imagine you are lying on the beach on a hot day. All you have to drink is ice water. For the last hour you have been thinking about how much you would enjoy a nice cold bottle of your favorite brand of beer. A friend gets up to go make a phone call and offers to bring back a beer from the only nearby place where beer is sold [a small, run-down grocery store] [a fancy resort hotel]. He says the beer might be expensive and so asks how much you are willing to pay for the beer. He says that he will buy the beer if it costs as much or less than the price you state. But if it costs more than the price you state, he will not buy it. You trust your friend, and there is no possibility of bargaining with the bartender. What price do you tell him?*

Respondents who are well-off show a classic decision making bias, as Thaler had originally reported. They will pay more for the same beer in the context of a fancy resort. Much like Alex's behavior, this difference in willingness to pay is an inconsistency. A beer is a beer (and they'll be consuming that same beer on that same beach). That beer will quench your thirst equally whether it comes from the grocery store or the resort. The well off, however, not sure what to pay, use the context to come up with a value.

The poor behaved quite differently. Their reported willingness to pay was much closer in the two contexts. It is not that they gave larger or smaller amounts. They simply gave more consistent answers. Note that what subjects are being asked here is not what they would *expect* to pay. Both the poor and the well off report the same answer when you ask them: of course the resort will charge more. The two groups differ only in what they themselves would be *willing* to pay. This is what we would predict: the poor are able to make better sense of what to pay. Unmoved by context, they can rely on their own internal metric of what a dollar is worth.

This gives us a recipe of sorts for where to look to "overturn" traditional behavioral economics findings, namely, those findings that depend on construing value from arbitrary local context. Along these lines, people have been shown to think of money as compartmentalized into separate accounts. For example, studies have found that when gasoline prices go up, people substitute lower quality gasoline. We act as if we're "poorer" even when the added cost of gas does not materially affect our overall budget. And even then, we act as if we're poorer "in gasoline." (Think about it—if money were the problem, you could just as easily save by buying cheaper cookies or by golfing less.) This is because money is kept in local accounts: a negative shock to the gas account (higher prices) leads to penny pinching (and lower quality) in that account. This idea of mental accounting has many implications. For example, it is the reason we might spend a $2,000 tax refund very differently from a $2,000 increase in the value of our stock holdings. We are wealthier by $2,000 in both cases, but we treat the two accounts ("free money" versus "retirement account") as separate and unequal, often with very different propensities to consume from the two accounts. The poor should be less prone to show this effect.

OPPORTUNITY COSTS

The confusion about the value of things comes about because we do not make trade-offs—perhaps do not even know how to make these trade-offs—when we have abundance. To look at this directly, we asked subjects to imagine the following scenario:

> *You purchase a season ticket package for your favorite sports team. The package includes tickets to a set schedule of eight games. Although a single ticket for each game costs $30, your season ticket package costs only $160, or $20 for each ticket. You like the set of games included in the ticket package, so you decide to buy it.*
>
> *Now imagine that the season is almost over, and you only have one game left to see. In fact, this game has a lot of buzz around it, and tickets are currently selling for $75 around town. You are about to go to the game. Imagine how you feel about the cost of attending the game.*

Subjects were asked to rate how much each of the two following statements captures their feelings about the cost of attending the game:

> *I feel like this costs me $75, the current worth of the ticket and the price I could have gotten had I chosen to sell.*

> *I feel like this costs me $20, the price I paid for the ticket.*

What's the right answer here? Economists view $75 as the real cost: if you skip the game, you can sell the ticket and get $75. (This doesn't even include the time trade-off.) Economists call this the opportunity cost—the trade-off of what else you could have spent the money on. Well-off people get this wrong. They are much more likely to say $20. Many of them would even choose a third option: $0 because the ticket is already paid for. You can see why it feels this way to the well off. When you have slack, arguably $0 (or $20 because that's something you can anchor on) feels "right." With slack, you are not giving up anything to go—selling that ticket really wouldn't buy you anything you wouldn't already buy.

In contrast, the poor have a clear idea of what they could do with $75. As a result, we find that the poor are much more likely to report that it feels as if the ticket costs them $75. Once again, they appear much closer to the economic ideal.

Every year many economists from around the world gather in one place to present research. (Sound like fun? Tickets are still available.) In 2005, two economists, Paul Ferraro and Laura Taylor, decided to turn the tables. They presented a question similar to the one above to more than two hundred professional economists. The responses were (somewhat predictably) far from the economic ideal. As the economist Alex Tabarrok blogged, "I have a hard time believing that this is possible but 78 percent of the economists gave the wrong answer! This is not a hard question. There is no trick. Opportunity cost is central to economics, the people asked were among the best economists in the world, a large majority of them have taught intro econ and yet the correct answer was the least popular."

Is it so surprising that the world's leading economists do not think about things this way? After all, they are well paid and have plenty of slack in their budgets. Not accustomed to facing minor trade-offs, why should they be prone to calculate minor opportunity costs? Measured against economics textbooks, these economists gave the wrong answer. But measured against everyday human behavior, they gave the right answer. Many well-off people—including these economists—do not think about trade-offs for modest amounts.

One could interpret our results as suggesting that being poor makes people better at economics than professional economists. One may also be tempted to conclude that economists would be better at economics if they were paid less, but at least one of the authors disagrees with this conclusion.

Behavioral economics was born from the empirical observation that people violate several basic predictions of economics. They do not consider opportunity costs. Their willingness to pay for items is too easily moved. But economics is meant to follow the logic of scarcity. It is fitting then that its predictions are truer for those who actually have the scarcity mindset.

We are, of course, not proposing that the poor are always more rational. What they have is a specific skill: they are better at making ends meet today. They make a dollar go further. They become experts in the value of money. This expertise can make them appear more rational, less prone to inconsistencies, in some contexts. But this local expertise also becomes a hindrance. Along with the focus that brings expertise comes tunneling. And with tunneling comes a slew of negative consequences.

5

BORROWING AND MYOPIA

*There is nothing in the prospect of a sharp,
unceasing battle for the bare necessities of life, to
encourage looking ahead, everything to discourage
the effort.*

—JACOB RIIS, *HOW THE OTHER HALF LIVES*

A recent report by the Center for Responsible Lending featured the
story of Sandra Harris:

> *Once a student in the Head Start child development program for
> low-income families, Sandra had come to serve on the board that
> administers Head Start in New Hanover County. She was honored as
> 2003 Employee of the Year for her work at the University of North
> Carolina, Wilmington (UNC-W), and Wilmington residents knew her
> as a radio personality on WMNX. But all was not well for Sandra
> underneath the surface. Her husband had lost his job as an executive
> chef. The couple, who had always been a month ahead on their rent
> and bills, found themselves in a cash crunch. Their car insurance was
> due, and Sandra simply could not pay the bill.*

Then Sandra came across a solution: a payday loan. The idea was
simple. She'd get cash now and pay it back along with a fee when
her paycheck arrived in a couple of weeks. Exactly what she needed.

She took the loan and paid her insurance bill on time. And on her next payday, Sandra was ready to pay off the small loan and the $50 fee.

> "You know, you can renew," the payday clerk told her, and the thought of her unpaid light bill flashed into her head. Sandra thought, "You're right. I do need it."

Sandra had started a chain. Next month was no easier than this one. Money was even tighter, and because of the fees, the amount she owed was even bigger. In the coming months, she kept rolling over the loans—taking a new loan to pay off the previous one. On some months she would even roll over the fees.

> After a round of rollovers, the first lender demanded full payment of the loan. Sandra could not pay it off, so she went to another payday lender, Urgent Money Service, and took out a loan to pay back the first lender. She kept getting in deeper. Within six months, Sandra was paying rollover fees on six different payday loans. In June 2003, Sandra and her husband were close to being evicted from the apartment they had lived in for six years. Sandra wrote, "Basically, we ended up having to use one loan to pay off another loan, and ended up paying $495 to $600 per month in fees, never paying the loans down."
>
> This went on for at least six months. This money did not support a lavish lifestyle, Sandra said. "People think you're living above your means," she said. But she was paying bills, not buying clothes. Sandra was working diligently to manage her family's bills during a tough financial time. . . .
>
> Sandra bounced checks. Her car was repossessed. She increased her tax exemptions so she'd have more money to pay her bills and ended up owing thousands of dollars in back taxes. She finally broke and spent a shift at the radio station wiping tears away between segments.
>
> "It takes a lot for me to cry," she said.

The data suggest that Sandra's story is fairly typical. In 2006, there were more than 23,000 payday lender branches in the United States, which was more than all the McDonald's (12,000) and Starbucks (almost 9,000) locations combined. Sandra's practice of rolling over and accumulating fees is also common. Three-quarters of all payday loan volume comes from rollovers, ultimately accounting for $3.5 billion in fees each year.

Why do those strapped for cash take on such extreme loans that they cannot afford to pay back? Why do they allow themselves even to start down such a slippery slope? Such questions typically lead to debates about the importance of personal responsibility or about how unscrupulous businesses prey on low-income individuals; they fuel discussions about the myopia of the poor and the need for financial education. Consumer advocates bemoan the payday loan industry as predatory and push to ban these loans. Others point out that when you're in real need, a loan, however expensive, can be better than no loan. We raise this example not because we want to enter this debate. We raise it because it provides an important window on scarcity.

The problem is more than just with payday loans. The cash-strapped borrow in many ways, not just through payday loans. They "borrow" by paying their bills late. About one of every six families in the lowest income quintile (the bottom 20 percent) pays at least one bill late in any given year. At the extreme end of this are "reconnect" fees. One study found that 18 percent of the poorest families have had their phone disconnected and 10 percent have had a utility shut off within a twelve-month period. Paying $40 to have your phone service reconnected after failing to pay the bill in time is similar to paying a $40 fee for a loan to avoid the disconnection in the first place. A 1997 study estimated that nearly 5 percent of the annual income of the poor was spent on reconnections and servicing and late fees, a number that we suspect has risen dramatically since then. Sandra Harris also "borrowed," first by reducing her tax withholdings and then by falling behind on her tax payments. The poor around the world borrow, often from informal moneylenders who charge rates every bit as extreme as the payday lender (and sometimes more). And yet poor borrowers pay these rates, not once but continuously, setting in motion the same slippery slope of rolled-over debt.

This phenomenon is not unique to the poor. Busy people borrow time, often at similarly high rates. To make room for a project due soon, the busy borrow by putting off other work. And just like a payday loan, the bill comes due: the work that was postponed must now get done. And there is often a "fee" for borrowing time as well: putting off work can increase the time it takes to do it. Mailing your tax returns via certified mail would have taken minutes, but on the last day, there's a line around the block at the post office. Because of an impending deadline, you put off typing up your handwritten notes from an interview. Later, you must decipher those notes, which takes longer than it would have when the interview was fresh in your mind. And just like the payday borrowers, the busy also roll over their debts. Something you were going to do today now needs to be put off because of something you postponed till today from yesterday. How many tasks are delayed time and time again before they finally get done? And for similar reasons—the next chance you get to do it, you find yourself with no more time than you had before.

Borrowing goes hand in hand with scarcity.

TUNNELING AND BORROWING

Why do we borrow when we face situations of scarcity? We borrow because we tunnel. And when we borrow, we dig ourselves deeper in the future. Scarcity today creates more scarcity tomorrow.

Take Sandra's example. That initial bill she could not pay created scarcity. She then tunneled on making ends meet that month. Within that tunnel, the payday loan proved eminently attractive. Its benefits fell inside that tunnel: it helped her make it through the month. The costs of the loan—the repayment and the fees—all fell outside this tunnel. The loan seemed to offer a solution to the problem she was fixated on.

Our own qualitative fieldwork supports the view that tunneling makes the payday loan particularly attractive. Ask a borrower at the time of borrowing, "How do you plan to pay it back?" and you usually get cursory answers such as "Well, I get paid in a week." Probe a bit—"But don't you have other expenses?"—and you encounter exasperation, as if you just don't get it. "Don't you understand? I've got to make my rent payment *this* month!" The subtext being "I'm focusing on what needs to get done now!" Next month's budgeting is an abstraction, something to turn to later. Like all the worthy goals that do not matter when you're speeding to the hospital, the long-term economics of the payday loan do not matter at that moment. This is why payday loans are so attractive—people turn to them when they are tunneling on putting out a fire. And their best feature is that the loans put out this fire, quickly and effectively. Their worst feature—that the fire will return in the future, possibly enlarged—is obscured.

Of course, none of this is unique to payday loans or to money. Think about putting off answering an e-mail. When we take on this time debt, we focus on the benefits: "Right now I need to get other things done." We do not spend much time asking ourselves, "How will I make time for this later?" It is not that we are blind to the costs; they just do not get much attention.

There is an important implicit assumption here about what we tunnel on. Sandra is short of cash today and still expects to be short of cash next month. The perpetually busy are busy this week and next. Those who experience scarcity experience it not only now but typically also later. Yet people tunnel on their immediate scarcity; knowing you will be hungry next month does not capture your attention the same way that being hungry today does. The bill that is due now generates threatening notices; the bill in two months' time is nowhere to be seen. Even if you were to think carefully about tomorrow's scarcity, you'd really only "know" it in the abstract; you wouldn't *feel* it, and thus it wouldn't capture your mind in the same way. One reason for this is the bandwidth tax. The present presses automatically on you. The future does not. To attend to the future requires bandwidth, which scarcity taxes. When scarcity taxes our bandwidth, we become even more focused on the here and now. We need cognitive resources to gauge future needs, and we need executive control to resist present temptations. As it taxes our bandwidth, scarcity focuses us on the present, and leads us to borrow.

We have already seen data that support this assumption. Recall the deadline study from chapter 1 in which one group of students had three weeks to finish an assignment while a second group faced a deadline every week. We attributed the second group's boost in performance to the focus dividend. But, of course, the first group also faced a deadline, one that was three weeks away rather than one week. This tells us that the three-week deadline was not as pressing. In fact, initially, each one-week deadline may not have felt very pressing either. But we can guess what happened. The deadline only mattered once it got close. Until then, it was an abstraction; it failed to evoke the scarcity mindset. But that mindset arose three times for those who had one-week deadlines and only once for those who had three weeks. All this, incidentally, should be familiar. It is why we experience a rush of productivity shortly before a deadline that was always there.

Tunneling this way creates a bias toward borrowing. Because only the most immediate scarcity enters the tunnel, loans are particularly attractive.

Of course, taking a loan need not be a bad choice. When you really do have more time next week, putting off things is eminently sensible. Borrowing to pay rent if you are facing eviction can be sensible if you have a paycheck coming soon. When resources today—time or money—can truly provide greater benefit than they would in the future, a loan is a good idea. When we tunnel, though, we borrow above and beyond what is dictated by this cost-benefit calculus. When faced with scarcity, we borrow when it makes sense in the long run and when it does not.

LET'S PLAY THE FEUD

This explanation for borrowing is different from the usual ones. To explain why the poor borrow excessively, we do not need to appeal to a lack of financial education, the avarice of predatory lenders, or an oversized tendency for self-indulgence. To explain why the busy put off things and fall behind, we do not need to appeal to weak self-control, deficient understanding, or a lack of time-management skills. Instead, borrowing is a simple consequence of tunneling. To test this idea, we resort to one of our favorite tools: creating artificial scarcity in the lab.

This time we turn to *Family Feud*, an American TV game show that our colleague Anuj Shah was curiously familiar with (not what you'd expect from a time-pressed Princeton PhD student, which he was at the time). Contestants on *Family Feud* are asked to name items that belong to categories like "Things Barbie could auction off if she needed money fast." Prior to the show, a hundred random Americans are presented with these categories, and they give their favorite answers. Contestants must then guess the most common answers, earning more points for those that are more popular. The answer "Barbie's dream car" earns 35 points because 35 out of the 100 people gave that as an answer. ("Ken," Barbie's friend, earns 21 points.) Many quiz shows ask trivia questions that require esoteric knowledge, leaving the audience wondering whether the contestants read almanacs for fun. The questions in *Family Feud*, by contrast, are accessible and engrossing because there is no correct answer, only popular ones. It democratizes truth—you could call it the first postmodern game show.

Shah realized that *Family Feud* contestants experience scarcity:

they must respond under time pressure, with very limited time to think. Regular trivia questions require that you *recall* an answer—either you know it or you don't. On *Family Feud,* the questions require a different, more creative approach. When asked, "Name something Barbie would sell," you sort through various candidate responses. You might think of things associated with Barbie and see if any of them might be sold. You could also think of things people typically sell and see if Barbie owns any of those. Each path leads to different answers, from "Ken" to "car." These answers are mere guesses: the potential popularity of each must then be contemplated. Time pressure means fewer paths can be followed, and less time can be devoted to gauging each answer's potential. Unlike busy people who measure scarcity in days or hours, *Family Feud* contestants measure it in seconds. Instead of deciding which project to work on first, they must quickly decide how to come up with the most popular answers.

We recruited Princeton undergraduates to play *Family Feud* in a controlled setting. Participants played several rounds in a fixed amount of time—the amount of time they were allocated determined their "wealth." The "rich" had more time; the "poor" had less. In every round, they saw a new question. At the end of all the rounds, the total number of points they accumulated was converted to dollars.

Having created the rich and the poor, we added the element of real interest to us: we gave them the option to borrow, with interest. Each additional second they chose to use on a round cost them *two* seconds deducted from their total time. We also allowed them to "save": if they finished a round early, the remaining time was "deposited" back into their total.

The poor focused. Per second, they were more effective than the rich; they made more guesses and earned more points. This was especially true in the later rounds, as they were running out of total time: the poor made 50 percent more guesses per second and earned more per guess. Had the rich stayed as intensely focused as the poor, they could have earned many more points. Since we gave the rich more than three times as many seconds, they could have played three times as many rounds and earned three times as many points. Instead, they only earned 1.5 times as much as the poor. Further analyses confirmed that none of the reasons that might come to mind—that the rich, who played longer, were getting bored, or that the best guesses come in early in each round—could explain these results.

The poor were more effective because they tunneled. As a result, they borrowed much more than the rich. Despite the high interest rate, loans looked extremely attractive in the tunnel, much more attractive than a view from the outside would warrant. So the poor resorted to borrowing often, to help themselves right now. But in the end they were hurt by it. When we took away the ability to borrow—you now played each round as best you could and then moved to the next one—the poor earned 60 percent more points; the rich were unaffected.

In another version of the experiment, we re-created a payday loan trap akin to Sandra's experience. The *Family Feud* poor rolled over the loans just like payday borrowers. Their debt would start getting repaid on the next round, making it just a tiny bit shorter. As subsequent rounds got shorter and shorter, subjects felt the need to borrow more seconds. Early borrowing created a vicious cycle for the poor. Pressed for time, too rushed to make productive guesses, they borrowed more. Most of their time was just going to paying off early loans (plus interest). And as before, when they were permitted to borrow, the poor did much worse than when they were not allowed to borrow, an effect that was missing for the rich.

This study shows the intimate link between success and failure under scarcity. The contestants in *Family Feud* borrowed most when they were being most productive, when they were most engaged, when they really felt they needed more time. In a sense they were right to borrow: those extra seconds had a good chance of paying off. In another sense, they were wrong to borrow because that pay-off did not compensate for the interest rate incurred. What they noticed in the tunnel—an extra second could really help right now—was accurate. Their mistake was to neglect what was outside the tunnel: how much would this extra second cost later in the game? It is worth noting that both the rich and the poor showed this pattern of borrowing when they were particularly productive and pressed. It's just that the poor, with their fewer seconds, were in that state a lot more often.

So why did the poor borrow more? Are these results due to tunneling or to something else? Perhaps time pressure leads people to borrow in a panic. After all, it's not every day that you find yourself having to answer questions in fifteen seconds. We have replicated these findings in numerous other contexts. In the Angry Blueberries study from chapter 1, we also allowed for borrowing. And we found that the blueberry-poor subjects—facing no time pressure—borrowed more blueberries and were hurt by the ability to borrow. Focus again played a role: those who took more time on each shot were more likely to borrow: the more engaged, the more they borrowed. We have tried this in many such games, and the results are consistent: scarcity, in whatever form, always leads to borrowing.

Or perhaps our results are due to a general myopia. For example, researchers have documented a bias toward the here and now, which they call *hyperbolic discounting*, or *present bias*. We overvalue immediate benefits at the expense of future ones: this is why it is hard to save, to go to the gym, or to do your taxes early. Of course, present bias would also generate borrowing. Perhaps the poor borrow simply because they are more present biased. In fact, some have tried to explain actual borrowing in the world using this argument. What is striking in our data is that subjects were *randomly assigned* to be poor: they were no different from the "rich" except for the flip of a coin. Clearly, both groups in this study, rich and poor, should show an equal amount of present bias. In fact, any attempt to analyze myopic thinking at the level of personal differences between rich and poor—whether differences in present bias or otherwise—would need to somehow explain how scarcity led to borrowing in our present contexts, where rich and poor were created at random and could not have been more alike.

These studies support our more general hypothesis about the world: the reason the poor borrow is poverty itself. No need to resort to myopia or to financial ineptitude for an explanation. Predatory lenders may certainly facilitate this type of borrowing, but they are not the source. The powerful impulse to borrow, the demand for high interest and potentially spiraling borrowing, the kind that creates a slippery slope and looks so ill advised, is a direct consequence of tunneling.

Scarcity leads us to borrow and pushes us deeper into scarcity.

NEGLECTING THE FUTURE

Imagine you are working under a tight deadline. Suddenly, after weeks of planning, your report is due tomorrow, and you are not quite there. You scramble all night, do all you can, but there are a couple of references you just can't trace. Not in time for tomorrow, anyway. So you submit the report to your boss as is, hoping for the best. And you move on to other pressing matters. The following week, hours before an important trip, you receive a note from your boss: "There are missing references in the report—I need them immediately!" Like a boomerang, that quick fix has come back at you, at the worst moment. Like borrowing, behaviors such as these look attractive inside the tunnel but have potentially spiraling consequences outside it: they can dig you deeper into scarcity.

Two organizational researchers illustrate this with the story of a steel cord manufacturer.

*Because machine uptime was important, the company encouraged maintenance engineers to respond to breakdowns as **quickly** as* *possible [emphasis added]. Even so, overall performance didn't improve. Only after the company started keeping and analyzing records machine by machine instead of person by person did it realize [why]. Engineers . . . would make a quick fix and move on to the next machine. Each . . . breakdown [was] patched three times before it was finally solved.*

In a way the engineers were doing exactly as asked: they were solving problems quickly. Management, you might think, had committed a classic mistake. As organizational researchers would describe it, they were "paying for A while hoping for B." They were asking for speed while hoping for speed and quality. However, this was not simply a case of misaligned incentives; the workers in this case would likely have taken this quick fix even if they were their own bosses. When working to finish things quickly, the engineers tunneled. Inside their tunnel, a quick fix was just the thing needed. Cutting corners was the perfect solution; the cost would only show up later. Much like an expensive loan, a hastily patched solution looks attractive within the tunnel. It saves us something today even as it creates greater expenses in the future. And we will then have more to do, more things to fix, more bills to pay. Patching is a lot like borrowing, a failure to invest and to commit the resources now so that the job is done correctly.

People short on money also patch together short-term solutions. You need a washer but are short on cash? Buy the cheapest appliance. It is, of course, less durable, but that problem falls outside the tunnel. When your tire goes flat, you may literally opt for a cheap patch rather than get a new tire. You know that a patched tire is less advisable, less safe, and less durable than a new tire. But that, too, is outside the tunnel. For now, inside the tunnel, the patch makes life a lot easier. Like a quick fix that saves time now, these are all quick fixes that economize on money today. And as the patches accumulate—for the engineers, the report writers, and the poor—so too do the long-term costs.

The author Steven Covey finds it helpful to classify tasks according to whether they are important and whether they are urgent. He notes that busy people spend their time on tasks that are both urgent and important. This is what it means to be working on a deadline. We get a burst of output working on the tasks that matter and that are due very soon. We would call this a focus dividend.

At the same time, he argues, busy people tend to neglect the *important but not urgent* tasks. These are tasks that can always be put off until later. And so we do. Nowhere do we see this more clearly than in the state of our offices or our homes. When we get very busy, our homes and offices become very messy. There is always something more pressing than keeping order, which is never truly urgent. Of course, we don't make a conscious decision to have a messy life. Instead, the messy surroundings just "happen" while we attend to what's urgent. The messy home or office is the result of a sequence of small choices, mostly passive, effortless, and unnoticed. Rushing to a meeting, you drop a stack of mail on top of another stack of papers. Getting to the phone, you leave the book you're reading open on the sofa. Lots of little things, at the end of which there's a mess. While not urgent, it is important. It is less productive and less pleasant to work and live in a messy space.

Putting off an important but not urgent activity is like borrowing. You gain time today by not doing it. But you incur a cost in the future: you will need to find time (possibly more time) to do it at some later point. In the meantime you may pay a cost for not having done it or lose the benefits that taking care of it could have brought. Having a messy office makes your work just that much less productive. You spend a whole lot of time trying to find those papers under the mail. Every day you incur a little cost. The cost is never big enough to make the thing urgent, as a deadline might. Instead, the neglected office bleeds you by a thousand little cuts.

Scarcity, and tunneling in particular, leads you to put off important but not urgent things—cleaning your office, getting a colonoscopy, writing a will—that are easy to neglect. Their costs are immediate, loom large, and are easy to defer, and their benefits fall outside the tunnel. So they await a time when all urgent things are done. You fail to make these small investments even when the future benefits can be substantial.

The tendency to put off important but not urgent choices shows up in money as well as time. Here is one example. Rag collectors in India travel around town looking for old clothes and cloth pieces being tossed away that can be sold for reuse. It is, as you might imagine, a low-income job: a typical collector earns less than a dollar a day. But it is also a low-investment job: besides labor, the only equipment is a pushcart, which might sell for $30. And yet most rag collectors do not own their pushcart; they rent it, for $5 to $10 a month. Most collectors would like to save up for a pushcart but never quite manage to do that.

Investing in a pushcart is an important but not urgent activity. Like keeping your office clean, it has benefits in the future, but it can always wait; it is not essential right now. The irony, of course, is that if a rag collector had the pushcart, he would have one less expense (the rent), and some of the other pressing expenses wouldn't be as hard to deal with. Of course, that is true for your office as well—if it were better organized, you'd be saving time and end up less rushed. (And with more time to clean the office.) The pushcart is but one of many examples that poverty researchers can point to: even when returns are high, the poor, who need those returns more than anyone, fail to invest in ways that cannot be explained by weak financial institutions or a lack of skills.

If all this sounds vaguely familiar, it may be because you have heard it discussed in politics. A similar focus on the urgent at the expense of the important has long been observed in the workings of governments that, over decades of tight budgeting, have slashed spending on infrastructure. The upkeep of bridges, for example, is a critical investment. Yet it is one that is all too easy to put off when budgets are tight and cuts are needed. Decaying bridges are important but not urgent, and so, according to a 2009 report issued by the American Society of Civil Engineers, approximately one in four rural bridges and one in three urban bridges in the United States are deficient.

FAILING TO PLAN

These various behaviors share one obvious feature: people are behaving myopically. This leads to the most basic implication of tunneling. When we focus so intensely on making ends meet now, we plan less effectively for the future. Of course, studies have shown that planning is a problem for all people. But scarcity makes this problem a whole lot worse.

Think of it this way. On a good day, you might start by looking at your calendar, taking a moment to gauge what's ahead of you today, maybe even getting a sense of what the week holds. Being aware of what is coming allows you to mentally prepare for it, to anticipate a challenging conversation or remind yourself of details so you don't walk into a meeting cold. In contrast, on a busy day you dive right in. You do not step back and scope out the day. You are not quite sure who's at the meeting or what it's about. And it's not only for lack of time. You may have a little time to work, but your mind is so focused on everything that needs to get done that your vision is obscured. You do not look past the first few meetings to what follows later.

Stepping back, detaching from the moment, and thinking ahead requires a wider perspective and some cognitive resources. Thinking about the bills due next month, the other income sources you might anticipate, the new time commitments that might arise, all require some leftover cognitive capacity. With the mind focused on present scarcity, looking ahead risks becoming yet another casualty of the tunneling tax.

Could we re-create this in *Family Feud* as well? As before, subjects were asked to play several rounds. Once again, some were rich (they had many seconds per round to play) and some were poor (they had only a few seconds). But now we gave subjects a chance to look ahead a little, to prepare for future rounds. Half were given a preview of the next round's question. They could think about that question in parallel to thinking about the current one. They could look at it and decide to save or borrow because they think they ought to spend more or less time on it.

The previews helped. To be more accurate, they helped the rich, who looked ahead, took advantage of the information, and scored more points. The poor, on the other hand, did no better with the previews. They were so focused on the current round that they did not expend the mental resources required to look ahead. Scarcity kept them tied to the present, unable to benefit from a glimpse of what the future might hold.

A common theme stretches across many forms of the tunneling tax. Scarcity brings about behaviors that make us shortsighted. We ignore the (future) health cost of eating out when we are busy. We do not think about the implications of paying back payday loans (in the future) when we are tight on cash. We do not consider the (future) benefits of keeping our offices clean when working on a deadline. Of course, there will be exceptions, things that grab our minds no matter where we are. You may forget a meeting today while busy contemplating your wedding a year from now. That's part of the beauty of the human mind. But by and large, the problems of scarcity press on us today. Tomorrow we may also be poor (in time or money), but that is another problem, left for another day. The scarcity that captures us is now, and it yields a tunneling tax and makes us act myopic.

But what is remarkable in this account is that myopia is not a personal failure. Tunneling is not a personal trait. It would be foolhardy, after all, to call Sandra myopic. She rose from a Head Start program to become employee of the year at UNC-W and a board member of Head Start. Similarly, we would not describe the busy people we know as myopic. And the students in our lab studies probably didn't get to Princeton through shortsightedness. Many of the busiest people who borrow time are the same people who have invested years in demanding careers and planned carefully how to get ahead. In fact, as far as personality traits go these people are anything but myopic; rather, it is the context of scarcity that makes us all act that way.

Tunnels limit everyone's vision.

6

THE SCARCITY TRAP

Everywhere is walking distance if you have the time.

—STEVEN WRIGHT

Koyambedu market in Chennai, India, is a spectacle. Sprawling over forty acres, it is crammed with 2,500 shops that sell everything from mangoes to marigolds. Tens of thousands of buyers flow through its colorful displays like one long rush hour on the subway. There is a lot to catch the eye. But perhaps the most interesting thing there is also the easiest to overlook.

In the hours before dawn, the street vendors arrive at the market. Anyone who has been to the world's poorer cities has seen and probably bought from a street vendor. In Chennai, they sit on the roadside, sometimes with a small stall but more often with only a blanket, hawking vegetables, fruits, or fresh flowers. Their business model is simple. A typical vendor buys about 1,000 rupees ($20) of stock in the morning. She sells it throughout the day for about 1,100 rupees, turning a gross profit of 100 rupees (a little over $2). Her business uses two inputs: her own labor and the 1,000 rupees she needs to buy stock every day. Some vendors have 1,000 rupees of their own money, although most (in our data over 65 percent) borrow this money. And the loan does not come cheap: the median vendor pays 5 percent *per day* on what she borrows. In other words, at the end of the day, half of the 100 rupee gross profit goes to paying interest. This, the interest rate that the vendors pay on their loans, is perhaps the most fascinating story in Koyambedu.

You might think that only an economist could use the word *fascinating* in conjunction with the words *interest rate*, but consider this. Nearly every vendor has a small amount of slack in her budget, something she can cut back on. She may buy a cup of tea, a small food treat like a *dosa,* or some candy for a child or grandchild. Suppose that instead of spending, say, 5 rupees on these items every day, she used those 5 rupees to purchase her goods. This way, she borrows 5 rupees less each day. It might seem that it would require two hundred days for the vendor to become free of her 1,000 rupee debt this way. In fact, it would only take *thirty* days. This is the power of compounding (especially when the interest rate is high). Five percent a day compounds quickly.

The magnitude is striking. By cutting back a little, within thirty days the vendor becomes debt free. By becoming debt free, she *doubles* her income for the rest of her working days. A social program for the poor that doubled incomes in a month would be considered astonishing, too good to believe. And yet while every vendor has access to this "program," they fail to use it. And persistently so. In our sample, the typical vendor has been borrowing for 9.6 years.

The vendor is trapped. But what is particularly interesting is how she is trapped. We are used to thinking about scarcity as a slice of reality that is handed out. And in some cases, this is true. The difference between someone who lives in the developing world on $1 a day and someone who lives in the developed world on $100 a day has little to do with behavior and everything to do with the geography of birth. But some scarcity—as with the vendors—is partly the result of human behavior. The vendor could be much less poor if she behaved differently.

The vendor's condition is an example of what we will call a *scarcity trap*: a situation where a person's behavior contributes to her scarcity. People in scarcity traps, like the vendor, may inherit components of scarcity that are beyond their control. Had the vendor been born in New York, she would be significantly richer. But we are particularly interested in that part of scarcity that follows from our behavior. And more than that we are interested in how scarcity generates that behavior, in how scarcity perpetuates and often amplifies itself through what we do when in a scarcity mindset.

Imagine two students, Felix and Oscar. Felix spends a good amount of time on work due at the end of each week and turns in his assignments on time. He is busy but relaxed. Oscar, on the other hand, who is equally talented and taking the same classes, is crunched for time. He is working more hours, feels harried, and rushes to turn in his assignments late every week. What makes Oscar so much busier? He is not taking more classes. He is not a less productive person. Instead, Oscar is simply one step behind: he is working on *last* week's assignments. Unlike Felix, for whom the material is vivid because he just heard the lecture, Oscar takes extra time reminding himself what the class did last week and trying to keep it apart from (yet not forget) this morning's lecture. Oscar works harder but gets no more work done. Oscar is one step behind.

You can also be one step behind with money. Imagine now that Felix and Oscar are farmers, planting the same crop season after season. Felix uses his own savings to buy seed, fertilizer, and to cover living expenses until harvest time. Oscar borrows money for the same purposes. Just as Felix the student looked more relaxed, Felix the farmer now looks richer. Oscar has less to spend. Although both Felix and Oscar earn the same income, some of Oscar's goes to paying off the interest on his loan. Again the problem is that Oscar is one step behind. Felix's income goes to investing for the next season; Oscar's income pays off last season's loan.

These scenarios illustrate how scarcity is not merely about

physical resources. In both cases, Felix and Oscar have the same resources available, yet Oscar experiences scarcity whereas Felix does not. In the first case, Felix and Oscar have the same amount of work and time; in the second, they have the same amount of land and income. Their different outcomes come from how those resources are deployed.

This contrast between Felix and Oscar clarifies what we mean by a scarcity trap. Both face clear constraints, but Oscar is trapped into scarcity through his own behaviors. More generally, the scarcity trap is more than a shortage of physical resources. It is based on a misuse of those assets so that there is an *effective* shortage. It is constantly being one step behind, constantly paying off last month's expenses. It is a way of managing and using what you have so that it looks and feels like you have even less. An initial scarcity is compounded by behaviors that magnify it.

We often observe scarcity in the world and overlook this feature. We might observe Oscar the farmer continuously borrowing, and we might think, "He spends too much. He cannot save." We might see Oscar the student work long hours and miss deadlines, and we might think, "He works too much. He should slow down." But once we understood the logic of the trap, we could then just as easily say, "Oscar spends too little (remember, he is spending less than Felix who has the same land)" or "Oscar doesn't get enough work done (he works more, accomplishing no more than Felix)." The problem is not how much is being spent but *how* it is spent. The perpetual borrower is spending less on what he wants; a lot of his income is going to paying off loans. The person who is perpetually behind is spending less time on getting things done; a lot of his time is going to playing catch-up. More concretely, we might look at the vendors and think they have too little money to save. We might think they have too little income. This is of course true. But scarcity traps them for another reason as well.

In this chapter, we describe scarcity traps, how they operate and why we fall into them. And why, like the vendor who does not put aside her 5 rupees a day, we do not do the things that would get us out of the scarcity trap.

CAUGHT JUGGLING

To understand why we stay stuck, we must first understand an overlooked feature of scarcity traps. In our own work we first encountered it while doing a project with the economist Michael Faye on jewel loans in the rural villages of Tamil Nadu, India. These loans are the equivalent of pawning jewelry. We were working with a bank in a poor village that was offering jewel loans at 13 percent annual interest, and we were surprised to discover that customers routinely preferred to do business with the local moneylender, who charged a much higher rate, more than 70 percent interest. The prevailing wisdom in the village was that jewel loans were used in emergencies; they were a "last-minute" resort. And the moneylender was always there. He had flexible hours. You could knock on his door on weekends and get a loan, whereas the bank was only open during the week and part of Saturday. But, of course, in an emergency you might not be able to wait. It's what you would do once you tunneled. It made sense, at least at first.

But then we saw the data on exactly what counted as an emergency. Number three on the list seemed reasonable: medical expenses. Numbers two and one were more puzzling: school fees and seed purchases. People presumably knew long in advance when school fees would be due and when they would need money for planting. How could that have been an emergency? In fact, when we dug deeper, even some of the medical expenses were not real emergencies; the money was being spent on planned surgeries such as cataracts or childbirth. Why were people reacting to these events only at the last minute? Why were they treating routine, scheduled events as if they were shocks?

Surely you must have experienced this before. When you are

focused on making ends meet this week, you are not dealing with the details of what next week holds. And then, when next week arrives, some things it brings, which you should have anticipated, surprise you. You missed the one-week-prior-purchase discount on an airline ticket you long knew you needed, or you report to your spouse with embarrassment that there are no longer any tickets available for a show you enthusiastically agreed to go to long ago. At work, after frantically finishing one project, you are stunned to realize you have only two days left to work on another. Only recently that deadline was weeks away. What you always "knew" is now a rude surprise.

Play this out over time and it leads to what we call *juggling*: the constant move from one pressing task to the next. Juggling is a logical consequence of tunneling. When we tunnel, we "solve" problems locally and temporarily. We do what we can in the present, but this creates new problems in the future. The bill today generates a loan, which becomes another (slightly bigger) bill in the future. The cheap medical treatment works for a while, but we will need more expensive medical attention later. With many balls in the air, we focus on the ball that is about to drop when we tunnel. Sometimes we solve the problem for good. More often than not, we catch the ball just in time, only to toss it back in the air again.

Juggling is why predictable events are treated like shocks. When you juggle, you tunnel on the balls that are about to drop, and you neglect those high in the air. When those balls "suddenly" descend, they are news to the tunneled juggler, a shock if you will. An observer might see the ball coming down for quite some time. As disinterested parties, we can see school fees looming. To the poor juggling their finances, they only become real when they are imminent.

This way of managing scarcity leads to a messy balance sheet. As we reach repeatedly for the most proximate solution to the most immediate problem, over time these short-term fixes create a complex web of commitments. The result is a messy patchwork of assets and obligations. For the busy, this means burdened and contorted schedules of the kind we talked about in the opening chapter, with "near toppling" piles of to-dos and double-booked appointments. For the poor, it means complicated financial lives. Detailed research in the fascinating book *Portfolios of the Poor* shows that the poor use about ten distinct financial instruments on average. In Bangladesh one instrument—a short-term interest-free loan—was used more than three hundred times by forty-two households in one year. At any point in time, the poor in these surveys owed and were owed money from numerous sources, a patchwork that was created through months and even years of tunneling on the moment's most pressing problem.

Decisions—whether about a new purchase or a new investment—must now navigate this increasingly complex patchwork. The legacy of previous choices makes each new one even more challenging. By juggling we—through our own behavior—make the problem more complex. The messy balance sheet of the scarcity trap increases the complexity and challenge of making ends meet.

Juggling is not about being busy in time. In some places, the poor hold multiple jobs and are truly busy. But in other places, they have plenty of free time, and they still juggle. In farming the end of the harvest cycle is when there is the most juggling. This is the time when the income from the previous harvest has run out. This is when, in our studies, people showed lower fluid intelligence and diminished executive control. At the same time, this is when farmers have little to do other than wait for the crops to be ready. Time-use data suggest they work very few hours those days. And yet there is a lot of juggling happening. Juggling is not about being harried in time; it is about having a lot on one's mind. Much of one's bandwidth ends up being devoted to the balls in the air that are about to fall.

These two features—being one step behind and juggling—define the scarcity trap. Life in the scarcity trap is about having even less than you could have. It is about playing catch-up, dealing with each ball just before it lands and the messy patchwork that emerges as a result. And much of this is a consequence of behavior under scarcity, which raises an obvious question. Why? If there are several ways to manage a fixed resource, why do we get stuck with one that is so terribly inefficient? Why do we not get out of the trap?

GETTING OUT

We have already seen one primary reason we stay stuck in scarcity: tunneling leads us to borrow. And when interest rates are high—such as with the vendors—then this very basic impulse creates more scarcity. This is not just the story of the vendors; it is also the story of Sandra and her payday loans from chapter 5. Though this mechanism is powerful, the psychology of scarcity makes it hard to get out of the trap for other reasons as well.

Getting out of a scarcity trap first requires formulating a plan, something the scarcity mindset does not easily accommodate. Making a plan is important but not urgent, exactly the sort of thing that tunneling leads us to neglect. Planning requires stepping back, yet juggling keeps us locked into the current situation. Focusing on the ball that is about to drop makes it terribly difficult to see the big picture. You would love to stop playing catch-up, but you have too much to do to figure out how. Right now you must make your rent payment. Right now you must meet that project deadline. Long-term planning clearly falls outside the tunnel.

And, of course, perhaps most important, future planning requires bandwidth, which scarcity taxes heavily. The Koyambedu vendor is preoccupied each day with a dozen considerations. How much of each vegetable and fruit should she buy and at what quality? What goods does she have left to sell, and can this stock keep overnight? Why has this been a slow day, and will it stay that way? Every business owner has these kinds of thoughts. The well-off business owner, who can afford the occasional mishap, makes these decisions and moves on. For the vendor, though, these thoughts linger. They burden her bandwidth, and as such her mind keeps going back to them even after she thought she had made a choice. Should she really stock up for next week's festival? Is she taking a big risk? Thoughts like these tug at her mind. They create, as we have seen, a very real bandwidth tax. It is hard under those circumstances to focus on formulating a plan for escaping her scarcity trap.

To make matters a lot worse, the actual plan needed is significantly more complicated than the simple one we sketched. Is putting aside 5 rupees every day the right strategy? Should she put aside more on some days? What about days where she really needs the money? As always, this is not unique to the vendor. In the introduction, we described a simple "plan" for Sendhil and Shawn to get out of their predicaments: say no to all new commitments or new purchases. A real plan would be much more difficult to formulate. Should Shawn really not incur any new expenses? What about expenses that might save money in the long run, like a dental checkup or new tires for the car? And which debts get paid down first? The most immediate? The oldest? The biggest? Juggling and the scarcity trap make for a messy patchwork of obligations. Unraveling the best way out is no trivial challenge.

Finally, even if a plan were formulated, implementation can prove difficult. As we have seen, the best of intentions often fail to be realized. In the moment, faced with a particularly appealing project or purchase, we often can't resist saying yes. Following through on a plan requires bandwidth and cognitive control, and scarcity leaves us with less of both.

Juggling makes getting out even harder. The unexpected happens. You have finally made a plan to climb out, and suddenly you are hit with a ticket for an expired car registration. Reregistering had been put off, one of the many balls tossed back in the air. Now it has landed. One more obligation, and you are back into the scarcity trap.

All this is complicated by the lack of slack. Suppose the vendor judiciously avoids spending on almost everything, day in and day out. She is vigilant and controlled and is accumulating cash as described. Then one day, out of so many days, she slips and makes one impulse purchase. She gets distracted, she miscalculates, something looks so worthwhile; after all, the money is there. And now weeks of mental effort and physical restraint are all lost. Escaping the scarcity trap does not merely require an occasional act of vigilance. It requires constant, everlasting vigilance; almost all temptations must be resisted almost all the time.

Now, might not willpower build up with practice? Might not the poor, having to exercise it constantly, develop stronger willpower? There is little evidence to show that willpower capacity increases with use. (Think of how ironic this would be relative to common belief: the poor having *greater* willpower!) And even if poverty did increase willpower, there is reason to think that this still may not suffice to yield the near infallibility required. Be that as it may, there is instead fairly good evidence to the contrary.

Recent research shows that self-control may actually get depleted as we use it. One study, for example, put dieters in a room with some highly tempting snacks (Doritos, Skittles, M&Ms, salted peanuts) and gave them a computer task to perform. For some, the snacks were placed, highly visible, on the table right next to them. For others, the snacks were far away, out of mind. Having completed the computer task, subjects were given access to large containers of ice cream. Those who had been sitting next to the snacks, continuously resisting the urge, finally caved. They ate significantly more ice cream than those who were less tempted by the distant snacks. Researchers in this field have likened willpower to a muscle, which fatigues with use. By this account, a persistent need to resist temptation would deplete, making it all the more difficult to escape the scarcity trap.

THE ROOT OF THE PROBLEM

Scarcity traps are particularly poignant because there is a feeling that with just one infusion, having just once gotten rid of all debt, a person can break free of the cycle. "If only I had a bit more time," bemoans the person who is perpetually behind, "I could get things done and then stay ahead." For the vendor, if only she could get the cash to buy the fruit (rather than having to save it up in tiny install- ments), she would be out of the debt trap, and her income would double. In all these cases, a one-time infusion of resources would appear to solve the problem.

To see what happens, we decided to give the vendors at Koy- ambedu the cash they needed. Working with the economist Dean Karlan, we ran a study with hundreds of vendors. Half of them we simply followed for a year, recording their finances. We gave the other half a way out of the trap: we bought out all their debt. Over- night, we converted them from borrowers to potential savers. And their incomes effectively doubled.

We wanted to understand the how and why of scarcity traps. Con- sider, for example, some of the explanations usually given for why the vendors find themselves in a debt trap. One possible explanation is they would rather borrow than save because they have nowhere safe to put their savings. They may be unbanked and may worry about the safety of cash sitting around, easily to be stolen or expro- priated by family members. If that were the case, then when we gave them the cash, they ought to have quickly bought something durable and safe with it, and then gone on borrowing. Which might have returned them to the scarcity trap eventually.

Another possible explanation is that the vendors are simply myopic: they are stuck in the debt trap because they do not think enough about the future. This view, it seems to us, cuts against the grain. The vendors wake up at 3 a.m. to ride in a crowded auto rickshaw for forty-five minutes to buy their wares; they spend all day in the hot sun. These hardly sound like the actions of a myopic person. Still, one might argue that at least in their finances the ven- dors focus too little on the future. If that were the case, then once we gave them the cash, the money would be squandered. You can imagine how quickly someone who is myopic would spend a large sum of money. The vendor would quickly find herself back in the debt trap.

For a third explanation, suppose the vendors simply failed to understand the power of compounding. After all, the fact that it would take only thirty days to become debt free—how quickly the interest payments add up—was a surprise to us; perhaps it would also be a surprise to the vendor. To a vendor who would rather borrow and who does not appreciate the cumulative cost of her borrowing, the daily loan appears cheaper than it is. Since giving her the cash will not have altered her perception of compounding, she should continue to find the loan cheap and will soon fall back in the debt trap.

We thought there was quite a bit to be learned by simply giving the vendors the one-time infusion needed to break free of the debt trap. We then tracked the behavior of the now debt-free vendors over the following year.

During the first few months, the deft-free vendors did not fall back into the debt trap. They did not blow the cash on unwise expenses. They did not decide to store it in some other format for safety. They did not start borrowing again. It looked as if they now saw the hazards in the debt trap and persisted in staying out of it. This largely accords with the qualitative data: the vendors seemed to fully understand that being one step behind was costly. Like the busy person behind on his obligations, they seemed to be fully aware that they were paying a steep price for living in the scarcity trap.

But that was not the full story. In the ensuing months they fell back, bit by bit. Or, rather, we should say one by one. By the end of the year, they all had accumulated as much debt as those whose debt we had left alone. So while the standard explanations are not supported by the data—the vendors do not fall back right away— neither is the view that those in a scarcity trap just need a one-time infusion to rid them of the debt.

How are we to explain this behavior? Why do the vendors eventually fall back? What is it about the scarcity trap that operates so dramatically to alter their lives again, even after they have been given enough money to double their incomes?

SHOCKS

The core of the problem is a lack of slack. Even after our cash infusion, the vendor is still living on less than two dollars a day. After all, her income must feed more than just herself. When packed so tightly, suppose she hits a bump in the road—a relative's wedding comes up and she has to buy a gift. In a place like India, social custom dictates buying a big-enough gift, so how this bump is managed partly depends on whether the vendor is in a debt cycle or a savings cycle.

In a debt cycle, the vendor faces a difficult challenge. She must make trade-offs: what to give up to buy the gift? Or perhaps she'll simply buy a smaller gift. She tunnels, but credit is not much of an option; she is already using the moneylender to buy fruits and vegetables. She weathers the storm by sacrificing what little she can. She may feel the pain of what she has to sacrifice to buy the gift and may feel ashamed at the meager gift she is able to afford.

Now picture the vendor in a savings cycle, after we've absolved her of the debt. When she faces the sudden need to buy a gift, she also tunnels. She must address this pressing need. And for her there's an "easy" solution at hand: she has cash sitting around. Of course, it is for emergency needs only, but this is one. She can borrow her working capital and use the available cash to handle the wedding gift. How will she exit another debt cycle? What are the costs? By now we know the answer to those questions: "I can't worry about that now." Those concerns fall strictly outside the tunnel.

In this view, the vendor falls back into the scarcity trap because she did not have enough slack in her budget to weather the shocks she faces. Shocks bigger than her slack push her right back into the psychology of scarcity. And once there, one of the first casualties is savings. Though such evidence is never direct, the data from the vendors support this interpretation. The vendors do not fall back immediately but gradually, one by one, as if being picked off, exactly what you would expect as shocks hit them sporadically. In many cases the vendors reported a shock as the trigger for their renewed borrowing and eventual decline.

All this should be very familiar, when you think of it in the context of time. Imagine we give someone who is very busy and perpetually behind a gift of time: overdue obligations disappeared, all outstanding time commitments resolved. This formerly overwhelmed but now just very busy person might stay ahead for a while. But eventually she, too, will likely slip up: an unexpected glitch on a large project, a medical setback at home, just plain lethargy and a momentary loss in productivity—and she suddenly finds herself behind again.

Any slight instability is a threat hovering over a life lived at the edge of a scarcity trap, because with little slack to absorb it, instability is almost certain to be felt. In *Portfolios of the Poor*, the authors observe that the lives of the poor are full of instability and shocks; that those living on $2 a day are not able to come by $2 every day. They have some $3 days and some $1 days. Life at the bottom is volatile. In the United States and other developed nations, that volatility may be lower, but it is still pronounced. The poor face variable income from many sources. They often have multiple jobs, all potentially intermittent. Many of their jobs are by the hour, and hours vary quite a bit. And, of course, job loss is always a serious possibility. Sudden expenses—a broken-down car or illness—also pose a problem. Consider the following account, drawn from interviews at a community college in New Mexico:

> [Automotive] repairs themselves are unexpected expenses. These respondents describe repair bills in the hundreds of dollars, which represent a significant percentage of their reported monthly incomes. To pay for these repairs, respondents borrow money from friends and relatives, seek financial assistance . . . or wait for anticipated, lump-sum financial windfalls, like academic financial assistance.

What matters most is the slack available to weather each new shock. This is why instability can have such an impact. Without enough slack, where do you get the money to fix your car when it breaks down? If you had liquid savings, you would use those. If you were well off, you would just cut back on other consumption, perhaps forgo that expensive dinner you'd been planning for the weekend. If you had a second car, you would perhaps delay making the repair until you carefully secured the money to fix this one. These are all easy or cheap options. But when you lack savings or a second car, and have no dinners to cancel, this becomes a serious challenge: where will you get the money? At that moment, you tunnel. You borrow. You start on a path back into a scarcity trap.

All this suggests that we should deepen our notion of scarcity. Scarcity is not merely the gap between resources and desires *on average*. Even if, as in the case of the vendor, there are many days with slack, it is the days of scarcity that matter. To be free from a scarcity trap, it is not enough to have more resources than desires on average. It is as important to have enough slack (or some other mechanism) for handling the big shocks that may come one's way at any moment. Social scientists—and especially economists—have understood for quite some time the importance of uncertainty in affecting outcomes. We know that uncertain returns can reduce investments, that uncertain income streams can create anxiety and reluctance. The present discussion, however, places a different perspective on uncertainty and instability in the context of scarcity. It says that periods of scarcity can elicit behaviors that end up pulling us into a scarcity trap. And with scarcity traps, what would otherwise be periods of abundance punctuated by moments of scarcity can quickly become perpetual scarcity.

This, incidentally, does not mean that the only way to avoid scarcity traps is to have wealth large enough to weather all shocks. It does not mean that the only way to solve the vendor's problem is to give her even *more* money. Rather, this discussion highlights the need for instruments for buffering against shocks. If the vendor had a low-cost loan or a liquid savings account—to be accessed solely for emergencies—that would give her the slack she needs in those critical moments of no slack. Similarly, insurance against some of these shocks would also solve the problem. Of course, many have realized the benefits of such buffers. But the benefits appear to be far larger than we had anticipated. These become buffers not merely for managing risk. They are also bulwarks against slipping back into the scarcity trap.

FEAST AND FAMINE

We can blame the vendor's relapse into a scarcity trap on the shocks that befell her, but we can also look to the lack of a buffer. Since she knows she faces a volatile environment, why not put money aside as a precaution during better times? Of course, vendors in India are not the only ones guilty of this mistake. The poor around the world have far too little *liquid* savings. As we mentioned earlier, studies report that half of all Americans say that they cannot get $2,000 in thirty days if they faced an emergency. And the data show that the poor, who are exposed to more shocks, tend to have even less liquid savings.

Looked at this way, the vendor's problems began well before the shock. The seeds of the scarcity trap were sown during a period of at least relative abundance. And the same dynamic appears to happen with time as well. You work feverishly to finish a project; you are behind, and life is miserable, and you vow never to do this again. When the deadline passes, you finally come up for air. The next deadline is weeks away. Thank goodness, you can now relax. A few weeks later, you wonder where the time went. You are once again frantically working against the clock. Like the vendor's scarcity, your scarcity originates with mistakes made during periods of relative abundance.

During periods of abundance, we waste time or money. We are too lax. In the harvest study from chapter 2, the farmers were poor before harvest, but they didn't have to be. Had they managed their money better after the harvest, they would not have found themselves lacking toward the end of the harvest cycle. They were poor right before this harvest only because they had mismanaged their finances when they were still flush. This is different from the problem of borrowing while poor. This is about waste when money is abundant. The result is an avoidable cycle punctuated by recurring periods of abundance followed by threatened periods of scarcity.

We have so far focused on problems caused by the scarcity mindset. We tunnel and we neglect. Our bandwidth is taxed, and we are less farsighted and more impulsive. All this might inadvertently suggest that during periods of abundance we are perfectly calculating and farsighted. Of course we are not. Decades of research have shown that even—no, *especially*—at the best of times we are prone to procrastination, an exaggerated focus on the present, and bouts of fuzzy optimism. We put off work that needs to be done. We squander money that should have been saved. We misallocate our abundance, saving and accomplishing too little sufficiently to insulate from scarcity that might come. Of course, both the rich and the poor do this. But the rich, because they have slack, come out fine, whereas the poor and the busy, carrying on with too little slack, are one shock away from falling into a scarcity trap.

Staying clear of the scarcity trap requires more than abundance. It requires enough abundance so that, even after overspending or procrastinating, we still leave enough slack to manage most shocks. Enough abundance so that even after extensive procrastination, we still have enough time left to manage an unexpected deadline. Staying out of the scarcity trap requires enough slack to deal with the shocks the world brings and the troubles we impose on ourselves.

Tying all this together, we see that scarcity traps emerge for several interconnected reasons, stretching back to the core scarcity mindset. Tunneling leads us to borrow so that we are using the same physical resources less effectively, placing us one step behind. Because we tunnel, we neglect, and then we find ourselves needing to juggle. The scarcity trap becomes a complicated affair, a patchwork of delayed commitments and costly short-term solutions that need to be constantly revisited and revised. We do not have the bandwidth to plan a way out of this trap. And when we make a plan, we lack the bandwidth needed to resist temptations and persist. Moreover, the lack of slack means that we have no capacity to absorb shocks. And all this is compounded by our failure to use the precious moments of abundance to create future buffers.

A DIFFERENT KIND OF SCARCITY TRAP

Picture someone in a new city. In his old town he has many friends, but in this new town he knows no one. After a few days, the solitary existence begins to weigh on him. He talks on the phone with his friends back home, but it's not the same. He dines in front of the TV, feeling sheepish about going out to eat alone. How does one go about meeting people? He decides to try a dating website, and after a few e-mail exchanges he sets up a date. But as the day approaches, he finds himself increasingly nervous, more nervous than he has ever been before about a date. The date starts badly. He tries to make jokes, but his delivery is strained, and the evening falls flat. He is so preoccupied with what he will say next that he finds it hard to pay attention to what his date says. He realizes he is just trying too hard. The date is a disaster.

This person, you might say, is trapped by social scarcity. His loneliness is making it hard for him to meet new friends and creating behaviors that perpetuate his loneliness. But this scarcity trap is different from what we have considered so far. There is no borrowing; there is no failure to save for shocks. Instead the problems—ruining a punch line or failing to listen—come from trying too hard to be liked, from focusing too much on scarcity.

Studies have shown that the lonely overfocus. In one study, researchers asked people who rated themselves as lonely to talk into a recorder. They had no specific task. They were simply to describe themselves and be interesting. All they knew was that someone else would listen to them later and rate them. Predictably, when raters listened to what the lonely had to say, they were not impressed. They rated the lonely as significantly less interesting than those who were not lonely. This is hardly surprising. You might say, "That is probably why they are lonely."

Another version of the experiment shows that this interpretation misses something important. In this version, the lonely participants talked into a recorder with one important difference. This time they did not expect anyone to listen and to judge them. They were just talking, being themselves. In these recordings, independent judges now rated the lonely to be just as interesting as the nonlonely. The problem of the lonely was not that they were boring or otherwise unappealing. Their problem was that they performed badly when they thought it mattered. It was not a lack of knowledge, either. Remember the study mentioned in the introduction: the lonely were better at deciphering others' emotions—that was their focus dividend. But when the stakes are high, they do not use these skills well. You could say the lonely choke. Think back to the situations where you have felt tongue-tied or particularly inept. If you are like us, you probably still remember some of those social situations that you botched exactly because you wanted them to go particularly well.

Of course, choking is not unique to the lonely. Nowhere is choking more transparent than in sports. In basketball, the free throw is among the easiest shots to make. It is not far from the basket and you get to attempt it at your own pace, with no one guarding you. The name itself suggests how easy a free throw is. The world record was once held by a seventy-two-year-old man who made 2,750 free throws in a row. Shooting over 90 percent in principle should not be hard for anyone with enough practice. Yet some players find it inordinately difficult. In the 2002–3 season, the professional basketball player Bruce Bowen typified the problem. That year, he made only 40 percent of his free throws. The problem for Bowen was not a lack of skill, as he was able to make much harder shots. That same season he led the league in three-point shooting, making 44 percent of those shots. A three-point shot is from much farther away and often from a weird angle. It must be shot quickly and often you have another player in your face or running toward you. Yet that season Bowen shot these shots better than free throws.

Any sports fan knows endless stories of the choking player. The basketball player who fails to sink a simple free throw that would have won the game. The golfer whose simple putt somehow goes errant at the time when it is most important. No matter how stellar the play to date, there is always trepidation in those moments. The drama is high exactly because we fear, or perhaps even anticipate, choking.

Researchers now better understand the psychology of choking. Many actions in sports can be done either consciously or automatically. You can think about your arm's movement while shooting a free throw. You can focus on the follow-through motion of a golf swing. Or you can just do it automatically, with your mind blank. For professional athletes, these activities are so routine that they are remarkably good at doing them automatically. In fact, they are *better* at doing them automatically. (Next time you run down the stairs, think about the movement of your feet. But please do not hold us accountable if you come close to tripping. Though you are a professional stair user, thinking about the task will make you much less effective at it.) For a beginner, remembering to pull the elbow in on a free throw (or to follow through on a tennis shot) improves performance. The conscious attention helps. For a professional, these are all actions to be done automatically. At this level of skill, extra focus prevents muscle coordination from happening in the quickest, most natural way. Athletes choke *because* they focus.

Choking is the tip of a much broader phenomenon. Psychologists have found across a wide variety of tasks that performance and attention, or arousal, are linked by an inverted U-curve. Too little attention and performance is weak. Too much attention and the excessive arousal worsens performance again.

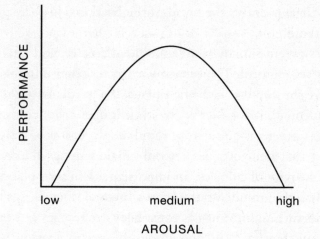

For tasks where we are far to the left of the peak, more attention is good. For other tasks—free-throw shooting, if you're a pro—we can find ourselves on the other side of the curve, giving too much attention. Free throws are hard for some good players because they focus too much. Bruce Bowen did not have time to think about his three-point shots. But free throws gave him far too much time to think. To make matters worse, the more you try not to think about it, the more you do. Psychologists call this an ironic process. When asked to not think of a white bear, people can think of little else.

Returning to the lonely, we now see why they do so badly. They choke exactly because scarcity focuses them. There is an inverted U-shaped curve for conversation as well. Someone who is distracted and unfocused on a conversation is uninteresting. Someone who is far too focused can seem clingy or needy. The lonely do badly exactly because they cannot think about anything besides managing their loneliness. They do badly because they are past the peak of the inverted U. Instead of listening to their partner and making small talk, they are attentively focused on "Do they like me?" or "Will this be the funniest story?" Just as expert free throw shooters do better when focusing less on the free throw, the lonely could do better by focusing less on their social need. Yet scarcity prevents that. It draws the mind of the lonely to just the place they need to avoid.

Dieters face a similar problem. One of the biggest challenges of dieting is self-control. The easiest way to resist an impulse is if you never have the impulse in the first place. If a particular treat does not cross your mind, it is easier to avoid. If it does cross your mind, the sooner you can get it out of your mind the easier it is to resist. Thinking about that delicious dessert only makes things harder. Dieting creates a scarcity of calories, and that scarcity in turn places the dessert firmly top of mind. Studies have shown that food ends up top of mind of dieters and not just because they are hungry but because of the scarcity they face. In one study, the preoccupation with food grew only more intense among dieters who had just eaten a chocolate bar. Physiologically, they had more calories; psychologically, they had now exacerbated the trade-offs they needed to make. Diets prove difficult precisely because they focus us on that which we are trying to avoid.

In both of these cases, the key feature of scarcity—that it grabs attention—turns into a hindrance. Dieters and the lonely struggle with their scarcity precisely because scarcity makes them focus on every detail.

THE SILVER LINING

The poor stay poor, the lonely stay lonely, the busy stay busy, and diets fail. Scarcity creates a mindset that perpetuates scarcity. If all this seems bleak, consider the alternative viewpoint: the poor are poor because they lack skills. The lonely are lonely because they are unlikable; dieters lack willpower; and the busy are busy because they lack the capacity to organize their lives. In this alternative view, scarcity is the consequence of deep personal problems, very difficult to change.

The scarcity mindset, in contrast, is a contextual outcome, more open to remedies. Rather than a personal trait, it is the outcome of environmental conditions brought on by scarcity itself, conditions that can often be managed. The more we understand the dynamics of how scarcity works upon the human mind, the more likely we can find ways to avoid or at least alleviate the scarcity trap.

7

POVERTY

Before you criticize someone, you
should walk a mile in their shoes. That
way, when you criticize them, you're a mile
away and you have their shoes.
—JACK HANDEY, *SATURDAY NIGHT LIVE* WRITER

Poverty is surely the most widespread and important example of scarcity. The breadth and depth of poverty in the modern world is striking. UNICEF estimates that 22,000 children die each day due to poverty. Nearly one billion people are so illiterate that they cannot even sign their names. Half the children in the world live below the global poverty line. Roughly 1.6 billion people live without electricity. Even in a country like the United States, poverty is stark. Nearly 50 percent of all children in the United States will at some point be on food stamps. About 15 percent of American households had trouble finding food for the family at some point during the year.

We have thus far treated the varieties of scarcity as if they were interchangeable. We have bounced from dieting to deep poverty to time pressure with little concern for the differences. This, after all, is our thesis. If scarcity evokes a unique psychology irrespective of its source, then we are free to treat the varieties of scarcity all the same. If there is a common psychology of scarcity, shouldn't everything we observe about the poor also hold for the busy or for dieters?

Just because the different forms of scarcity share common ingredients does not mean they will have similar outcomes. In chemistry, the same basic elements can produce different compounds, depending on the proportions. Carbon and oxygen can form carbon dioxide—an essential ingredient for the cycle of life—or they can form carbon monoxide, a deadly pollutant. Same ingredients, very different outcomes. Our analysis of scarcity follows a similar logic. There are the common ingredients: tunneling, borrowing, a lack of slack, the bandwidth tax. But these play themselves out in different ways, depending on the context. In the case of money scarcity, borrowing is an obvious feature. In the case of loneliness, however, it is unclear what borrowing even means. That particular ingredient, like that additional atom of oxygen, is simply missing in the case of the lonely. The ingredients of poverty create circumstances that are particularly hostile to the scarcity mindset.

A well-to-do professional who is very busy is in that situation because he has taken on many projects. He would be less busy if he simply took on fewer. He could, in effect, choose to have less scarcity. The extent of his scarcity is, to some extent, discretionary.

This discretion provides a critical safety valve that can limit scarcity's stress and damage. The tourist frantically trying to see Italy in a week can only get so worked up about her scarcity of time. At some point, she may simply say, "Forget this, I'll just see the Colosseum on another visit," or, "I'll stay another day in Rome and see less of the south." This safety valve limits the damage and depth of the scarcity trap. For those who have some discretion, the scarcity trap threatens but only so much. The overcommitted can miss a few deadlines. Dieters can take a break from their diet. The busy can take vacations.

One cannot take a vacation from poverty. Simply deciding not to be poor—even for a bit—is never an option. There is no equivalent in the world of poverty to the dieter deciding to live with being overweight or the busy person giving up on some of his ambitions. It would be silly to suggest that the rural poor in India should cope with money scarcity by simply moderating their desires. Basic desires, for clothing, freedom from disease, even modest toys to bring joy to one's children, are significantly harder to cast off. The poor are not alone in having mandated scarcity. The dieter who faces a serious medical condition, the profoundly lonely, and those who are busy because they must work two jobs to pay the rent all have little choice. A lack of discretion makes for a particularly extreme form of scarcity.

This discussion clarifies what we mean by poverty. We mean cases of economic scarcity where changing what you want, or think you need, is simply not viable. Some of these hard-to-change needs are biological, such as hunger for the subsistence farmer, and some are socially constructed. What we feel we need depends on what others have and on what we've gotten used to. Indoor plumbing, for example, would hardly make anyone in the developed world feel terribly lucky these days, yet it was pretty much inconceivable until the last quarter of the nineteenth century, and it is still a dream in many places today. To the subsistence farmer, it is a luxury; to someone living in New Jersey, it is a necessity. Driving a car was a status symbol in the fifties and remains so in many parts of the world. In other parts of the world today, it is a necessity. A deep and complicated question is: How exactly do these needs compare? Does the poor American who cannot afford adequate plumbing really feel a lot like the poor farmer who cannot afford a shirt or the poor European who cannot afford a car? There is too little evidence to know how comparable these two forms of poverty—absolute versus relative—are psychologically. For our purposes, they are all examples of poverty.

Poverty is extreme in another way. Consider the parents of a newborn, who are suddenly time scarce. They also do not have the option to "want less"; the baby needs to be taken to the doctor, and fed, and changed, and cuddled, and bathed, and rocked (forever) to sleep. There are just so many nondiscretionary activities to juggle. But if you are a parent with money, your time scarcity can be alleviated in another way. You can hire a nanny or a maid, order in food rather than cook, use an accountant, employ a gardener, all of which will free up time. Similarly, if you are on a diet, with plenty of money, you can buy tasty but healthy food. Money, because it is fungible, can be used to compensate for other forms of scarcity.

The reverse—trying to alleviate the scarcity of money—is much harder. Sure, you can try to work a few more hours, but in most cases you don't have much to give, and it will bring limited extra wealth and leave you even busier and more exhausted. Less money means less time. Less money means it is harder to socialize. Less money means lower quality and less healthy food. Poverty means scarcity in the very commodity that underpins almost all other aspects of life.

We have used the psychology of scarcity to create an empathy bridge. We have used experience with one form of scarcity (say, time) to connect to another form (money). Having known what it's like to badly need a little more time, we might start to imagine what it's like to desperately need a little more money or even more friends. We used this bridge to draw a connection between a busy manager fretting about insufficient time before a deadline and a person short on cash fretting about insufficient funds to pay rent.

This empathy bridge, though, only goes so far. After all, the manager can say, "Forget it. I'll just strive less and alter my work–life balance," whereas the person stressed for cash can't simply say, "Forget it. I don't need the apartment after all." So while both time and money can tax bandwidth, the *magnitude* of those taxes—their gravity—can be very different.

THE ELEPHANT IN THE ROOM

Most conversations about poverty feature an elephant in the room.

Take the case of diabetes, which affects 285 million people worldwide. It is a serious disease with consequences that include coma, blindness, limb amputations, and death. Luckily, it is now a manage-able disease. Drugs taken regularly—sometimes in pill form, some-times with an injection—can prevent diabetes from doing too much damage. Yet diabetes remains a major problem. Part of the problem is pharmacology: medicine has not fully cured the disease. But a big-ger part of the problem is psychology. For any medicine to work, people must take it. Yet diabetics take their medication only 50 to 75 percent of the time, greatly reducing its efficacy.

Think of how striking this is. Decades of medical research trans-form a debilitating, deadly disease into a manageable one. But we trip up on the last mile, on the most trivial step: taking a pill or shot. This last mile plagues much of medicine. Twenty years ago, we would have been ecstatic to have the antiretroviral drugs for the treatment of HIV that we have today. Yet millions have died because they did not take the medications consistently. For tuberculosis, the problem is so large that the standard delivery protocol in developing countries, DOTS (directly observed therapy), is designed just to address this problem: someone comes every day to watch you take the pill. In some countries, we cannot afford to provide tuberculosis medica-tion. Not because the pills are expensive—they are cheap antibiotics—but because the cost of DOTS is too high. One remarkable medical achievement after another stumbles on nonadherence, this vagary of human behavior.

Nonadherence affects many people, but it is particularly concen-trated in one group: the poor. While people at every income level may fail to take their medications, the poor do so most often. Dis-ease after disease—HIV, diabetes, tuberculosis—the same pattern repeats itself. No matter the location, the kind of medication, or the side effects, one thing stays the same: the poor take their medication least consistently.

Moving to a very different context, consider the case of agricul-tural yields. The amount of crop that can be grown on a plot of land affects all of society. It determines food prices, world trade, environ-mental impacts, and even the feasible population of the planet. It matters perhaps most of all to the farmer: his entire income depends on his yield. As with medicine, technology has made terrific strides in improving yields and sustainability: better seeds, farming techniques, and organic farming methods. Yet like the doctors above, agricultural scientists who work on these issues are continuously vexed by one thing: farmer behavior.

For thousands of years, farmers have known that weeding dramatically improves crop yields. Weeds suck away nutrients and water from the main crop. Weeding requires little skill or machinery, merely some tedious work. Yet farmers in the poorest parts of the world fail to weed. Some estimate that losses from not weeding in parts of Africa are more than 28 percent of total yield. In Asia, uncontrolled weed growth has been estimated to cost up to 50 percent of total rice output. It's possible that these estimates are too large. But even a 10 percent increase in yield would be a fantastic return for a couple of days of tedious work. Besides, since weeding increases output without using more money or land, a 10 percent increase in yield means a 20 to 30 percent increase in earnings, a pretty hefty sum. Nonetheless, many farmers leave this money on the table by failing to weed regularly or enough. And even within these areas, the biggest offenders are again the poorest farmers.

To move to yet another example, take parenting. Researchers have now spent a great deal of time studying how people raise their children. Do parents raise their voices needlessly? Do they show love and support in times of need? Are they consistent in their application of rules, or do they make demands that are haphazard and arbitrary? Do they give positive feedback when the child does well? How much do they engage with the child as opposed to plopping her in front of the TV? Do they help with homework?

One broad theme emerges from decades of this research: the poor are worse parents. They are harsher with their kids, they are less consistent, more disconnected, and thus appear less loving. They are more likely to take out their own anger on the child; one day they will admonish the child for one thing and the next day they will admonish her for the opposite; they fail to engage with their children in substantive ways; they assist less often with the homework; they will have the kid watch television rather than read to her. We now know more about what makes for a good home environment, and poor parents are less likely to provide it.

The poor fall short in many ways. The poor in the United States are more obese. In most of the developing world, the poor are less likely to send their children to school. The poor do not save enough. The poor are less likely to get their children vaccinated. The poorest in a village are the ones least likely to wash their hands or treat their water before drinking it. When they are pregnant, poor women are less likely to eat properly or engage in prenatal care. We could go on. And on.

These facts follow like a tedious argument of insidious intent (to butcher T. S. Eliot). The overwhelming question in this case is an old, almost tired one. Why do the poor fail so badly and in so many ways?

This is the elephant in the room.

CONFRONTING THE ELEPHANT

When we do confront the disturbing facts, it is natural first to question their interpretation. Perhaps the poor are not "failing" to take their medication; perhaps these pills are simply too expensive. Why do they not weed? Because they are too busy. Why do they not parent better? Because they grew up in similar circumstances and have not been taught other parenting skills. Surely, all these issues of access and cost and skills play some role. But time after time, when you look at the data, these factors alone cannot explain the failures. For example, the poor in the United States who are on Medicaid pay nothing for their medications, yet they fail to take them regularly. The poor in rural areas report that their time is abundant between harvests, yet they do not weed. These failings cannot be dismissed as merely circumstantial: at the core there is a problem of behavior.

Another instinctive response is to question the facts themselves. Whether the poor fail or not is really in the eye of the beholder. Perhaps they are not failing. Perhaps those who created the data are biased. There is plenty of compelling psychology to back up such assertions. In one study, for example, subjects watch a video of a young girl, Hannah, taking a test. Her performance is ambiguous: she gets some hard questions right and some easy ones wrong. One group of subjects sees Hannah against a background that suggests she comes from a poor family; another sees a background suggestive of an upper-middle-class family. Both groups watch her take the test and then gauge her performance and abilities. Those who observed "poor" Hannah saw more errors, judged that she did worse, and guessed she was at a lower grade level than those who observed "rich" Hannah.

It seems easy to be biased in our interpretation of the data about the poor. Given that we hold highly negative stereotypes about the poor, essentially defined by a failure (they are poor!), it is natural to attribute personal failure to them. Is it a surprise then that researchers "see" the disadvantaged failing? Unfortunately, when you look closer, the elephant cannot be taken out of the room so easily. Most of these data are genuine correlations, not just biased perceptions.

Nor can the data be dismissed as the result of researchers' political bias. The data are often collected by researchers without an agenda, and when they have one, it is often contrary to what they find. Other times, the findings are incidental to their research, not something they were looking for. Agronomists and medical researchers collect large data sets where income is but one variable; they report this among many other correlations. They neither went looking for findings about the poor nor do they trumpet them. Moreover, when researchers finally do focus on poverty, they often come to the subject with a pro-poor bias. Scholars working on families or obesity or any number of other domains that focus on poverty tend to have a natural affinity for their subjects, and they report discomfort with what they find. Perhaps most compelling is the sheer breadth and depth of this evidence. It comes not from an isolated study or polemic piece of research. Many efforts have accumulated quite a bit of data. And together they present quite a large elephant.

If we cannot dismiss the elephant, how can we make sense of it? One way is to assume that the causality runs from failure to poverty; that the poor are poor precisely because they are less capable. If your earnings depend on making good choices, then it follows naturally that those who fail end up poor. There are obvious complications to this view. Accidents of birth—such as what continent you are born on—have a large effect on your chance of being poor. Still, one prevailing view explains the strong correlation between poverty and failure by saying failure causes poverty.

Our data suggest causality runs at least as strongly in the other direction: that poverty—the scarcity mindset—causes failure.

PARENTING

One study on parenting focused on air traffic controllers. What made air traffic controllers interesting is that their jobs change daily and can be intense. Some days there are many planes in the air, weather conditions are bad, and there are congestion and delays. On those days the cognitive load—tunneling for long hours on landing all planes safely—is very high. Other days are more relaxed, with not many planes in the air or on the mind. What the researchers found was that the number of planes in the air on a particular day predicted the quality of parenting that night. More planes made for worse parents. Or, if you don't mind a more vulgar framing, think of it this way. The same air traffic controller acted "middle class" after an easy day at work and acted "poor" after a hard day's work.

Of course you know this yourself. You come home from work after a long, frustrating day. All you want is some peace and quiet, but your kids are enthusiastically watching cartoons. The TV is not terribly loud but certainly enough to grate on your nerves. You implore your kids to turn the thing off, happy you managed not to be brusque. They respond that this is their television time, that you had explicitly promised that they could watch TV at this hour if they had finished their homework, which they have done. You hesitate for a second but the noise is too much. "Just turn the damn thing off!" you bark. Later you feel bad. It is not how you'd like to be with your wonderful children, but you couldn't stop yourself.

And you would have good reason to be upset. While research on child rearing is murky, there are a few things that emerge as clearly good, and they are pretty intuitive. Consistency is near the top of the list. It is tough and anxiety-producing for children to learn things—discipline, rules of conduct, a sense of comfort—if parents are inconsistent in their statement and application. Yet this is easier said than done. Being a good parent, even when you know what to do, is hard. Consistency requires constant attention, effort, and steadfastness.

Good parenting generally requires bandwidth. It requires complex decisions and sacrifice. Children need to be motivated to do things they dislike, appointments have to be kept, activities planned, teachers met and their feedback processed, tutoring or extra help provided or procured and then monitored. This is hard for anyone, whatever his resources. It is doubly hard when your bandwidth is reduced. At that moment, you do not have the freedom of mind needed to exercise patience, to do the things you know to be right. A crowded airspace during the day leaves a crowded mind that night. A difficult day as an air traffic controller at work makes for a worse parent at home.

The poor have their own planes in the air. They are juggling rent, loans, late bills, and counting days till the next paycheck. Their bandwidth is used up in managing scarcity. Just as air traffic controllers might have their heads buzzing, so do the poor. An outside observer in their living room who didn't know about all those planes in the air would indeed conclude that these parents lacked skills.

A recent study showed some evidence of this. As we have seen, poor parents receive food stamps once a month, but by the end of each month they are running short. The end of the month is when their bandwidth is most taxed, the time when parenting is likely to be toughest. The economist Lisa Gennetian and her colleagues showed that these are also the times when children of parents who receive food stamps were most likely to be acting out and end up being disciplined in school.

Being a good parent requires many things. But most of all it requires freedom of mind. That is one luxury the poor do not have.

POOR IN MORE THAN ONE WAY

The poor are not just short on cash. They are also short on bandwidth. This is exactly what we saw in the mall studies and in the harvest studies. The same person when experiencing poverty—or primed to think about his monetary troubles—did significantly worse on several tests. He showed less flexible intelligence. He showed less executive control. With scarcity on his mind, he simply had less mind for everything else.

This is important because so many of our behaviors, not just parenting, rely on bandwidth. For example, an overtaxed bandwidth means a greater propensity to forget. Not so much the things you know (what psychologists call declarative memory), like the make of your first car, but things that fall under what psychologists call prospective memory—memory for things that you had planned to remember, like calling the doctor or paying a bill by the due date. These tasks must be maintained alive in your head, and they get neglected when your bandwidth is reduced. Is it any surprise then that the poor fail to take their medications? Some may find this hard to believe: how can you forget something so important? But memory doesn't work that way. You don't remember as a function of long-term value. Certainly no one forgets to take painkillers: the pain is a constant reminder. Diseases such as diabetes, though, are "silent"; their consequences are not immediately felt. There is nothing to remind a person with an overburdened bandwidth to take those medications.

Another consequence is reduced productivity at work. Nearly every task—from processing drive-thru orders to arranging grocery shelves—requires working memory, the capacity to hold several pieces of information active in our minds, until we use them. By taxing working memory, poverty leads us to perform less well. It makes us less productive because our mental processor is occupied with other concerns. This creates a tragic situation where the poor, who most need the wages of their labor, also have their productivity most heavily taxed.

An overtaxed bandwidth means a reduced ability to process new information. How much of a lecture will you absorb if your mind constantly gets pulled away? Now think of a low-income college student whose mind keeps going back to making rent. How much will she absorb? Our data above suggest that much of the correlation between income and classroom performance may be explained by the bandwidth tax. And learning is impeded not only in the classroom. Many public health programs rely on the poor to absorb new information. Campaigns try to educate the public about the importance of eating healthier, smoking less, obtaining prenatal care, getting screened for HIV, and so on. In poor countries, extension workers reach out to farmers to educate them about the latest crops or the latest pests. It should not come as a surprise that these efforts are less successful with the poor, largely failing to get them to smoke less, eat healthier, or adopt the latest farm practices. Absorbing new information requires working memory.

The bandwidth tax also means that you have fewer mental resources to exert self-control. After a long day hard at work, are you likely to floss? Or will you say, "Never mind, I'll do it tomorrow." To make matters worse, we have seen how the constant struggle with poverty (and scarcity generally) further depletes self-control.

When you can afford so little, so many more things need to be resisted, and your self-control ends up being run down. Now picture yourself as a farmer preoccupied by thoughts of how you will make ends meet this week. You go to sleep preoccupied by how you'll afford the dentist for your son who's been complaining of toothache. You may need to forgo the night out with friends that you've been looking forward to. And you need to weed soon. You wake up, tired and still anxious. Like failing to floss, it is all too easy to imagine how you might decide, "I'll just weed tomorrow."

We see this in the data on smoking: smokers with financial stress are less likely to follow through on an attempt to quit. The poor will end up fatter too; eating well is a substantial self-control endeavor. One study found that when low-income women were moved to higher-income neighborhoods, rates of extreme obesity and diabetes dropped tremendously; other factors may have played a role, but a reduction in stress is almost certainly part of the story. Being a good parent requires self-control. Showing up at work even when you are sick requires self-control. Not snapping at your boss or at a customer requires self-control. Regularly attending a job-training program requires self-control. When you live in a rural village, ensuring that your kid gets to school every day requires self-control. So many of the "failures" surrounding poverty can be understood through the bandwidth tax.

Finally, think about the following. You have a big presentation tomorrow, for which you have prepared intensively. You know the value of rest, so you make sure to finish work by 5 p.m. You go home, have a good dinner with the family, and turn in early. But your mind is buzzing with thoughts of the presentation. So despite the need to sleep, you do not sleep well. Sleep research shows you are not alone. In one study, thirty-eight good sleepers were instructed to go to sleep as quickly as possible. Some of them were told that after the nap they would be giving a speech. Most people really do not like to give speeches. Indeed, this group had far more trouble falling asleep and slept less well when they did. Other data on insomniacs show that they are more likely to be worriers. Put simply, it is hard to sleep well when you have things on your mind.

This is perhaps the most pernicious, long-term detrimental way in which scarcity may tax bandwidth: thoughts of scarcity erode sleep. Studies of the lonely show that they sleep less well and get fewer hours. These effects are quite strong for the poor: they too have lower-quality sleep. And not sleeping enough can be disastrous. The U.S. Army has shown how lack of sleep can lead soldiers to fire on their own troops. The oil tanker *Exxon Valdez* crashed in Alaska in 1989 arguably in part because of the crew's sleep deprivation and sleep debt. These effects cumulate. Studies show that sleeping four to six hours a night for two weeks leads to a decay in performance comparable to going without sleep for two nights in a row. Insufficient sleep further compromises bandwidth.

One of the things the poor lack most is bandwidth. The very struggle of making ends meet leaves them with less of this vital resource. This shortfall is not of the standard physiological variety, having to do with a lack of nutrition or stress from early childhood hindering brain development. Nor is bandwidth permanently compromised by poverty. It is the present-day cognitive load of making ends meet: when income rises, so, too, does cognitive capacity. The bandwidth of the farmers was restored as soon as crop payments were received. Poverty at its very core taxes bandwidth and diminishes capacity.

Bandwidth underpins nearly every aspect of our behavior. We use it to calculate our odds of winning in poker, to judge other people's facial expressions, to control our emotions, to resist our impulses, to read a book, or to think creatively. Nearly every advanced cognitive function relies on bandwidth. Yet a tax on bandwidth is easy to overlook. Perhaps the best analogy is this: Think of talking to someone who is clearly doing something else, say surfing the web, while talking to you. If you did not know what they were doing, how would they seem to you? Daft? Confused? Uninterested? Not all there? A bandwidth tax can create the same perception.

So if you want to understand the poor, imagine yourself with your mind elsewhere. You did not sleep much the night before. You find it hard to think clearly. Self-control feels like a challenge. You are distracted and easily perturbed. And this happens every day. On top of the other material challenges poverty brings, it also brings a mental one.

In this light, the elephant in the room no longer seems so puzzling. The failures of the poor are part and parcel of the misfortune of being poor in the first place. Under these conditions, we all would have (and have!) failed.

IS BANDWIDTH TAX THE CULPRIT?

We began with a small sample of observations all pointing at the elephant in the room. In a great variety of circumstances, poverty appears to correlate with failure. We have given one explanation for these findings: the bandwidth tax. But how do we know that this, in fact, is the explanation? You might wonder, for example, whether the bandwidth tax is large enough to explain everything from failed adherence to forgotten weeding. We think it is. In the mall study from chapter 2, where the low-income group would not even qualify as truly poor, the bandwidth tax was sizable: roughly thirteen to fourteen IQ points, with an equally large effect on executive control. In the harvest study in India, we found an eight-to-nine-point effect on IQ and an even larger effect on executive control. These are, as we have pointed out, very large effects on cognitive function. In terms of the standard IQ classification, they can take you from "normal" to "superior" intelligence, or from "normal" to "dull," or even "borderline deficient." Not only is the bandwidth tax large, but the fact that we find it in two very different contexts is powerful confirmation. The poor in rural India are quite different from low-income shoppers at a New Jersey mall, yet they exhibit broadly similar bandwidth taxes. It is therefore not unreasonable to expect that the bandwidth tax plays a similarly large role in the lives of the poor everywhere.

The bandwidth tax is an appealing explanation because it accounts for a diverse set of phenomena. Explanations of the poor's failure are normally piecemeal. Perhaps farmers do not weed for cultural reasons; perhaps diabetics do not take their medications because of side effects; perhaps poor parents just lack the knowledge. These explanations are scattered because the circumstances of the poor are so very different. What people don't know in Trenton they might know in Nairobi. And what is a norm in Nairobi might not be so in the rural Philippines. In contrast, a single, fundamental mechanism—bandwidth—can make sense of this diverse set of empirical facts across behaviors, time, and place. Surely the specific circumstances also matter for understanding the lives of the poor, but bandwidth is fundamentally important and applies across all of them.

Understanding the role of bandwidth also helps us to better understand the specific circumstances of the poor. Disease, noise, and malnutrition are no longer simply sources of misery but also additional forms of bandwidth taxation. Take the idea that the poor lack certain basic skills. Rather than viewing this as an established fact, we may consider how a bandwidth tax can be one reason for this skill shortfall. Any form of skill acquisition, whether it be learning social skills or developing good spending habits, requires bandwidth. If the poor lack bandwidth, they will be disadvantaged at acquiring useful skills.

All this proposes a new lens through which to understand poverty. We need to look at data that have already been collected—on drug adherence, weeding, parenting, and other behaviors—with a cognitive lens, informed by scarcity considerations. Rather than isolated behaviors, each requiring its own account, these ought to be viewed as predictable consequences of overtaxed bandwidth. This perspective also suggests a new focus for collecting data. When we study poverty, we tend to focus on material conditions, but we also ought to look at psychological conditions—at band-width. In this way, existing puzzles may become less puzzling. To understand the poor, we must recognize that they focus and they tunnel and they make mistakes; that they lack not only money but also bandwidth.

PART THREE

Designing for Scarcity

8

IMPROVING THE LIVES OF THE POOR

During World War II, the United States military was troubled by the recurrence of "wheels-up" crashes: after landing, pilots would retract the wheels instead of the flaps. And, as you can imagine, retracting a plane's wheels while on the ground is not a good idea. To solve the problem, they brought in an expert. Lieutenant Alphonse Chapanis was a psychologist by training, ideally suited to get inside these pilots' heads. Why were they so careless? Were they fatigued? Were they relaxing too soon, thinking they could "let go" after a stressful mission? Was it a problem of training?

One clue quickly surfaced: the problem was limited to bomber pilots, those flying B-17s and B-25s. Transport pilots did not make this mistake. This clue helped Chapanis break free of his own biases. He decided not to look inside the pilots' heads but instead inside their cockpits. In these bombers, the wheel controls and the flap controls were side by side and looked nearly identical. Transport planes, by comparison, had very different controls. What separated the bomber pilots from the transport pilots were the cockpits. One type of cockpit made it too easy to make a mistake.

This experience transformed how cockpits are designed. Chapanis and others came to realize that many pilot errors were really cockpit errors. Until then, the focus had been on training pilots and ensuring alertness, on producing "excellent pilots" who make few mistakes. But Chapanis's conclusions changed this. Of course pilots must be trained; of course you must select for the best. But no matter how well you train them or pick them, they will make mistakes, especially if put in confounding contexts.

Error is inevitable, but accidents are not. A good cockpit design should not facilitate mistakes and, more important, should prevent errors from becoming tragedies. Chapanis solved the bombers' problem by placing a small rubber wheel on the end of the landing gear lever so the pilots could tell which lever they were touching. A good cockpit provides feedback in case one *might* make a mistake. A low-altitude alarm next to the altimeter helps to ensure that a low-flying pilot actually intends to fly low. Planes are much safer today not just because we have built better wings or engines but also because we have gotten better at handling human error.

POOR BEHAVIOR

Chapanis started off stymied by the pilots' behavior. Many analysts are similarly stymied by the behavior of the poor. Low-income training programs in the United States, for example, suffer from absenteeism, dropouts, and a failure by the intended recipients to sign up. Microfinance programs in the developing world bemoan the fact that their clients do not invest enough in high-return activities: instead, loans are used to pay off other debts, to fight "fires" (like school fees that have come due), or simply to buy consumer durables. And vaccination programs suffer when people fail to show up to get vaccinated, with the result that debilitating but preventable illnesses still rage through much of the developing world.

We have seen this in our own work. We once served as advisers to a welfare-to-work program in the United States that sought to help men and women on public assistance find jobs. One of the biggest challenges were the clients themselves. Despite repeatedly being advised to report to the worksite in professional clothes, they would often show up not wearing the right clothing. Many had substandard résumés, badly formatted and with typos. While sometimes this was due to lack of knowledge or skill, much of it was a failure to follow through, to execute as planned. Even after receiving instructions, few would avail themselves of the computers on site to format their résumés or of the offers to procure more appropriate clothing. When interviews were finally scheduled, clients would arrive without résumés and would not bring their "A" game. In many cases they simply failed to show up.

But the designers of these social programs rarely take the perspective that Chapanis took. Rather than look inside the cockpit, they have assumed that the problem lies with the person. They assume the problem is a lack of understanding or of motivation. So they follow up with attempts to educate or to sharpen incentives. In developed countries, this leads to a discussion of a "culture of welfare." One solution has been to place a lifetime limit on the number of years that a person can receive welfare. This is driven by a simple impulse: to motivate the unemployed to look for work. It has also led to the chastising of aid programs, and it has occasionally motivated public officials to move away from simple transfers—for example, by charging people for clean water rather than giving it to them for free. It has also occasionally led to programs with strong incentives, such as conditional cash transfer programs, where the amount of aid one receives depends on performing assorted "good" behaviors.

But why not look at the design of the cockpit rather than the workings of the pilot? Why not look at the structure of the programs rather than the failings of the clients? If we accept that pilots can fail and that cockpits need to be wisely structured so as to inhibit those failures, why can we not do the same with the poor? Why not design programs structured to be more fault tolerant?

We could ask the same question of anti-poverty programs. Consider the training programs, where absenteeism is common and dropout rates are high. What happens when, loaded and depleted, a client misses a class? What happens when her mind wanders in class? The next class becomes a lot harder. Miss one or two more classes and dropping out becomes the natural outcome, perhaps even the best option, as she really no longer understands much of what is being discussed in the class. A rigid curriculum—each class building on the previous—is not a forgiving setting for students whose bandwidth is overloaded. Miss a class here and there and our student has started a slide from which she is unlikely to recover. The programs' design presumes that if people are motivated enough, they will make no mistakes. Those who cannot be bothered to get to class on time, goes the implicit argument, must not care: they do not "deserve" the training.

But the psychology of scarcity predicts that errors like this will be all too common, perhaps even unavoidable, no matter how motivated the person. Imagine you come home from a day at work, worried about where you will find the money to make this month's rent, cover all the bills, and pay for your daughter's birthday party. You have not been sleeping well. A few weeks ago, you signed up for a training program in computer skills that one day could help you move up to a better job. But this evening the benefits of such training are abstract and distant. You're exhausted and weighed down by things more proximal, and you know that even if you go you won't absorb a thing. Now roll forward a few more weeks. By now you've missed another class. And when you go, you understand less than before. Eventually you decide it's just too much right now; you'll drop out and sign up another time, when your financial life is more together. The program you tried was not designed to be fault tolerant. It magnified your mistakes, which were predictable, and essentially pushed you out the door.

But it need not be that way. Instead of insisting on no mistakes or for behavior to change, we can redesign the cockpit. Curricula can be altered, for example, so that there are modules, staggered to start at different times and to proceed in parallel. You missed a class and fell behind? Move to a parallel session running a week or two "behind" this one. Miss a module and you can get back on track on the next round. Sure, it will take you a bit longer to finish, but at least you will get there. As it is, training programs are built with no mistakes in mind, as if the participants are not expected or allowed to stumble. But the poor—even, or perhaps especially, when they are unemployed—have a lot going on. And much of it does not sit so well with being a student. Skipping class in a training program while you're dealing with scarcity is not the same as playing hooky in middle school. Linear classes that must not be missed can work well for the full-time student; they do not make sense for the juggling poor.

It is important to emphasize that fault tolerance is not a substitute for personal responsibility. On the contrary: fault tolerance is a way to ensure that when the poor do take it on themselves, they can improve—as so many do. Fault tolerance allows the opportunities people receive to match the effort they put in and the circumstances they face. It does not take away the need for hard work; rather, it allows hard work to yield better returns for those who are up for the challenge, just as improved levers in the cockpit allow the dedicated pilot to excel. It is a way to ensure that small slipups—an inevitable consequence of the bandwidth tax—do not undo hard work.

INEFFECTIVE INCENTIVES

Remember the lifetime limits on welfare payments discussed earlier? They were based on a belief that cycling in and out of welfare was due to a lack of motivation on the part of the poor. People went on and off of welfare, it was said, because the system made it too easy not to work. To fix this, in the United States a lifetime cap was imposed for the primary welfare program (now renamed Temporary

Assistance for Needy Families). A person could now only be in the program for a total of five years over her lifetime.

A lifetime limit may not be foolish. Limits create scarcity, the logic goes, which might lead to better management of how the resource is "used." This almost relies on the psychology of scarcity. But it is flawed. We have seen that deadlines work when they are pressing, when they are top of mind. A long-term limit, like a distant deadline, becomes pressing only as it approaches, toward the end. To those who are currently juggling and tunneling, the limit, years away, will reside outside the tunnel, until it is very near. Until the limit becomes a pressing threat, it will be neglected and will rarely cross the person's mind. And by then it will be too late. This is almost certainly not what was intended by those who devised the plan—years of neglecting the deadline, followed by last-minute panic and eventual failure to receive further aid. In a way, it is the worst of all possible arrangements: it penalizes but fails to motivate.

Limits can be made more effective once we understand tunneling. For a limit to affect behavior it must enter the tunnel. One way would be to send a salient reminder of the months that are remaining. By calling attention to it we can try to force this distant problem into the tunnel. Another way is to change the structure of the limit. We have seen that frequent interim deadlines have a greater impact than a single distant deadline. So a better solution would be to create smaller but more frequent limits. (Perhaps, instead of so many years in a lifetime, only so many months in a given few-year period.) And to make the consequences of going over the limit smaller but immediate, easy to detect and to survive—perhaps a drop in payments rather than cutting off welfare altogether.

There is a general lesson here for how (and how not) to structure incentives. Incentives that fall outside the tunnel are unlikely to work. Imagine you are trying to encourage the vaccination of children whose parents are struggling to make ends meet *this* month. Which is more attractive to them, a payout in a month or two or a payout now? In one study in rural Rajasthan, India, a mere kilogram of lentils proved particularly effective in getting people to come in and get vaccinated. Rewards and penalties in some distant future are less effective for those who tunnel. A hefty subsidy in a savings program that pays out years from now is nice, but it renders those savings an "important but not urgent" matter, one that falls outside the tunnel and can be neglected indefinitely. For an incentive to work, people must see it. And most incentives, unless designed well, risk falling outside the tunnel, rendering them invisible and ineffective.

BANDWIDTH COMES AT A PRICE

Conditional cash transfers are an increasingly popular way to transfer money to the poor: the amount of cash a person receives depends on the good behaviors she exhibits. Studies show that these programs work; clients respond to the cash incentives. But that's only one side of the coin. The other side is that many potential clients fail to respond. Here again, the incentives often fall outside the tunnel; the payments come in the future and the desired behaviors are not what is tunneled on now. But this raises another question: Even if we could bring those incentives into the tunnel, should we? Each additional incentive taxes bandwidth. To capitalize on a bonus payment for a child's medical checkup, a parent must set up the appointment, remember to keep it, find the time to get there and back, and coerce the child to go (no child likes the doctor!). Each of these steps requires some bandwidth. And this is just one behavior. Conditional cash transfer programs seek to encourage dozens, if not hundreds, of these good behaviors. Just understanding those incentives and making the necessary trade-offs—deciding which are worth it for you and which are not, and when—requires bandwidth.

We never ask, Is this how we want poor people to use their bandwidth? We never factor in this cost in deciding which behaviors are most worth promoting. When we design poverty programs, we recognize that the poor are short on cash, so we are careful to conserve on that. But we do not think of bandwidth as being scarce as well. Nowhere is this clearer than in our impulse to educate. Our first response to many problems is to teach people the skills they lack. Faced with parenting problems, we give parenting skills programs. Faced with financial mistakes—too much borrowing at too-high rates—we provide financial education classes. Faced with employees whose social skills are lacking, we offer "soft skills" classes. We treat education as if it were the least invasive solution, an unadulterated good. But with limited bandwidth, this is just not true. While education is undoubtedly a good thing, we treat it as if it comes with no price tag for the poor. But in fact, bandwidth comes at a high cost: either the person will not focus, and our effort will have been in vain, or he will focus, but then there is a bandwidth tax to pay. When the person actually focuses on the training or the incentives, what is he *not* focusing on? Is that added class really worth what little quality time he managed to spend reading or with his children? There are hidden costs to taxing bandwidth.

And even when we do decide that educating is the right thing, there can be ways to do so and still economize on bandwidth, as illustrated in a study by the economist Antoinette Schoar and her coauthors. They had been working with a microfinance institution in the Dominican Republic called ADOPEM, whose clients run small enterprises—general stores, beauty salons, food services—usually with no employees. ADOPEM felt that its clients were making mistakes in their accounting books and generally didn't understand finance as well as they should. The solution seemed simple: financial literacy education. So Schoar procured a standard financial literacy training module, of the kind typically given to microentrepreneurs worldwide. Her reaction upon seeing the material: Wow, how tedious! (And she's a finance professor at MIT.) The course was several weeks long and focused on traditional accounting techniques, teaching daily recordkeeping of cash and expenses, inventory management, accounts receivable and payable, and calculating profits and investment.

In a world of unlimited bandwidth, all this would be worth knowing. But in the real world, Schoar believed that she could do better for her clients. She gathered together a group of the best local entrepreneurs to look at how they managed their finances. They, too, were not engaged in complex accounting, but they did what the less successful entrepreneurs did not do: they followed good rules of thumb. For example, several would put the cash from their store in one register and pay themselves a fixed salary. This prevented the commingling of home money and business money that makes it difficult to determine how much they were spending at home versus how much the business was earning. (Some of the women kept one wad of cash in their bra's left cup, and the other in the right cup.) This is not quite double-entry bookkeeping, but it was effective and simple. It economized on bandwidth and preserved most of the benefits.

Schoar collected the best rules of thumb and designed a different "financial education" class based on them. Her class was shorter and much easier to grasp. It used a lot less bandwidth, and this showed up in the data. Attendance was much higher, and at the end of the rules-of-thumb class, clients were ecstatic and asking for more; many even said they would *pay for another class themselves.* Normally, you have to cajole people to come back to a class on financial education.

The reduced bandwidth also made the class easier to absorb and more effective. In follow-up surveys, students were more likely to implement the rules of thumb than the complex rules of accounting. And this showed up in the bottom line. Revenues—actual business sales—went up for the rules-of-thumb graduates, especially in bad weeks when improved practices can matter most: they had 25 percent higher revenues in those bad weeks. Traditional financial literacy training, in contrast, had no impact. The lesson is clear: economizing on bandwidth can yield high returns.

Whether it is in the trade-offs that people are led to make, the way education is structured, the incentives that are created, or how we handle failure, understanding the psychology of scarcity can dramatically alter the way social programs are designed. Of course, none of this provides a magic bullet to end poverty. The problems are deep. But an awareness of the psychology of scarcity and the behavioral challenges it yields can go some way toward improving the modest returns of anti-poverty interventions.

BANDWIDTH CAN BE BUILT

You are a working single mother who holds down two jobs. You have a lot to juggle. Besides the financial juggling we talked about already, you must also juggle daycare for your kids, which is expensive. You know of one program that is highly subsidized, but it will accept only one of your kids, and it closes much too early to help with your second job. So you use a patchwork of solutions. You arrange for your younger child to stay with your grandmother. You must also arrange transportation from school to your grandmother's for one child and from daycare for the other. And because you work in the service sector, your child care needs depend on the hours your staff supervisor gives you. She is nice and tries to help, but there is inevitable volatility.

Now imagine that we offer you a highly subsidized daycare program. What exactly are you getting for it? Surely we are saving you time shuttling your kids back and forth. We might be saving you money as well, either explicitly (this program is cheaper than your previous one) or implicitly (if we account for your grandmother's time). But we would be giving you something else, even more precious. Something you could spend on many things. We would be giving you back all that mental bandwidth that you currently use to fret, worry, and juggle these arrangements. We'd be taking a cognitive load off. As we've seen, this would help your executive control, your self-control more broadly, even your parenting. It would increase your general cognitive capacity, your ability to focus, the quality of your work, or whatever else you chose to turn your mind to. From this perspective, help with child care is much more than that. It is a way to build human capital of the deepest kind: it creates bandwidth.

Typically, when experts evaluate this child-care program, they will look at narrow outcomes: Was the mother able to work more hours; was she less tardy? This, however, may be far too narrow a perspective. What the program produces is freedom of mind, greater bandwidth, not something that's easy to measure. If the program is successful, its benefits should show up in many contexts. All else being equal, one ought to be able to look directly and see the mental impact of this program. Does working memory improve? Do impulse control and self-control improve? Some of our pessimism about existing programs might come from a failure to appreciate and therefore measure such impact. If we look too narrowly at this child-care program, we will miss many of its broader benefits. Taken together, a successful intervention may yield much more than a modest return. But if we fail to look where the deepest needs are and where the benefits accrue, we are bound to underestimate its impact.

There are, besides child care, many examples from around the world of how bandwidth might be built. The first comes from finance. Recall that a great deal of juggling among the poor comes from fighting everyday fires. If we can help people fight these fires, we will create new bandwidth. What is inherent to these fires is that they are acute—there is an immediate need for cash. The need is not for big investments; it is for small amounts—to buy a school uniform, for example. Put differently, the poor most want what the moneylender can easily offer: a small amount of money, provided quickly and repaid quickly to help out with an urgent need. Instead, the kind of finance that is offered to the poor is often built on the opposite principle: modest to large amounts of money provided judiciously and slowly. Such loans can be helpful for investing. But if people are busy fighting fires, they will not have the bandwidth for investments. Is it any surprise then that despite the presence of respectable microfinance institutions, people still prefer to go to moneylenders? In India, we tested one very short-term small loan product with KGFS, a full-service financial institution that serves the rural poor. And we were amazed by the high demand for loans that averaged less than $10. The product does not help build wealth; it does not turn people into entrepreneurs. On the surface, it does not look like the kind of sum that can transform a life. Yet it might do just that. The scarcity trap begins with firefighting and with tunneling, doing things that have tremendous costs lurking outside the tunnel. Change that and we can change the very logic of poverty.

We can also go back to the source. Income flows are often lumpy and volatile in the developing world, because workers lack formal, steady employment. Even in developed nations, many low-income individuals who are employed face a great deal of volatility in incomes and earnings. As we saw earlier, income volatility is a major source of the eventual need to juggle. Why not try to mitigate it? A greater focus on the creation of dependable jobs and stable incomes for the poor across the world could be psychologically transformative.

But we can go further. We tend to focus on big shocks, such as medical emergencies or rainfall insurance. Surely these are important. Yet when one is juggling, small shocks can have equally large effects. For a poor farmer, a sick cow can reduce daily income enough to cause a slide into a scarcity trap. We should therefore look to insure the poor against these apparently "small" shocks. In the United States, something as simple as inconsistent work hours (this week you work fifty hours, but next week you get only thirty) can cause juggling and perpetuate scarcity. A solution would be to create the equivalent of unemployment insurance against such fluctuations in work hours, which to the poor can be even more pernicious than job loss.

We have seen how most of the shocks that come from juggling and induce tunneling are generally quite predictable. On the one hand, suddenly needing money for fertilizer counts as a shock. On the other hand, it is entirely predictable. It happens every year, but when you are busy juggling, you do not see it coming. This points to the great potential value in finding ways to buffer against such shocks. One way is to create financial products that help the poor build savings slack. We could do that using some of the techniques for managing scarcity we discussed earlier. For example, we can use tunneling to our advantage. Offer high-fee loans to deal with current fires. These loans will be attractive in the tunnel, and we can use the high fees to build a savings account.

Better yet, create products that prevent the firefighting. We saw how scarcity traps and juggling often follow lax management during times of relative abundance. Why not help then? Build a financial product that takes a farmer's harvest payment and smooths it out, effectively yielding a monthly income. This is but one example. More broadly, we spend enormous resources on financial planning for retirement. Helping the poor escape a continuous life of juggling and firefighting could be similarly transformative.

All this reflects a deeper, and somewhat different, perspective on poverty. It focuses not just on the poor's obvious scarce resource, income, but on that other, less palpable but equally critical resource, bandwidth. Considerations of bandwidth suggest that something as simple as giving cash *at the right time* can have big benefits. If done correctly, giving someone $100 can serve to purchase peace of mind. And that peace of mind allows the person to do many more things well and to avoid costly mistakes. One cash transfer program in Malawi showed a 40 percent reduction in the psychological distress of low-income participants. Understanding how to provide transfers at the right time and measuring these broader impacts are more ways to move toward bandwidth-sensitive policies.

All this is a radical reconceptualization of poverty policy. It forces us to recognize the many ways in which different behaviors are linked. We understand that rent and food and school fees all form part of a household's budget. Now, rather than looking at education, health, finance, and child care as separate problems, we must recognize that they all form part of a person's bandwidth capacity. And just as a financial tax can wreak havoc in one's budget, so can a bandwidth tax create failure in any of several domains to which a person must attend. Conversely, fixing some of those bottlenecks can have far-reaching consequences. Child care provides more than just child care, and the right financial product does much more than just create savings for a rainy day. Each of these can liberate bandwidth, boost IQ, firm up self-control, enhance clarity of thinking, and even improve sleep. Far-fetched? The data suggest not.

A PERSISTENT PROBLEM

The fight against poverty has been an uphill struggle. Program after program has proved either unsuccessful or at best modestly successful. Social safety nets tend to be sticky. In the United States, once a person has fallen into the social safety net, she is bound to return to it again and again. And training programs appear to be only moderately effective. Researchers who have sought to estimate their impact have found some benefits: they are worth the investment, but they are not able to alter the course of poverty. Changing neighborhoods also only helps a bit. One experiment in the United States moved thousands of families from low-income to higher-income neighborhoods, and found modest impacts, primarily on stress and quality of life, but the underlying patterns of poverty did not change.

Internationally, the results are similar. Microfinance—providing small loans to help start small businesses—has been touted as highly transformative. While the impact of microfinance is likely positive, several studies now suggest that it is unlikely to change the fundamental logic of poverty. Feeding programs show some impact on children's learning. Education has a robust but quite limited return. For years, nonprofit organizations have tried to provide a variety of holistic packages to address the varied needs of the poor. Surely they are doing good work. But they, too, have observed only modest returns.

This is certainly not intended as a critique of current programs. Poverty is a difficult problem. Even modest returns can make for worthy social investments. This is, however, a suggestion for how we might do better. When we encounter programs that have had limited success, we may be tempted to infer that they deliver something people do not want or do not consider important. But perhaps the problem is not in what these programs are trying to deliver but with the actual delivery. Like the bomber cockpits of World War II, these programs might achieve greater success through better design. And a better design will have to incorporate fundamental insights about focusing and bandwidth that emerge from the psychology of scarcity.

9

MANAGING SCARCITY IN ORGANIZATIONS

St. John's Regional Health Center, an acute care hospital in Missouri, had a problem with its operating rooms. Some thirty thousand surgical procedures were performed annually in thirty-two operating rooms, and scheduling the rooms was proving difficult; they were always fully booked. In 2002, the hospital's operating rooms were at 100 percent capacity. So when emergency cases arose—and they were often 20 percent of the full load—the hospital was forced to bump long-scheduled surgeries. "As a result, hospital staff sometimes performed surgery at 2 a.m., physicians often waited several hours to perform two-hour procedures, and staff members regularly worked unplanned overtime," according to a study summarizing the remarkable events that happened next.

This was a classic case of scarcity: more surgeries than operating rooms. St. John's was stuck in a scarcity trap. The hospital was constantly behind, and because it was behind, it had to reshuffle surgeries, struggled with sleep and work regulations, and became even less efficient. Rearranging in circumstances like this can be costly. And, at least in the short run, these efforts can exacerbate scarcity because a portion of the already insufficient budget is "wasted" on the rearranging. The hospital was like the overcommitted person who finds that tasks take too long, in part because the person is overcommitted and cannot imagine taking on the additional—and time-consuming—task of stepping back and reorganizing.

But St. John's had to figure out what to do. The hospital administration brought in an adviser from the Institute for Healthcare Improvement who studied the problem analytically, with the luxury of not having to tunnel on the hospital's daily pressures. He came up with a rather surprising solution: leave one room unused. Dr. Kenneth Larson, a general and trauma surgeon at St. John's, responded as you might expect: "We are already too busy, and they want to take something away from us. This is crazy," he remembered thinking.

Yet there was a profound logic to this recommendation, a logic that is instructive for the management of scarcity. On the surface, what St. John's was lacking were operating rooms. No amount of reshuffling could solve that problem. But if you looked deeper, the lack was of a slightly different sort. Surgeries come in two varieties: planned and unplanned. Right now the planned surgeries took up all the rooms. Unplanned surgeries, when they showed up (and they did!), required rearranging the schedule. Having to move a planned surgery to accommodate an emergency came at a cost. Some of it was financial—overtime—and some may have been medical—more errors. But part of it was a cost in efficiency. Having people work unexpectedly late is less efficient. They are less proficient at their tasks, and each surgery takes longer.

Without the reshuffling imposed by emergencies—with everybody working the scheduled hours and taking less time—there were enough operating rooms to handle all the cases. The scarcity in rooms was not really a lack of surgery space; it was an inability to accommodate emergencies. There is a close analogy here to the indebted poor, whose money might often suffice to live a bit better if it were spent smoothly and without shocks. But much of that money goes to paying off debts. It is not just the tight budget. It is that a chunk of the money goes toward financing the need to catch up. In the St. John's case, it was not that the hospital was too "poor" in operating rooms. It's that when emergencies arrived, the tight space went toward accommodating them and then catching up again.

"Everyone assumed that because the flow of unscheduled surgeries can't be predicted, setting aside an OR just for 'add-ons' would be a very inefficient use of the space," said Christy Dempsey, vice president of the Emergency Trauma Center, who led the initiative. As it turns out, the terms "unplanned" or "unanticipated" surgery are a bit misleading: they imply that these emergency surgeries are unpredictable. Of course, while each individual surgery is not known in advance, the fact that there will be such surgeries, much like the shocks that hit the poor or the busy, is quite predictable. There is always a steady flow of "unanticipated" cases. Why not set aside an operating room to be used specifically for unscheduled cases? That way, all the other operating rooms could be packed well and proceed unencumbered by surprises, and all the unplanned surgeries would go into the one specially designated room.

It worked. Once one operating room was dedicated to emergency surgeries alone, the hospital was able to accommodate 5.1 percent more surgical cases. The number of surgeries performed after 3 p.m. fell by 45 percent, and revenue increased. The trial had lasted only a month before the hospital made the change permanent. In the two years that followed, the hospital experienced a 7 to 11 percent increase in surgical volume each year.

In fact, once the hospital began to appreciate the benefits of change, other insights followed. Surgeons had tended to schedule surgeries earlier in the week to ensure that postoperative rounds would not fall on weekends, a practice that had led to an uneven distribution of elective surgeries. This imbalance became transparent once there weren't emergency surgeries to hide it. Before long, St. John's started scheduling elective surgeries evenly over the entire week, and further improvement followed.

UNDERAPPRECIATED SLACK

The St. John's case illustrates something fundamental to the scarcity trap. The lack of rooms the hospital had experienced was really a lack of slack. Many systems require slack in order to work well. Old reel-to-reel tape recorders needed an extra bit of tape fed into the mechanism to ensure that the tape wouldn't rip. Your coffee grinder won't grind if you overstuff it. Roadways operate best below 70 percent capacity; traffic jams are caused by lack of slack. In principle, if a road is 85 percent full and everybody goes at the same speed, all cars can easily fit with some room between them. But if one driver speeds up just a bit and then needs to brake, those behind her must brake as well. Now they've slowed down too much, and, as it turns out, it's easier to reduce a car's speed than to increase it again. This small shock—someone lightly deviating from the right speed and then touching her brakes—has caused the traffic to slow substantially. A few more shocks, and traffic grinds to a halt. At 85 percent there is enough road but not enough slack to absorb the small shocks.

And yet, even those who should know better routinely undervalue slack.

You used to have an amazing assistant always ready to do the tasks you needed, on short notice, happily, and well. But then a management consultant discovered that your assistant had a lot of free time on his hands. The department was reorganized, and now you share the assistant with two other people. The office's time-use data show that this is much more efficient; now the assistant's schedule is packed as tight as yours. But now your last-minute short-notice requests can no longer be handled immediately. This means that, with your heavy schedule, even the smallest shock sets you behind. And as you fall behind, you start to juggle and fall behind further and further. The assistant was an important source of slack. He allowed for the handling of "emergencies" when all your regular venues were fully scheduled. The very fact that the assistant was "underused," like that room at St. John's, is what made the assistant valuable.

A standard impulse when there is a lot to do is to pack tightly—as tightly as possible, to fit everything in. And when you are not tightly packed, there's a feeling that perhaps you are not doing enough. In fact, when efficiency experts find workers with "unused" time on their hands, they often embark on making those workers use their time "more efficiently." But the result is that slack will have been lost. When you are tightly packed, getting stuck in the occasional traffic jam, which for others is only mildly annoying, throws your schedule into total disarray. You are late to meeting number one, and with no time in between, that pushes into meeting number two, which pushes into obligation number three. You finally have no choice but to defer one of today's tightly packed obligations to the next day, except, of course, that tomorrow's schedule is "efficiently" packed, too, and the cost of that deferral ends up being high. Sounds familiar? Of course it does. You have undervalued slack. The slightest glitch imposes an obligation you can no longer afford, and borrowing from tomorrow's budget comes at high interest.

We fail to build slack because we focus on what must be done now and do not think enough about all the things that can arise in the future. The present is imminently clear whereas future contingencies are less pressing and harder to imagine. When the intangible future comes face to face with the palpable present, slack feels like a luxury. It is, after all, exactly what you do not feel you have enough to spare. What should you do? Should you leave spaces open in your schedule, say, 3–4 p.m. Monday and Wednesday, just in case something unexpected comes up, despite the fact that there is so much you'd like to do for which you have so little time? In effect, yes. That's what you do when you allocate forty minutes to drive somewhere a half hour away, or when you salt away some money from your monthly household budget to save for a rainy day. When you face scarcity, slack is a necessity. And yet we so often fail to plan for it. Largely, of course, because scarcity makes it hard to do.

SLACK VERSUS FAT

The mishandling of slack is not only about individuals; it applies to organizations as well. During the 1970s and the early 1980s, there was a perception that many corporations were "bloated." Some industries were so awash with cash that the executives spent carelessly. They would overpay for real estate and business acquisitions, fail to bargain, and be unconcerned with the bottom line. Cash was spent so badly that some oil companies were worth less than the value of the oil they owned; the market anticipated they would simply waste their assets. The leveraged buyout wave in the 1980s was an attempt to solve this problem. The logic was simple: buy these companies and impose pressure by placing them in debt. Move them from abundance to scarcity. The discipline of debt—in our parlance, the focus that comes from scarcity—would improve performance. The executives would start paying attention, spend more prudently, and produce greater profits.

In fact, a raft of empirical studies showed that, whatever their other consequences, leveraged buyouts did improve corporate performance. One reason is that the "corporate fat" exacerbates the incentive problem of managers. They spend poorly because they are spending someone else's money. Fat, which is effectively free money, is spent on luxuries that management enjoys but are useless from the shareholders' perspective. By increasing leverage and reducing fat, managers spend more wisely.

Leverage also had an effect because of the psychology of scarcity. Companies became "lean and mean" in part for the same reason deadlines produce greater productivity, and low-income passengers know the price of cabs. Being a hypervigilant manager who keeps costs low can require a great deal of cognitive effort. You must negotiate diligently with suppliers and scrutinize every line item to decide if an expense is necessary. This kind of focus is easier to come by under scarcity and harder to come by under abundance. Even private companies, where managers are spending their own money, start acting "fat" when awash in cash.

But as we have seen, slack is both wasteful and beneficial. When cutting, it can be hard to separate out true waste from useful slack, and indeed, many of the leveraged companies were left at the brink of bankruptcy. Faced with that reality, they tunneled. If the 1980s were a lesson in the power of cutting fat, the 2000s were a lesson in the danger of managerial myopia. Perhaps these two were related. Cut too much fat, remove too much slack, and you are left with managers who will mortgage the future to make ends meet today.

MARS ORBITER

In December 1998, NASA launched the Mars Orbiter. Missions to Mars are fueled by centuries of human fascination with a planet so close, so similar in size to Earth (it even has a similar length of day) and with a tiny but tantalizing possibility of life. Orbiter was unlikely to make major findings by itself. But it was a spearhead. It would provide valuable data for future missions, perhaps even a manned landing on Mars. Its launch was the culmination of a $125 million project involving tens of thousands of hours of effort. As per its name, Orbiter was designed to enter a stable orbit close to Mars from which it would collect data.

Entering a stable orbit around a planet is tricky business. As the satellite approaches, gravity pulls it in. If the satellite approaches too slowly, gravity's pull is strong enough to crash it on the surface. If the satellite is traveling too fast, gravity does too little: the satellite skates by the planet and proceeds in a different direction. At just the right speed (and the right angle, of course) the pull of gravity is just enough to pull the satellite into a stable orbit. Needless to say, determining the proper speed requires complex and precise calculation. As Orbiter approached Mars, it would have to fire its reverse thrusters to slow down just enough to get caught in Mars's orbit. Since it takes about ten minutes for a signal to reach from Earth, this was all pre-programmed. All ground control could do was sit and listen (with a delay). Luckily, there are not too many surprises in the dead of space. Astrophysical calculations can be made with a precision that is the envy of earthbound engineers.

Nine and a half months after launch, on September 23, 1999, Orbiter reached Mars and began to execute its entry procedure. This would take it behind Mars, preventing any contact for several minutes. But then came the sign of trouble: no transmissions from the spacecraft at all, even though Orbiter was to have reemerged. With every tense second, a bit of hope dissipated. Eventually, the ground crew gave up. Orbiter was presumed to have crashed.

In the aftermath of such a public failure, scrutiny would follow. What happened? Why a crash? What could have been done to prevent it? Who was to blame? Failures, especially of complex systems, typically have many causes. In this case, however, the culprit was both newsworthy and obvious. The reverse thrusters had fired too strongly. But what was particularly intriguing was the degree to which the firing was off. NASA calculated that the ratio of desired firing to actual firing was a curiously familiar number, 4.45. This is the number used to convert between the metric and British measures of force. The embarrassing error quickly became apparent.

Satellites like Orbiter are built piecemeal by several subcontractors. The thrusters, built by one firm, were interpreting the input they were receiving in pounds, the English system measurement of force. The central processor, built by a different firm, was providing the input in newtons, the metric system measurement. Every time the processor said "X," the thrusters heard "4.45 times X." (When the processor said "10," that meant 10 newtons, but the thrusters heard "10 pounds," the equivalent of 44.5 newtons.) The result: Orbiter slowed down too much and got caught in the gravitational pull of Mars. For a project of this significance, this was a comical, if highly consequential, blunder.

Errors are inevitable. NASA engineers know this. This is why endless checks and tests are put in place. So what happened? In the months leading up to the launch, the entire team at the Jet Propulsion Laboratory was running behind schedule. They were understaffed and had failed to turn their attention fully to all the project details until it was late. Everyone falls behind, and it has been observed that organizations that are firefighting tend to allocate smaller teams to new projects, since much of the staff is still helping fight the last fire. Unlike workers in other industries, however, these engineers did not have access to the universal fallback of the tardy—an extension of the deadline. Celestial orbits drive the launch date: the locations of Mars and other bodies determine a narrow launch window. It is hard to negotiate with the astronomical calendar.

The tight deadline created long hours. But it also created tunneling. The focus was on making the launch date. Things directly unrelated to that goal were put off, and as it turned out, they were never returned to. The 4.45 mistake was one such casualty. The engineers' own data showed there was something wrong well before the launch. They noticed the inconsistencies. But figuring out the source of the inconsistencies was one more task on the to-do list, and with so much left to do, not everything can be done. Following up on apparent inconsistencies was one casualty. Another casualty was a joint simulation of thruster and processor, which would have revealed the problem directly. The usual checks and balances were sacrificed, potential signs of trouble were overlooked, all in order to make the deadline. By now you will recognize this as a logical consequence of tunneling.

This is not hindsight. A NASA report to the Jet Propulsion Laboratory *prior to the crash* highlighted the problem. Initial project delays (perhaps because of understaffing), it argued, were leading to shortcuts and workarounds. Staff were working long hours and making mistakes. The initial delay was generating more inefficiency. Worse, crucial checks—those that seemed less pressing—were being overlooked. The report essentially foretold the pattern that led to the mix-up and eventual crash.

This is more than a symptom of falling behind. Once they established the technical autopsy, the investigators of the Orbiter crash looked to organizational reasons for the failure. One reason, they concluded, was the "Faster, Better, Cheaper" paradigm that NASA had adopted. This paradigm put an emphasis on cost savings and schedule reduction. Teams started to run short on time and tunneled. And then they neglected. In this case crucial checks were neglected because they were important but not urgent; they were not crucial to the task at hand—to make the launch happen, on time.

THE FIREFIGHTING TRAP

Both St. John's and NASA had fallen into a firefighting trap. As the organizational researchers Roger Bohn and Ramchandran Jaikumar describe it, firefighting organizations have several features in common. First, they have "too many problems, not enough time." Second, they solve the urgent problems but put off the nonurgent ones, no matter how important. Third, this leads to a cascade so that the amount of work to be done grows. Put simply, time is spent on fighting the immediate fire, with new fires constantly popping up because nothing is being done to prevent them. At St. John's the surgeons were so busy dealing with patients right now that they could not step back and look at the overall patient mix. At NASA the engineers were so busy trying to make the deadline for each component that they did not look at how the components fit together. The firefighting trap is a special case of the scarcity trap.

A thorough five-year study of four top manufacturing firms in the United States documented multiple instances of firefighting. As one manager puts it: "If you look at our resource allocation on traditional projects, we always start late and don't put people on the projects soon enough . . . then we load as many people on as it takes . . . the resource allocation peaks when we launch the project." Based on their years of study, the researchers conclude, "There are few images more common in current discussions of R&D management than that of the overworked engineering team putting in long hours to complete a project in its last days before launch."

Firefighting does not just lead to errors; it leads to a very predictable kind of error: important but nonurgent tasks are neglected. Just as the name implies, you are busy fighting the urgent problem (the fire); other problems, no matter how important, are drowned by the most urgent (seatbelts on the way to the fire). As a result, structural problems—important, but they can wait—never get fixed. When Microsoft shipped its Windows 2000 software, it went out with 28,000 *known* bugs. The project team knew they were shipping a product with lots of problems, but they were already behind the deadline. As a result, they immediately began working on a first patch, which was to fix all the bugs they knew they had shipped out. Not a good place to be when reports of new bugs start coming in.

Firefighting traps involve a great deal of juggling. You are so focused on the looming deadline that when you finish you realize the next project is suddenly due. Most of us have found ourselves doing this at one point or another, and we know intuitively that firefighting is a trap for all the reasons scarcity is a trap. Once you start firefighting, it is hard to emerge unscathed. When teams are frantically working on a project that should have already been done, they start late on the next project, which ensures they will firefight there as well and stay perpetually behind.

Understanding the logic of scarcity and slack can reduce the chance that we enter a firefighting trap. Yet we know that tunneling makes it easy to overlook other considerations. One solution, at least in organizations, is to explicitly manage and ensure the availability of slack. There is a lesson in how banks have tried to manage risk. Banks have long recognized that managers, tunneling on the bottom line, do not sufficiently take risk into account. As the 2008 financial crisis demonstrated, this is an understatement. More recently, many banks have introduced "chief risk officers," who sit apart from the rest of the management team and report directly to the CEO. They must approve financial products, loans, and other transactions, viewing them through the lens of risk. Unlike the managers who focus (tunnel!) on the most appealing transactions and on making the big profits and the sales targets, these executives' sole goal is to monitor risk.

Similarly, as fat continues to be cut, and slack goes with it, organizations may want someone in-house who is not tunneled on stretching resources. Someone, removed from the daily tunneling, whose job is to ensure that the organization has enough slack and who focuses not on what needs to be done today but on what possible shocks may upset tight plans tomorrow. Someone must ensure that those who are focused on meeting immediate project targets are not borrowing from future projects, thereby exhausting any slack and digging the organization deeper into a bandwidth hole in the future. It is not a coincidence that the adviser that St. John's hired was clearly removed from the struggle for the next operating room.

MANAGE THE RIGHT SCARCE RESOURCE

> *The truly efficient laborer will be found not to crowd his day with work, but will saunter to his task surrounded by a wide halo of ease and leisure.*
>
> —HENRY DAVID THOREAU

There is another lesson to draw from the NASA experience. When the Jet Propulsion Laboratory crew started to fall behind, management did what most managers would do. They increased hours. They saw a scarcity of time—Orbiter must launch soon—and they deployed more time to address it. This is a common response to time scarcity. A project is running behind schedule? Put in more people on the problem to get caught up. And if an organization is stretched for employees—time is pressing, and hiring and training new people will take time—simply work your people more hours, at least until new employees can be brought in. On the surface this seems like an obvious solution and the easiest way to do more with a fixed amount of resources. Yet this response may not be as sensible as it seems. It recognizes one form of scarcity—time left to finish the project—but it ignores another form of scarcity—bandwidth. It neglects the consequences of reduced bandwidth on performance.

Consider the use of cell phones. Ten states now ban the use of handheld cell phones while driving. This makes some sense, and other states are sure to follow. After all, with only one hand on the wheel, you are bound to be a less efficient, less responsive driver. But this also makes a major, if hidden, assumption. As it turns out, drivers holding a cell phone are significantly more likely to get into an accident, but so are drivers using a headset. The hands are not the problem—the mind is. In one simulation study, drivers using hands-free phones missed twice as many traffic signals compared to those who were not on the phone. We naturally think of driving as an activity requiring physical resources, but safe driving requires more than two hands; it requires bandwidth as well.

Similarly, we often overlook bandwidth when arranging our time. What we naturally think of is the time it will take to complete our to-do list, not the bandwidth it will require or receive. Think of how the Jet Propulsion Laboratory engineers responded to the problem of the impending celestial deadline. They poured more engineer *hours* into the problem. But that did not necessarily provide more bandwidth, and one can argue that the overworked engineers may have given their work *less* total bandwidth despite the longer hours.

Nearly a century ago, Henry Ford recognized the distinction between hours and bandwidth. His decision to institute a forty-hour workweek for his factory workers was clearly motivated by profits as much as by humanitarian concerns. As one commentator observes:

When Henry Ford famously adopted a 40-hour workweek in 1926, he was bitterly criticized by members of the National Association of Manufacturers. But his experiments, which he'd been conducting for at least 12 years, showed him clearly that cutting the workday from ten hours to eight hours—and the workweek from six days to five

days—increased total worker output and reduced production cost.
Ford spoke glowingly of the social benefits of a shorter workweek,
couched firmly in terms of how increased time for consumption was
good for everyone. But the core of his argument was that reduced
shift length meant more output.

Finding the data on Ford's original experiments is difficult. But
several similar studies have been run in almost a century since Ford's
experiments. One study, on construction projects, found that "where
a work schedule of 60 or more hours per week is continued longer
than about two months, the cumulative effect of decreased productivity will cause a delay in the completion date beyond that which
could have been realized with the same crew size on a 40-hour
week." In a very different industry, a software developer notes that
when his staff began putting in sixty-hour weeks, the first few weeks
would see much more work getting done. But by week five, the
employees were getting less done than when they had been working
forty-hour weeks.

Another study looked at what happened in a cardiothoracic surgery department when the number of patients per medical service
worker increased. Again, there was an increase in productivity in the
short run. Patients were dealt with more quickly. But this came at a
cost. There was neglect. Dealing with more patients quickly lowered
quality: patients were more likely to die. In fact, even the benefits did
not persist. A sustained increase in workload eventually led to an
increase in the time it took to manage each patient.

The impact on productivity can also show up in other ways. Here
is one researcher discussing innovation in the workplace:

At the end of each interview I asked the interviewees what they
would do first to encourage innovation in their organization if they
were suddenly omnipotent. By far the most common answer was
time. But respondents often qualified this—they didn't want more of
the same kind of time, they wanted more unstructured time that did

not have specific outputs or procedures attached to it. The managing director . . . put this very well when she yearned for "time to play . . . time to gaze out the window . . . time to let things settle . . . time to read and react."

In a way, none of this should be surprising. Just as we get physically exhausted and need to rest, we also get mentally depleted and need to recover. Instead, with prolonged scarcity, bandwidth taxes tend to accumulate. To understand the mechanism, consider something as simple as sleep. People with time scarcity who are working more hours will try to squeeze more into the remainder of each day; they will neglect and patch things. Sleep is one obvious candidate. When you run out of time, you sleep a little less and squeeze in a few more hours of work. Yet the effects of sleep on productivity are striking. Studies have repeatedly shown that when workers sleep less they become less motivated, make more errors, and zone out more often. One clever study demonstrated this by looking at the start and end of daylight savings time, nights on which, because of the time change, people lose sleep. It found that people spent 20 percent more time cyberloafing—searching the web for unrelated content—for every hour of lost sleep on those evenings. And that is just one night of sleep. Research shows that the cumulative effects are far worse. As work hours accumulate and sleep time diminishes, productivity eventually goes down.

Yet most firms still manage hours, not bandwidth. One group of researchers describes a thirty-seven-year-old partner at a large accounting firm, married with four children:

When we met him a year ago, he was working 12- to 14-hour days, felt perpetually exhausted, and found it difficult to fully engage with his family in the evenings, which left him feeling guilty and dissatisfied. He slept poorly, made no time to exercise, and seldom ate healthy meals, instead grabbing a bite to eat on the run or while working at his desk. [His] experience is not uncommon. Most of us respond to rising demands in the workplace by putting in longer hours, which inevitably take a toll on us physically, mentally, and emotionally. That leads to declining levels of engagement, increasing levels of distraction, high turnover rates, and soaring medical costs among employees.

These same researchers tried a pilot "energy management" program. This included breaks for walks and focusing on key factors such as sleep. In the pilot study, they found that 106 employees at twelve banks showed increased performance on several metrics. Perhaps this sounds far-fetched. But how different is this from how we manage our bodies? To prevent repetitive strain injury, frequent computer users take mandated breaks. To help with computer vision syndrome, people are advised to look away from the screen every twenty minutes or so for about twenty seconds to rest the eyes. Why is it counterintuitive that our cognitive system should be so different from our physical one?

The deeper lesson is the need to focus on managing and cultivating bandwidth, despite pressures to the contrary brought on by scarcity. Increasing work hours, working people harder, forgoing vacations, and so on are all tunneling responses, like borrowing at high interest. They ignore the long-term consequences. Psychiatrists report an increasing number of patients who show symptoms of acute stress "stretched to their limits and beyond with no margin, no room in their lives for rest, relaxation, and reflection." There is nothing magical about working forty or fifty or sixty hours a week. But there is something important about letting your mind out for a jog—to maximize effective bandwidth rather than hours worked.

Of course, all of these mistakes—from firefighting to failing to cultivate bandwidth—are individual problems, to which any person can fall prey. But organizations can magnify the problem. When one member of a team begins to fall behind or enters a firefighting mode, this can contribute to the scarcity felt by others. When one person's bandwidth is taxed, especially at the top, a sequence of bad decisions can lead to further scarcity and to taxes on others' bandwidth. Organizations can create a domino effect, with each individual member pulling the team toward firefighting and reduced bandwidth. But organizations can also be insightful, creating environments conducive to the successful management of scarcity's challenges.

BENIHANA

Like many American entrepreneurs, Hiroaki ("Rocky") Aoki had a wild youth. As a rambunctious teenager in Japan in the 1950s, he sold pornography in school and started a rock band called Rowdy Sounds. He also showed discipline: as a flyweight wrestler his hard work earned him a spot in the 1960 Summer Olympics, an athletic scholarship to an American university, and eventually the U.S. flyweight title and a spot in the wrestling Hall of Fame. As he matured, his creativity, energy, and diligence increasingly turned to business. While competing as a wrestler, he studied for an associate's degree in restaurant management, and in his free time he ran an ice cream truck in Harlem.

Aoki's most successful venture started small. With $10,000 from his ice cream truck, he started a four-table Japanese steakhouse called Benihana, on West 56th Street in New York. The first few years were bumpy, but the restaurant began to draw buzz for its food and atmosphere, eventually becoming a hotspot for celebrities. (Muhammad Ali and the Beatles dined there.) Aoki capitalized on this success by expanding the restaurant into a chain, first throughout New York City and eventually to the rest of the country and the world. Today Benihana is in seventeen countries. At the time of Aoki's death in 2008, his empire was thought to be worth over $100 million. So thorough is his stereotype that it borders on parody, complete with his name, the paternity suits, intrafamily lawsuits, a collection of antique cars, an array of eccentric hobbies, and an ethnically flavored semi-mystical back story for the chain's name (after a single red flower—*benihana* in Japanese—that Aoki's father saw amid the rubble after a U.S. bombing of Tokyo in World War II).

Anyone who has been to a Benihana restaurant knows why it's unique: The chef cooks the meal right in front of you; in fact, "cooking" does not do justice to the performance. The chef is a virtuoso: he juggles his knives, tosses food from the spatula directly onto your plate, and creates onion ring volcanoes! Only at Benihana do meals end with a round of applause. Search for "Benihana" (or, better yet, "hibachi chef") on YouTube and you'll see hundreds of videos, with tens of thousands of hits, showing the theatrics. All this contributes to Benihana's success in a roundabout way. Aoki did more than create a bit of entertainment. He understood at a deep level the scarcity restaurants faced. And he solved it.

People think restaurants are about food, décor, and service. After all, this is what we experience as customers. Yet we all know wonderful restaurants that have shut down. Getting customers in the door does not ensure success in the restaurant business. Dry logistical and operational decisions drive profitability. The problem restaurants face is that much of their costs are fixed. Sure, they spend money on the food, but the ingredients do not cost as much as the overhead: salaries, rent, electricity, insurance, and so on. Whether you serve many customers or only a few, most of these costs must still be covered. As a result the business is all about "cream." After your revenues rise to a level that covers the fixed costs, a large percentage of the remainder goes directly to profits. This creates interesting math. Three seatings on a busy Saturday night is not just 50 percent more profitable than two seatings. If the first two cover your fixed costs and leave you with a small profit, then the third is "cream," mostly all profits.

What Aoki (and others) recognized is that the restaurant business is really about seating scarcity. How many seatings can you fit in? You get more seatings if you can squeeze in more tables. You get more seatings if you fit more people per table. You get more seatings if you can turn tables over faster, if you get four sets of customers out of a table each evening rather than three.

What appears to be theater at Benihana was really a very clever solution to scarcity. The chef's production involves people sitting at communal tables. And communal tables of eight mean a much more efficient packing of customers. No more waiting for two tables of two to open up side by side so you can seat a party of four. At communal tables you simply fill up the tables as people come in. A table of four merely means four chairs at the table. But even better, the tables turn over much faster. The chef cooks theatrically—and quickly—in front of you. You sit, the chef is there, the menu is small, and the time to order is limited. The chef then festively paces the meal for you. The food is tossed onto your plate, and you eat quickly because you can see the following course is about to be tossed next. Even the dessert—ice cream, which near the hibachi melts quickly—is designed for speed. And when the show ends, the chef bows and you applaud and it's over. What are you going to do, sit around and chew on your chopstick? It is hard to loiter when the chef is standing there, all done, the table has been cleared, and others are leaving. All this means that Benihana earns much more per table per night; some estimates suggest Benihana earns ten cents more in profit per dollar of revenue than other restaurants, making it far more profitable.

PACKING IN BUSINESS

Besides well-orchestrated meals, Benihana provides an important lesson for many organizations. Even when businesses are insightful enough to identify their true scarce resource, they often underappreciate the complexity of managing scarcity and the benefits that come from doing it just a little bit better.

Sheryl Kimes, an operations researcher at Cornell University, discovered this when she was hired by Chevys, a Mexican restaurant chain, to see if she could improve its profits. She started by talking to the staff to get a better feel for the challenges, and one problem was clear: long lines. In a way, this had to be good—the restaurant was popular. But it can also be a bad thing. Long lines can make you proud, but they bring in no money. You need people inside and eating, not outside and waiting. Customers can get disgruntled and not come back. You don't want it said of you, "Nobody goes there anymore; it's too crowded," as Yogi Berra put it. To understand what might be done—raise prices? expand?—Kimes conducted a thorough statistical analysis, which gave her a snapshot more precise than the staff's impressions: What was the income per table? Which tables were most occupied? What was the turnover? And so on.

What she found surprised her. The visuals showed long waits; the data showed low usage. Only during five hours each week were more than half the seats occupied. But there were many more hours with lines outside. What was going on? Two clues in the data helped crack the problem. First, there was enormous variability in usage time, and the biggest variation occurred after one meal ended and before the next one began. Even in busy times, there were long lulls between consecutive parties at a table. Second, even though restaurants like Chevys are considered places for friends and coworkers, the data told another story: 70 percent of parties were just one or two people. The restaurant didn't seem to have the right tables for the parties it was hosting. To see if this was right, Kimes took the data on parties coming to eat and ran it through an algorithm to look for efficient packing for Chevys, particularly for what tables ought to be used. This yielded a clear suggestion: more tables for two. Management implemented it, and the result was a financial windfall—a more than 5 percent increase in sales, approximately $120,000 a year in just one branch. Of course, purchasing new tables, remodeling the restaurant, and making other changes were not without cost, but after all the accounting, the profits exceeded the costs in the first year and turned into pure profits in the ensuing years. The investment on managing scarcity earned a high rate of return.

Until Kimes showed up, Chevys was failing to manage its scarcity because it was undervaluing scarcity's challenges. And those challenges were not trivial: serious computer analyses were needed for just one restaurant's problem. And restaurants are not alone. Businesses often succeed and fail as a function of how they manage scarcity.

10

SCARCITY IN EVERYDAY LIFE

Doctors and the cable guy have one thing in common. An appointment scheduled for three o'clock rarely happens at three o'clock. Staying on schedule can be hard. A slipup early on—perhaps a bit of procrastinating or something that has run unexpectedly long—gets magnified when there is no slack to absorb this shock. What first seemed like manageable tightness becomes a cascade of lateness. Every appointment becomes rushed. You tunnel on getting through this appointment. Predictably, you borrow from future ones. A time-debt trap forms. A tight calendar leaves you on the edge of being late to every meeting. And on most days you go over that edge early. (Why customers put up with it is another question.)

A colleague of ours—the president of a foundation—is no stranger to tight calendars. He has the distinct pleasure of spending most of his days in back-to-back meetings. He could easily fall perpetually behind like the doctor or the cable guy, every meeting more delayed than the previous one. And since people are coming to ask him for money, they would put up with it! But he does not run late.

About five minutes before a meeting is scheduled to end, his assistant shows up and announces, "Five minutes left." And at the end of the meeting, his assistant shows up again. This fairly obvious intervention—used by many executives lucky enough to have a skilled and dedicated assistant—prevents the cascade and the scarcity trap.

The assistant knocking at the door is not a particularly innovative intervention, but it illustrates something profound. Small changes to one's circumstances can short-circuit the consequences of scarcity. The psychology of scarcity is primitive, and changing it "from within" can be hard. But you don't need to change the psychology in order to get the right outcome. The foundation president is not tunneling any less. His trick is to change the environment to counteract the psychology. And not even drastically: the assistant does not create additional slack. Meetings are still scheduled back to back, and the president still tunnels during these meetings. All the assistant does is stand in the way, preventing the psychology of scarcity from doing harm. You can think of it as akin to a rumble strip on the side of a highway. It's a small change, yet it protects drivers against their wandering minds and fatigue; it's much easier than getting them to focus or to sleep more.

In the same way, we can "scarcity-proof" our environment. We can introduce the equivalent of rumble strips and helpful assistants, using our insights into why things go badly to build better outcomes. What matters is the logic of the enterprise—the appreciation of how understanding scarcity can help us think differently and manage enduring problems.

WHAT IS IN THE TUNNEL?

A simple yet often underappreciated tool for managing scarcity is to influence what's in the tunnel. This is one thing the assistant does well: she forcefully brings in the next meeting while the executive is still tunneling on this one. In work with the economists Dean Karlan, Margaret McConnell, and Jonathan Zinman, we tried to bring savings into the tunnel for poor individuals in Bolivia, Peru, and the Philippines. We built upon the insight that the poor fail to save partly because of tunneling. Saving is an important but not urgent task, the kind that nearly always falls outside the tunnel. At any point in time, there are more pressing things to do than save. So we brought savings back into the tunnel for a moment by making it top of mind. Having asked people what they were saving for and how much, we would send them, at the end of each month, a quick reminder—a text message or a letter. This benign reminder alone increased savings by 6 percent, a strikingly large effect given how infrequent and nonintrusive this was. (Messages, after all, are much less salient or vivid than an assistant standing in your doorway.) We were able to increase savings not through education or by steeling people's willpower but merely by reminding them of something important that they tend to overlook when they tunnel.

Tunneling gives us a new way to think about financial products. Some financial decisions naturally appear in the tunnel. Someone has an incentive to ensure that you repay your loan or pay your rent. That person or institution, like the assistant, will bring it into your tunnel no matter how tunneled you are. Savings, on the other hand, has no dedicated assistants to care for it, and—absent a behaviorally informed intervention like ours—will end up outside the tunnel most of the time.

Of course, insights about tunneling can also be used to exploit. You might set high late fees and then not remind people of the impending charges. Many of these effects, from reminders to the impact of late fees, will disproportionately affect the poor, since they are the ones who are tunneling—and suffering the consequences— the most.

Reminders, of course, are not limited to money. A busy person will too readily neglect the gym, which is important but never urgent. Signing up for a personal trainer reduces this problem. Now the trainer's calls bring fitness back into the tunnel. Now going to the gym becomes something that cannot be neglected: a trainer, intruding into your tunnel, is asking when you would like to come work out this week. The trainer is a constant presence, ensuring that the gym is top of mind.

Impulses, rather than reminders, are also easy to bring to the tunnel. Supermarkets have long understood this. They saw an easy way to make money: place candy bars at checkout counters. The candy intrudes into the tunnel in the form of an immediate urge: *I want chocolate.* Many urges are like this; however important or desirable they may be, they may be out of mind when they are out of sight because they are not pressing. But when they're in sight, they assert themselves, pushing other impulses—in this case your weight-watching impulses—out of the tunnel.

Given this observation, why not do the same for savings? We did this in another project, with a product we call "impulse savings." Much like candy bars, impulse savings cards are left to hang at prominent locations, such as next to cash registers. They have pictures on them that portray people's savings goals—such as college, a home, or a car—designed, like a candy bar, to create an urge. Except that when they "buy" these cards, people are actually saving: the dollars they pay get transferred into their savings accounts.

The cards not only combat tunneling by bringing a person's latent goal to the forefront; they also provide an easy way to act on it—"buy this card"—before the goal fades. In a small pilot program with IFMR Trust (a large provider of financial services to the poor), we found a surprising number of people eager to save in this way. A photo of one's family occasionally emerging on a busy person's desktop (irregularly enough to capture attention rather than becoming part of the background) may also work: make something top of mind that might otherwise be neglected.

Reminders can be powerful, yet they are often underappreciated, perhaps because they are so obvious. In 2008, the Massachusetts Registry of Motor Vehicles thought of a way to reduce costs. All the letters they were sending to remind people about their soon-to-expire car registrations were costly. So they got rid of these reminders. In a way this made perfect sense, but in light of our analysis, you can see why it might be foolish. Registrations expire at a fairly random time, solely a function of the last time you registered. Without a reminder, it is hard to remember the date. For the poorest and the most hurried, these reminders were likely the only thing that kept the registration from expiring and risking a ticket for the car owner. In effect, with this simple policy change the state had (inadvertently?) imposed a regressive tax.

Reminders are deceptively simple yet are often overlooked. Policy makers can spend millions of dollars in shaping attitudes toward savings but then fail to incorporate reminders urging people to save. We can spend hefty sums on gym membership yet never stop to consider what to do to ensure that the gym stays within the confines of our tunnel.

NEGLECT

Last year, we neglected our savings. In fact, it has been quite some time since either of us has thought about it. What causes this reckless behavior? (One of us even has kids!) Well, it's actually not terribly reckless. Our savings accounts—from retirement savings to college savings for the kids—have been growing quite comfortably. How did we save without actively saving? The same way most people do. Each of us enrolled a long time ago in a plan that automatically deducts 10 percent from our paycheck. Our savings balances show that we saved a lot, even though our daily behavior suggests total neglect: we spend our paychecks without ever thinking about saving. Automatic deduction allows us to save with full neglect.

This example highlights a simple insight. When there's neglect, it is often more effective to alter the outcome it leads to rather than fight it. Here is an example with retirement savings. When people in the United States start a new job, they need to fill out a form regarding their participation in a 401(k) plan. Typically, if they fail to fill out the form, they are not enrolled, which can be a recipe for disaster later in life. But when you have just been hired, with all the turmoil and anxiety that brings, you will often tunnel, and the form will get neglected. In one insightful study, researchers changed the consequences of neglecting the form. New employees received a revised form that said something along the lines of: "You are enrolled in a 401(k) at 3 percent. Turn this form in if you prefer not to enroll or to enroll at a different level." Now, when people neglected the form, they were saving. And better yet, for all those who thought about it and wanted to save, everything was set—there was nothing at risk by forgetting. The results were striking. Even three years later, there was a dramatic difference in enrollment rates. At those companies where new employees had to opt out, more than 80 percent had enrolled in the 401(k) plan. At those companies where new employees had to opt in, only 45 percent had enrolled. Changing the default— what happens when a decision is neglected—can have strikingly large effects.

Of course, there are a lot of tricky policy issues with *someone else* setting your defaults. But in many cases you can set the defaults on your own. Automatic bill pay is a prime example. A busy person who enrolls for automatic bill pay no longer runs the risk—in the tunnel of work—of forgetting to pay her bills. Or, rather, she is free to ignore her bills, but when she does, those bills still get paid. As a result, some of the most persistent tunneling problems for the busy these days—at least for those who have access to modern technology—are those tasks that cannot be automated, like a car registration, a driver's license renewal, or taxes. Worse yet are those that are not automated and do not have a natural deadline or reminder, like writing a will or getting a medical checkup.

This thinking applies more broadly, to things that are repetitive and predictable. Picture someone working at home and tunneled on a deadline. We know that they will neglect the quality of their eating; they will eat whatever they can find near at hand. In fact, distracted and depleted, they will tend to prefer the less healthy options, those most immediately tempting. With a pantry full of assorted options, this busy person will end up gaining a few pounds. In contrast, a pantry stocked with only healthy options can insulate the waistline from the deadline.

A recent Bank of America program called Keep the Change illustrates a constructive use of turning neglect to good purposes. As the bank explains:

> With the Keep the Change program, you can grow your savings automatically. After your enrollment, we'll round up all your Bank of America debit card purchases to the nearest dollar amount and transfer the difference from your checking account to your savings account. Every cup of coffee, tank of gas, and bag of groceries you buy adds up to more savings for you. What could be easier?

Keep the Change (which has been criticized on other grounds, including low interest and high fees) does one thing very well: it gets people to save not by trying to curb their impulses to spend but by harnessing these impulses. People do neglect to save, so this program gets them to save while doing what comes most naturally, namely, consuming.

VIGILANCE

For a busy professional, going to the gym with some regularity is much harder than signing up for a gym membership. One reason for this is obvious. The pain of signing up does not compare to the pain of stomach crunches or a half hour on the elliptical machine. But there is another reason. You only need to sign up for the gym once, whereas going regularly requires vigilance—doing the right thing again and again. We can think of choices as coming in one of two varieties: vigilance and one-off. Vigilance choices require that we continuously repeat the choice, like going to the gym, saving for a rainy day, eating the right foods, or spending quality time with our family.

Some even require hypervigilance. Miss a visit to the gym and you undo only a tiny bit of your hard work, but skip a dose of certain medications, and things quickly get a lot more serious. Slipping up just once and using your savings to buy a leather jacket can also undo many months of hard work. One-off choices only need to be done once (or at least very infrequently) to get the desired outcome: enroll in automatic bill payment and you are done with worrying about paying bills, buy a washer/dryer and you save a trip to the laundro-mat for years, enroll in some discount feature with your telephone provider and you take advantage of the savings until further notice.

Especially when you tunnel, it is much easier to do the right thing once than to have to repeat it. Yet so many good behaviors require vigilance: being a good parent, saving money, or eating right. To make matters worse, so many bad behaviors need be done just once to cause the pain: borrowing, taking on an ill-advised commitment, making an unwise purchase. You splurge or take a loan just once, and you have dug yourself a hole for the extended future, a hole that will require vigilance to climb out of.

This suggests a recipe: whenever possible, convert vigilant behaviors into one-time actions. Rather than having to be vigilant every time you grab a snack from the pantry, just be vigilant at the grocery store. Many banal tasks have this structure. Keeping your house clean requires vigilance, or (assuming you can afford it) just set up a maid service once. Paying your bills every month requires vigilance. Setting up automatic bill payment only needs to be done once. Remembering to have sufficient cash for tolls while you drive requires vigi-lance; signing up for E-ZPass, an automatic form of toll payment, is done once. More broadly, because tunneling induces neglect, con-verting those things that tend to get neglected into one-time solu-tions can be very powerful. Spending time with your kids invariably suffers when it depends on your vigilance, but if you sign up for a weekly activity together, that one-time action ensures that you will have a minimum amount of quality time together each week.

The other direction also works. Convert questionable one-time behaviors into the kind that demands vigilance. Some policy makers have proposed "cooling off periods" for car purchases, and similar arrangements may be wise for loans of every variety (money, time, calories, and so forth). Essentially, you are setting up a system that requires you to confirm the decision several times before you actually commit to it. (Imagine that any time you receive a tempting invitation, your e-mail is set up to send the following response: "Thank you. I may be able to do this. I will let you know in a week.")

Occasionally, you may also want to turn automatic renewals into acts of vigilance. When was the last time you checked if there might now be more affordable car insurance than the one you so meticulously chose years ago? Options change, and some one-off choices may also have been misguided. When we signed up for a movie-rental service, we thought we'd be watching several movies a month and returning them promptly. As it stands, it scares us to think of how much we must be paying per movie. Instead of automatically renewing, it might be wise occasionally to confirm the ongoing wisdom of that old one-off choice.

So what about loans? Should we ban quick loans, one-time choices with potentially bad consequences? In the *Family Feud* experiment from chapter 5, we saw how removing poor participants' option to borrow improved overall performance. But, of course, this is where life gets more complicated than the lab. Some loans are bad, but some are good. How do we decide which are which? Even within our own theory, some loans provide needed slack. When your car breaks down and you need cash to fix it, a loan (even an expensive one) may prevent a worse cascade—arriving late to work, risking job loss, and so on. Paradoxically, scarcity increases the chance you'll need a quick fix, as well as the chance that some such fixes will hurt you.

One insight of the psychology of scarcity is the need to prepare for tunneling and to insulate against neglect: navigate so that bad choices are harder to make in a single moment of tunneling, and arrange it so that good behaviors require little vigilance yet are occasionally reevaluated.

LINKING AND THE TIMING OF DECISIONS

In a world of tunneling and neglect, a lot depends on timing. Some of our biggest mistakes happen when deciding for the future, when things far removed from any tunnel look distant and fuzzy. Things we'd never agree to today ("Too busy today!"), we readily commit to a month from now ("Sure! Calendar looks wide open!"). Our needs today are pressing; those a month away are abstract and unrealized. This, as we have seen, is how we end up overcommitted. It's how those strapped for cash end up buying items they eventually cannot afford. The washing machine that was so appealing six months ago, when it came with 180 days of no payments, now has become a major weight.

But once we understand the psychology, we can use it for some good. There is no reason that the very same feature—a lack of appreciation of scarcity in the future—cannot be harnessed to help. A willingness to commit to a less scarce future underlies the well-known Save More Tomorrow program, through which people who felt they were not currently able to save agreed to increase their savings deductions whenever their salary increased. There would be no new sacrifices now; only later, in that fuzzy future. The results have been stunning. In one firm, more than 75 percent of those offered the plan chose it over trying to save on their own, and only a minority ever opted back out. By the third pay raise, individuals had more than tripled their savings rates.

What's particularly clever here is the linkage between something you expect to happen (the salary raise) and something you would like to happen (the increased savings). This arrangement automatically links the two. You can do something similar with borrowing. Consider the following thought experiment. In an attempt to curb predatory lending, one state forces payday lenders to charge lower fees—say, $25 instead of $50 on a $200 loan. Assume the industry remains profitable and survives. In another state, a different program is created: fees remain at $50, but only $25 goes to the lender;

the remaining $25 goes into an account in the borrower's name. Once $200 has been accumulated in this account—in this case, after eight loans—the person no longer needs to borrow. When she needs a loan, she can use these savings instead. In effect, by saving $25 of every $50 they would have paid for fees, the borrowers can quickly become "lenders to themselves."

Put simply, the truth about all those good decisions you plan to make sometime in the future, when things are easier, is that you probably won't make them once that future rolls around and things are tough again. So preempt and link wisely. At a moment of focus on the importance of exercise, buy a membership, hire a personal trainer, bet a friend, do what you can for this motivation to linger once you're tunneled elsewhere. If you're focused enough on healthy foods while shopping, make sure to fill the pantry with the right stuff, for those times when your mind is no longer food conscious. And when something—a book, a commercial—happens to focus you for a moment on life in old age, take action. Arrange for an automatic deduction into savings; call your lawyer to arrange a meeting to write a will. Otherwise, you'll plan to do it sometime soon, but you'll be in another tunnel then.

ECONOMIZE ON BANDWIDTH

Because scarcity taxes bandwidth, a key concern in the management of scarcity is to economize on bandwidth. Just as the busy are concerned with every minute of the day, and the poor focus on money, everybody under scarcity is profoundly influenced by how their bandwidth is distributed and spent.

Bandwidth is about allocating our limited information-processing abilities. In that sense, decisions that demand more information processing have immediate bandwidth implications. Every manager stretched for time values assistants who are good at synthesizing decisions, who can distill choices into their essential components and present them clearly. A subordinate who delivers large amounts of unprocessed data is far less useful. Clear and simple syntheses are a terrific way to economize on cognitive capacity.

Yet we often fail to appreciate this when presenting information. This was illustrated in a study of payday loans conducted by economists Marianne Bertrand and Adair Morse. The researchers divided customers who were about to take a payday loan into two groups. One group was shown a table that listed the annual effective interest rate they would be paying (443 percent) compared to comparable loans (16 percent on a credit card). Another group was presented with similar data, but instead of interest rates, they were shown how many dollars they would pay on the loan if they were to repay in two weeks ($45), one month ($90), and so on, as compared to how many dollars they would pay if the same amount were borrowed on a credit card ($2.50 for two weeks, $5 for a month, and so forth). In other words, similar data were presented in slightly different ways: In one case, interest rate, an abstract measure of something, the precise implications of which may be hard to gauge. In the other, dollars paid, familiar units that you need to take out of your pocket. What Bertrand and Morse found was that far fewer customers took the payday loan when they were shown the cost in dollars. Those who come for payday loans are accustomed to seeing, thinking about, and needing dollars. Interest rates, by contrast, are exotic financial instruments that few of us use in daily life and which require substantial intellectual effort to turn into something more palpable. When your bandwidth is taxed, a concrete sum carries a lot more meaning than some abstract term.

Nutrition labels present a similar problem. They inundate people with a great deal of exotic information. Consumers now get not just calorie information but also information on calories from fat, good fats versus bad fats, essential nutrients (are you getting your omega-3 fatty acids?), percentage daily allowance of several vitamins and minerals, and so on. All this makes for serious information-processing demand, and without an easy way to process the information, it's hard to know how to act. How bad is a bagel? It is hard to tell.

Simply making trade-offs can be taxing. Picture yourself with a lot of work to get done. A good friend is leaving town and there is a going-away party that you really should attend, despite all the work. You decide to squeeze it in by going but not for very long. You will decide how long to stay when you get there, depending on the atmosphere and on what feels right. You arrive at the party, and after an hour you start wondering, "Should I go?" The party is fun and your departure could be misinterpreted, but work calls. Is an hour enough time? Will you look rude? You vacillate. You stay a bit longer, but really your mind is no longer at the party. The trade-off—what you are giving up for being at the party—makes it hard to be truly present. You thought you were helping yourself by remaining flexible, but what that really meant is giving way to lingering and distracting trade-offs.

The busy are desperate for time to devote to family and friends. Squeezing this time into a busy schedule is challenging—it ends up a predictable victim of neglect—and even when it is squeezed in, the pleasure is often gone, while the mind is elsewhere, contemplating what could be done instead. One of the wisest interventions we know of for dealing with scarcity's trade-offs is the Jewish Sabbath. The Sabbath is an old concept. You do not work on the Sabbath, or e-mail, or write, or cook, or even drive. It is a day of tranquility, serenity, rejuvenation of the kind that many of us might not experience for years. And it's ingenious for at least two reasons. One is that there are no options, no dilemmas; it's a day of nothing but time off, no trade-offs. And the other is that it happens at the same time every week, right when Friday exits, no matter how busy you might be, no questions asked, no need to plan. The Judaic scholar Abraham Joshua Heschel wrote a book about the Sabbath, which he considered God's gift of time.

The Atkins diet is reminiscent of the Jewish Sabbath. Most diets encourage trade-offs. They allot a certain number of calories, a certain number of grams of carbs, and other assorted constraints. Dieters are then asked to pick the mix of foods that they prefer, while satisfying the overall restrictions. It gives them the "flexibility" to contemplate their own preferences. But, like the partygoer above, this only condemns the bandwidth-taxed dieter to prolonged bouts of trade-off thinking. And trade-off thinking is both distracting and particularly bad for dieting since focusing on food makes it harder to resist. One study randomly assigned participants to diets that differed in their rule complexity and concluded, "Perceived rule complexity was the strongest factor associated with increased risk of quitting the cognitively demanding weight management program."

The Atkins diet (in its many incarnations) helps resolve this problem. Instead of constant trade-offs, it imposes a very small budget for carbohydrates. This makes some choices quite easy: some foods are so low in carbs that you can eat them without trade-offs. It makes other choices—a very big dessert—a virtual impossibility because they simply have too many carbohydrates. This leaves some room for trade-offs—a small dessert or a few slices of bread—but far less than in a standard diet. Now, there are those who are not convinced the Atkins diet is particularly good for you. But psychologically, it has one distinct advantage. Instead of having to ration your caloric intake and calculate at every meal what you would do, the Atkins diet is closer to the Sabbath, with its simple prohibitions and very few trade-offs.

BANDWIDTH VARIES

Another important thing about bandwidth is that it doesn't remain constant over time. Recall the sugar cane farmers we studied in chapter 2. Right before harvest they were poorer and right after harvest they were richer. But more important, right before harvest they had less bandwidth and right after harvest they had more. In a similar way, because of the failure to smooth their consumption, low-income workers who are paid monthly, as well as food stamps recipients, will likely have the least bandwidth near the end of the month and more bandwidth right at the beginning. And it would be wise to exploit this timing in implementing policy and program design. If you had a program trying to teach almost anything where some bandwidth is required, from health practices to business accounting, when would it be most effective? Right before or right after harvest, if you are teaching farmers? Right before Christmas, when the poor are scraping together money for gifts, or right after? Once you understand the bandwidth timeline, you can mark the calendar for those weeks in which you will find people listening and absorbing and those in which you'll encounter mind wandering.

The importance of timing bandwidth is that it also allows you to link events to better bandwidth moments, as illustrated by the following telling study. Fertilizer has been shown to have high economic returns for farmers—over 75 percent, for example, for maize farmers in Kenya. And yet many Kenyan farmers do not use it. The problem does not appear to be a lack of knowledge; most farmers report that they plan to buy fertilizer, yet fewer than a third actually do. They often cite that they have run out of money. What they really mean is that they did not have the money *when they needed it*. They get paid right after harvest, and the fertilizer needs to be purchased many months later, at a time when they are cash-poor and bandwidth taxed.

To bridge the gap between when there's money and when fertilizer is needed, some researchers created a simple and clever intervention. They had the farmers prepurchase the fertilizer, buying it during harvest, when they were flush with cash, for delivery at planting time. With this simple change, the percentage of Kenyan farmers who bought and used fertilizer rose to 45 percent from 29 percent—a dramatic increase. Failure was averted by relocating an important decision from a time when the farmers were cash-poor and, more important, bandwidth-poor to a time when they were cash-rich and bandwidth-rich.

Being aware of the natural variation in bandwidth can also help those with busy lives. The busy often schedule their activities based on time available—a task requires a certain amount of time, and I have that kind of time right here, Wednesday at 11 a.m. But beyond time, tasks also use bandwidth, some more, some less. Monitoring a conference call to make sure all goes as planned requires a lot less bandwidth than a tense in-person meeting with a boss or a client. Yet we often focus on available time slots without this recognition. Clearly, our bandwidth varies throughout the day. Are we allocating our tasks wisely, ensuring that high-bandwidth tasks get assigned high-bandwidth slots?

Exploiting bandwidth might include not only timing tasks and events but also setting the best order. For the longest time, as we struggled to write this book, we would put aside a block of time every morning. And we protected it ferociously, sometimes even when it was painful to do so—for example, when you're the only one holding up the scheduling of a six-person meeting. We were not simply protecting time; we were protecting *high-bandwidth* time. But this did not work very well; our writing sessions were not particularly effective. And then we realized what we had done wrong. Before sitting down for our ferociously protected writing time, we quickly looked over e-mail, to take care of any urgent business before we withdrew. By nine o'clock we would force ourselves to quit even if sometimes this required extreme action, like turning off the wireless router! But, as it turned out, we hadn't fully quit. One message about a delayed project highlighted how seriously behind we really were. Another would remind us about the urgent need to raise some money. We weren't sitting down to write so quietly. We had begun a series of mental, and noisy, trains of thought. We had acted like dieters exposing themselves to donuts every morning just before sitting down to think about other things.

SNAGS

Many low-income high school graduates do not go to college. And many generous financial aid programs, driven by the assumption that the reason is a lack of money, are geared toward helping low-income individuals. Yet these programs are severely underutilized; few applicants show up. This is surprising, so a group of researchers set out to find out why. They divided eligible high school graduates (and their families), who had come for help with their tax filing, into three groups and gave them all the forms needed to apply for financial aid to college. For the first group, they simply observed the tendency to apply. For the second, they tried to bridge the information gap. Perhaps eligible high school graduates didn't know about the money they were eligible for, so the tax professionals told them. For the third group, the researchers did something inspired. Tax professionals not only told the eligible graduates what they were eligible for, but they also actually filled out the forms with them. Simply telling people the exact benefits they were eligible for had no noticeable effect. But the help filling out the forms did have a remarkable effect: not only were they more likely to apply for financial aid, they were also 29 percent more likely to enroll in college.

Having to fill out forms is a potential snag for anyone, a chance to procrastinate and to forget. But with their bandwidth taxed, and with perhaps a bit of stigma attached, it is a bigger snag for low-income people. Families with no college experience *tripled* their submission rate if they received help in filling out the forms.

There is a deeper insight here about how to manage scarcity. Misplanning, procrastination, and forgetting can turn seemingly minor steps into major stumbling blocks. Yet we overlook these snags when structuring our lives or crafting policies for others. Give someone a form to take home and she may forget it; have her fill it out on site and enrollment goes way up. Of course, filling out a form is a "minor" step, but it is also one that is too easy to stumble on, like having to compute interest or remembering to renew the registration. When our bandwidth is taxed, the simplest snags can do a lot of damage.

Those on public benefits, for example, often are required to "recertify"—to complete a series of forms—every year to show that they are still eligible. As you might imagine, it is during these periods of recertification that people drop out of the program. And this requirement appears often to screen out the *most* needy: those who are most taxed are also those most likely to delay in recertifying and, unfortunately, the ones in greatest need of the benefit.

To see the logic of taxing bandwidth, think about it this way. Imagine we imposed a hefty financial charge to filling out applications for financial aid. We would quickly realize that this is a silly fee to impose; a program aimed at the cash stretched should not charge them much cash. Yet we frequently design programs aimed at people who are bandwidth-stretched that charge a lot in bandwidth. To use another vivid metaphor, it's like going to a juggler who is in need of help and tossing one more ball in the air for him to juggle.

This, incidentally, is not an argument for removing all snags. Sometimes there is a reason for their existence. Financial aid forms are complex because a lot of information is needed. Recertification happens because circumstances change, and programs need to target those who are eligible. But there are alternatives: for one, many forms could be automatically filled using tax data. The mistake we make in managing scarcity is that we focus on one side of the calculus—removing snags can be costly—while we underestimate the other—the bandwidth tax. But the data suggest that this tax can be unreasonably large. Small snags can be the difference between a successful program and an unsuccessful program, between receiving benefits or not, between being and not being a college graduate.

THE PROBLEM OF ABUNDANCE

As we contemplate the better management of scarcity, we should remember that scarcity often begins with abundance. The crunch just before a deadline often originates with ample time used ineffectively in the weeks preceding it. The months just before harvest are particularly cash tight because money was not spent well in the easy months following last harvest.

Remember the study from chapter 1, where participants did better at proofreading essays when they were given tighter deadlines? Although most people realize that deadlines can help them work better, deadlines are often underappreciated. In another version of that experiment, some participants were allowed to choose their own binding deadlines. The option to pick a deadline helped: participants voluntarily imposed strict deadlines that helped them earn more than the no-deadline group. But their freely chosen deadlines were not as aggressive as they should have been. They earned 25 percent less than the group that had no choice, whose deadlines were imposed on them. We have seen this with our own students. In one of our classes, we let students pick their deadlines for the final paper. Some wisely chose deadlines much earlier than the end of the semester. But many did not, causing themselves to cram for this paper right when all their other papers were due.

In a world of scarcity, long deadlines are a recipe for trouble. Early abundance encourages waste, and by the time the deadline approaches, tunneling and neglect settle in. Breaking a long deadline into progressively earlier chunks can cut this arc. The same thing happens with money. A farmer paid in one lump sum is being set up on a similar cycle of early abundance followed by eventual scarcity. And as with time, dividing a payment into incremental pieces can help. What if the farmer were to get paid not in one lump sum but more regularly? The same is true of food stamps. Recall that food stamps recipients were not able to smooth out their income over the month. Lots of bandwidth must now be used to plan, remember, control, and make trade-offs. Why not pay the benefits weekly? Or, if needed, some combination: a large initial payment to take care of big monthly expenses and then smaller payments for week-to-week expenses. A way to fight the abundance-then-scarcity cycle is to even it out—to create long periods of moderation rather than spurts of abundance followed by heightened periods of scarcity.

THE NEED FOR SLACK

The reason why the abundance-then-scarcity cycle is so bad is that, as we have seen, scarcity can get us trapped. It is not merely that we fail to smooth our activities under abundance; it is that we fail to leave slack for the future. We saw with the Koyambedu vendors in chapter 6 what having too little slack can do. When hit with a shock, they got themselves right back into a debt trap, one that could have been avoided given earlier abundance. This is the danger of not leaving enough slack, not enough buffer for potential shocks. It is not merely that the shocks hurt us but that they put us in a position for the psychology of scarcity to kick in. We begin to tunnel and to borrow, and soon we are one step behind and perpetually playing catch-up.

Yet despite this, it is striking how often we fail to build a buffer stock. While direct research on this question is scant, there are some good hints. For one, the data suggest that we tend to underappreciate the likelihood of many low-probability events. That's why we underinsure for floods and earthquakes. When everything is going smoothly, we can, of course, imagine dark clouds, but we undervalue their possibility and thus do not prepare properly. And it's a lot worse when any of many possible shocks can trip us. Technically, we are facing a disjunction of low-probability events. What could interfere with your plans are not just floods or earthquakes, but you may get sick, or a family member could get sick, or there could be a break-in, or a car theft, or a war, or the loss of a job, or a surprise wedding, or an unexpected birth. All of these, of course, are possible but highly unlikely. But the problem is that any one of these is enough to count as a shock, for which you should have built some buffer stock.

And that buffer stock needs to be built *during times of abundance*. If time is where you expect scarcity, this means leaving some extra room in your schedule, for "no good reason," other than being able to move your many projects and obligations around at no cost. With money, it means having and building a rainy day account, even if you do not feel terribly flush. All this does not come easy, does not feel natural, because even when you know that shocks and scarcity can happen, it doesn't *feel* that way when there's abundance.

The tug of scarcity can be strong. But understanding its logic can minimize its negative consequences. We can go some way toward "scarcity proofing" our environment. Like investing in a smoke alarm or setting up a college savings account for your new baby, a singular moment of insight can have lasting benefits.

CONCLUSION

As our island of knowledge grows, so does the shore of our ignorance.

—JOHN A. WHEELER

This book offered an invitation to read about a science in the making. We hope that this first glimpse of the science of scarcity has helped to change the way you think about many things, from the occasional bouts of feeling overworked to persistent problems like loneliness and poverty.

Looking at the familiar in a new light can lead to unexpected observations, sometimes in unexpected places. The two of us often play a game on our phones called Scramble. It's a break from work, a way to fill time, and, yes, a tool for procrastination. The game is simple, and brief, and we got pretty good at it. But while working on the book, we noticed that our Scramble scores took a precipitous drop. Tense days of writing under deadline led to remarkably weak scores. This was a vivid illustration of how pervasive the bandwidth tax can be. Even though we had conducted the studies and had seen the data, the magnitude of the drop was surprising. We had the vague sense of being "cognitively tired," but the 30 or 40 percent drop in scores was more than we would have anticipated. And the game was a simple and fun task. We suspected that our minds were not operating at full capacity, but we did not appreciate how taxed we were.

You might try to think of comparable moments in your experience. What activities in your life might create a large bandwidth tax? And where would these have a noticeable impact? Are you a worse driver then? You know to avoid driving when sleepy, but did it ever occur to you not to drive after a day of hard thinking at work? Are your jokes less funny then? Are you less friendly? Are you making worse decisions? Have you ever said, "I don't want to make this important decision now; my bandwidth is taxed?"

People overlook bandwidth. When you're busy and must decide what to do next, you might take into account the time you have and how long it will take you, but you rarely consider your bandwidth. You might say, "I only have half an hour. I will do this small task." You rarely say, "I have little bandwidth. I will do this easier-to-accomplish task." Of course, you sometimes do this implicitly, such as when you switch to another task when you fail to make progress. But this just means you paid a tax on an already scarce resource.

We schedule and manage our time but not our bandwidth. And it is striking how little we notice or attend to our own fluctuating cognitive capacities. Contrast this with physical capacity, where we are attuned to the potential effects of eating, sleeping, exercise. Like most workers in modern society, we use our minds to make our living, yet we know remarkably little about our minds' daily rhythms. If our job were to move boxes from one place to another, we'd have a better sense of how best to maximize our efficiency—when to exert more effort, when to rest. But for a job focused on moving ideas rather than boxes, we know little about how to maximize our limited cognitive capacity.

And just as we as individuals know little about our own fluctuating bandwidth, we as social scientists know little about the fluctuating bandwidth of society. Scientists tend to measure what their theories tell them to measure. Social scientists therefore measure the material dimensions of scarcity: how many people are unemployed, what was produced in a particular quarter, what earnings were, and so on.

Yet we know next to nothing about the cognitive side of the economy. Just as our own individual bandwidth appears to fluctuate, it is likely that society's bandwidth fluctuates as well. Might we find that the economic recession in 2008 also produced a profound cognitive recession? Perhaps bandwidth dropped significantly. What if while unemployment was climbing, the quality of decisions was dropping? We do not have the data to answer these questions. And while it is too late to gauge this for 2008, it is not too late to collect these data for future booms and recessions. There has been an effort in recent years to measure societal well-being, to create a measure of Gross National Happiness to go along with Gross National Product. Why not also measure Gross National Bandwidth?

From this, we might learn not just about our country as a whole but also about how different subgroups in our country are doing. When the unemployment rate jumps from 5 percent to 10 percent, that means an additional one in twenty working-age people are now struggling financially. A look at bandwidth might suggest that the effects of this increase are more widely felt. It is possible that, in times like these, many more individuals have money on their mind as a result. Perhaps even those who have had only a small tightening of budgets have lost enough slack to be experiencing some scarcity. And perhaps those individuals who are close to the newly unemployed—friends, relatives, neighbors—are showing the effects, too. It is possible that the cognitive impact is more widespread than the financial one.

This is not just about recessions. Take productivity, a driver of economic growth. Productivity depends crucially on bandwidth. Workers must work effectively. Managers must make wise investment decisions. Students must learn in order to build human capital. All of this requires bandwidth, and it is possible that a drop in bandwidth today further reduces productivity in the future.

It is also not just about economics. Bandwidth is a core resource.

We use it in parenting, studying, getting ourselves to the gym, and navigating our interpersonal relationships. It affects the way we think and the choices we make. When the economy enters a financial recession, we can buy fewer things. When we enter a cognitive recession, all aspects of our lives can potentially be affected, from parenting and exercise to savings and divorce.

Of course, bandwidth measurements need not be confined to countries. Companies could do bandwidth inventories: how are their employees doing? Individuals can conduct their own. Perhaps before a big decision, you would want to confirm that you are functioning at full bandwidth. We have seen several related tests already, and more can be drawn on and new ones developed. Some would be focused on scarcity. How best to measure slack? How most effectively to determine whether people are engaging in trade-off thinking? But we can go further, perhaps measure fluctuating cognitive capacity more generally.

One can also use these measures to better evaluate social programs and public policies. In a program for the unemployed, we focus on reemployment. Undoubtedly, that is important. But why not also gauge its impact on bandwidth? After all, if the unemployed have greater bandwidth, the benefits will be felt more broadly. The data show that the children of parents who are unemployed do significantly worse in school. If bandwidth is the culprit and we can do something to alleviate it, then these programs may have benefits far outside their initial scope.

A focus on bandwidth leads to more than just better measurement. Take the problem of the fast-food manager from chapter 2, the one lamenting the time he must spend managing his underperforming employees. What might he do? Should he spend his time and energy motivating them? Should he resort to threats of firing? Greater incentives? More training? Additional conversations? The manager's problem is not unique. Many employers of low-wage workers face problems of productivity and absenteeism. And they invariably try these assorted interventions.

But a focus on the psychology of scarcity suggests that this manager may want to tackle a different problem. Rather than motivating or training, threatening or enticing, perhaps he can focus on increasing bandwidth. Low-wage workers have volatile financial lives. We have seen their effects. We have also seen that incentives can be less effective in circumstances like this. When you're tunneling, many rewards can fall outside the tunnel. Why not instead think about financial products, logistical interventions, or working conditions that help workers deal with financial volatility and help clear some bandwidth?

Here is a stark example. Many workers, as we saw in chapter 5, resort to payday loans. Yet it's worth observing that a payday loan is often simply a loan against work that has already been done. The worker who takes a payday loan halfway through the pay cycle has already earned half her paycheck. The need for a loan is largely due to the fact that payment happens with a delay. Why should an employer have workers taking these loans, potentially falling into scarcity traps, taxing bandwidth, and resulting in lower productivity, especially when the employer can himself give pay advances at low cost? How valuable would it be for employers to improve productivity by offering the right financial products and creating bandwidth?

The case of employers is just one example of how thinking about bandwidth may prompt us to ask different questions and solve problems in different ways. Take the simple example of adherence: the poor, more than others, fail to take their medication as prescribed. We could say, "This is a fact of life," and move on, no longer trusting the poor to do what's required. Or we could build a product like GlowCaps. This pill bottle kicks into action whenever it has not been opened the right number of times that day. It starts by glowing, and if it still hasn't been opened, it beeps, eventually sending text messages to the user's phone. Little by little, it makes its annoyance known, preventing the neglect that comes with tunneling. With GlowCaps the poor have been shown to adhere to their medication schedules at dramatically higher rates. Similar products and interventions can solve adherence and other problems through an understanding of the psychology of scarcity. GlowCaps illustrates how cheaply, unobtrusively, and effectively we can use technology to address problems created by bandwidth. Naturally, similar insights are bound to prove equally dramatic in other places.

When we think about increasing farm productivity around the world, perhaps we should focus not on new crops or farmer training. Perhaps we should be thinking about how to get the farmers to do those small activities, such as weeding, which they surely already know about but so often remain outside their tunnel. What should be the farmers' GlowCaps, to remind them about weeding or about pest control?

ABUNDANCE

In thinking about scarcity, we have encountered several new puzzles. This book, for example, was not completed on time. Why? Besides all the obvious reasons, two stand out as we reflect on the last few years. First, some of the work was done when we were facing a sharp deadline. And when we wrote against a sharp deadline, we experienced scarcity. On many days we benefited from this, as our theory suggests. We were focused and more efficient.

But much of the time was not spent feeling as if we had a sharp deadline. During long periods, we worked with the feeling that we had plenty of time. And during those periods, predictably, time was frittered away. Not wasted exactly, but the per day productivity— say measured in words written—was far from where it could have been. You could say we were suffering from not having scarcity. But is that all? Or was it something about the psychology of abundance?

We have treated abundance as merely what happens when scarcity is absent, as if that's the "standard" state, when all is fine. But introspection tells us that there have been periods when we felt real abundance and that those periods feel distinct, not only from scarcity but from other, less marked times. There are times when a psychology of abundance kicks in. And what makes the psychology of abundance so intriguing is that it seems to have in it the seeds of eventual scarcity.

Many of us end up tight for time right before a deadline because we wasted the preceding period of abundance. Our students inevitably write their papers in the two days (or in many cases one night) before the papers are due, and this is often preceded by weeks when time was abundant. This was not their intention going into the semester; their last-minute scrambling is a microcosm of the time-management problems experienced by executives who live the good life just before they end up firefighting or by vacationers who don't know where the day went.

The experience of scarcity near the deadline often emerges because of how time was managed during abundance. This intimate link between scarcity and abundance repeats itself in many places. The farmer is strapped for cash before harvest because of how he spent his previous harvest's proceeds. How he behaved during abundance contributes to his eventual scarcity. We fail to save when cash is plentiful. We loll around when the deadline is far away.

Consider the financial crisis of 2008. Many have speculated that one reason for this crisis was a cognitive blind spot. Housing prices were rising throughout the late 1990s and early 2000s. During these boom times, a sudden fall in house prices seemed a remote possibility, difficult to imagine, and hardly worth the concern. This belief affected a great many choices. If house prices were destined to keep going up (or at least not tank), highly leveraged transactions seemed sensible, mortgages with high loan-to-value ratios seemed safer. Of course, prices did fall—dramatically, in some cases. And all of the investment decisions predicated on the assumption that they would not fall led to a financial cascade that nearly brought down the global financial system. In this case as well, the acute scarcity of the financial crisis had its roots in the lax behavior that characterized those preceding years of abundance.

Of course, we could write off all of those as merely the usual behaviors. People waste time. They are overconfident. But the good times and the abundance before the financial crisis magnified these tendencies—they boosted overconfidence, and reinforced complacency.

Follow the thread of scarcity far enough and it leads back to abundance: the recession that is caused by our behavior during the boom; the last-minute cramming that can be blamed on our inaction in the weeks prior. While scarcity plays a starring role in many important problems, abundance sets the stage for it.

Just as with scarcity, could there also be a common logic to abundance, one that operates across these diverse problems?

We ought to answer this question. Now that this book is done, we have plenty of time not to.

NOTES

INTRODUCTION

1   *If ants are such busy workers*: This quote is attributed to Marie
     Dressler. See, for example, Marie Dressler—Biography. IMDb.
     Retrieved November 6, 2012, from http://www.imdb.com/name
     /nm0237597/bio.
2   **"Illusion is the first of all pleasures"**: T. Smollett and J. Morley,
     eds., *The Works of Voltaire: The Maid of Orleans (La Pucelle
     d'Orléans)*, vol. 41 (New York: E. R. DuMont, 1901), 90.
4   **By scarcity, we mean:** This definition of scarcity is inherently
     subjective. One person with a lot of wealth but many desires can
     in principle experience the same scarcity as another with less
     wealth (and fewer desires). This subjective definition of scarcity
     is essential for understanding the psychology. Of course the *con-
     sequences* depend on both the psychology and the material real-
     ity. We are taking this subjective approach only to understand
     the psychology. When we analyze problems—poverty, for exam-
     ple, in chapter 7—we will combine both the subjective and the
     objective.
4   **people having too few social bonds:** In his seminal book, Robert
     Putnam showed across a diverse set of data a trend in Americans'
     participation in civic institutions. See Robert D. Putnam, *Bowling*

Alone: The Collapse and Revival of American Community (New York: Simon & Schuster, 2000). Since then, the field has been transformed by the influx of large amounts of data on social interaction. See Jim Giles, "Computational Social Science: Making the Links," *Nature* 488 (August 23, 2012): 448–50. Of course the importance of social capital—the inverse of social scarcity—by now is discussed in a wide variety of problems from economic development to the value of cities.

5   **the Allies realized they had a problem:** Todd Tucker, *The Great Starvation Experiment: Ancel Keys and the Men Who Starved for Science* (Minneapolis: University of Minnesota Press, 2008).

5   **a team at the University of Minnesota:** A. Keys, J. Brožek, A. Henschel, O. Mickelson, and H. L. Taylor, *The Biology of Human Starvation*, 2 vols. (Oxford: University of Minnesota Press, 1950).

6   *The men became impatient waiting in line:* S. A. Russell, *Hunger: An Unnatural History* (New York: Basic Books, 2006).

8   **One recent study asked subjects to come to a lab around lunchtime:** R. Radel and C. Clement-Guillotin, "Evidence of Motivational Influences in Early Visual Perception: Hunger Modulates Conscious Access," *Psychological Science 23*, no. 3 (2012): 232–34. doi:10.1177/0956797611427920.

8   **fast enough to remain beyond conscious control:** B. Libet, C. A. Gleason, E. W. Wright, and D. K. Pearl, "Time of Conscious Intention to Act in Relation to Onset of Cerebral Activity (Readiness-Potential): The Unconscious Initiation of a Freely Voluntary Act," *Brain* 106, no. 3 (1983): 623–42.

9   **One study finds that when subjects are thirsty:** H. Aarts, A. Dijksterhuis, and P. de Vries, "On the Psychology of Drinking: Being Thirsty and Perceptually Ready," *British Journal of Psychology* 92, no. 4 (2001): 631–42. doi:10.1348/000712601162383.

9   **the size of regular U.S. coins:** P. Saugstad and P. Schioldborg, "Value Size and Perception," *Scandinavian Journal of Psychology* 7, no. 1 (1966): 102–14. doi:10.1111/j.1467-9450.1966.tb01344.x.

9   **The coins "looked" largest to the poorer children:** In visual perception, a greater focus does not necessarily mean greater accuracy. Several studies have found that both motivation and attention

can penetrate and guide early visual processing. Psychophysical, neurophysiological, and behavioral evidence suggests that attention changes the strength of a stimulus by increasing its salience, and thus can enhance its perceptual representation, improving or impairing various aspects of visual performance. For example, observers report perceiving the attended stimulus as being higher in contrast than it really is. Marisa Carrasco, Sam Ling, and Sarah Read, "Attention Alters Appearance," *Nature Neuroscience* 7 (2004), 308–13; Yaffa Yeshurun and Marisa Carrasco, "Attention Improves or Impairs Visual Performance by Enhancing Spatial Resolution," *Nature* 396 (Nov. 5, 1998), 72–75; Rémi Radel and Corentin Clément Guillotin, "Evidence of Motivational Influences in Early Visual Perception: Hunger Modulates Conscious Access," *Psychological Science* 23, no. 3 (2012), 232–34.

9   **the coins captured the focus of poor children:** In this study, the poor children value the coins more than the rich children. Of course many other features vary between poor and rich children. More recent work has experimentally induced value, rather than taking population level differences in value. For a recent paper using this approach see Brian A. Anderson, Patryk A. Laurent, and Steven Yantis, "Value-driven Attentional Capture," *Proceedings of the National Academy of Sciences* 108, no. 25 (2011): 10367–71.

9   **"subjective expansion of time":** P. U. Tse, J. Intriligator, J. Rivest, and P. Cavanagh, "Attention and the Subjective Expansion of Time," *Attention, Perception, and Psychophysics* 66, no. 7 (2004): 1171–89.

9   **flashed pictures of faces for one second:** W. L. Gardner, Valerie Pickett, and Megan Knowles, "On the Outside Looking In: Loneliness and Social Monitoring," *Personality and Social Psychology Bulletin* 31, no. 11 (2005): 1549–60. doi:10.1177 /0146167205277208.

10   **their loneliness might imply social ineptitude or inexperience:** This is not to say that the lonely have greater social skills all around. Quite the opposite. We must be very precise about what we mean by "social skills." This study measures capacity to decode social cues. On the other hand, numerous studies have shown the lonely do show a lower capacity to regulate behavior in social settings. In chapter 6, we will argue that this diminished performance in

regulating their behavior in social settings is also a predictable consequence of scarcity. A wonderful book explores these ideas in much greater detail: John T. Cacioppo and William Patrick, *Loneliness: Human Nature and the Need for Social Connection* (New York: W. W. Norton, 2008).

10   **One study asked people to read from someone's diary:** See W. L. Gardner, C. L. Pickett, and M. B. Brewer, "Social Exclusion and Selective Memory: How the Need to Belong Influences Memory for Social Events," *Personality and Social Psychology Bulletin* 26, no. 4 (2000): 486–96. doi:10.1177/0146167200266007.

10   *Suddenly, Bradley cannot escape noticing connections:* W. L. Gardner, Valerie Pickett, and Megan Knowles, "On the Outside Looking In: Loneliness and Social Monitoring," *Personality and Social Psychology Bulletin* 31, no. 11 (2005): 1549–60.

11   **European paleontologists in nineteenth-century China:** K. Vitasek, M. Ledyard, and K. Manrodt, *Vested Outsourcing: Five Rules That Will Transform Outsourcing* (New York: Palgrave Macmillan, 2010).

12   **the feeling of scarcity depends:** A. F. Bennett, "Structural and Functional Determinates of Metabolic Rate," *American Zoologist* 28, no. 2 (1988): 699–708.

12   **we are unhappy:** The word *scarcity* is also used to describe a different effect in psychology. The *scarcity principle*, as it is often called, captures the idea that when there is less of something people want more of it. Marketers use this idea extensively, for example, with limited-time offers, by making sure the shelves are only partly stocked for online offers that say "only 3 left." See chapter 7 of this book for a nice description of the scarcity principle: Robert B. Cialdini, *Influence: Science and Practice*, vol. 4 (Boston, Mass.: Allyn and Bacon, 2001).

12   **Scarcity leads to dissatisfaction and struggle:** In economics, this is the principle of increasing utility. Having more of a resource provides greater utility or well-being. In the vast majority of economic analyses—as in our work—these preferences, the utility functions, so to speak, are also taken as given.

12   **mindsets created by particular instances of scarcity:** One study on dieting and mood is Peter J. Rogers, "A Healthy Body, a Healthy Mind: Long-Term Impact of Diet on Mood and Cognitive Function," *Proceedings—Nutrition Society of London* 60, no. 1 (CABI Publishing, 1999, 2001). A more recent study has examined the

physiological pathways: Doris Stangl and Sandrine Thruet, "Impact of Diet on Adult Hippocampal Neurogenesis," *Genes and Nutrition* 4, no. 4 (2009): 271–82. For a discussion of culture and poverty, see the recent collection of articles in David J. Harding, Michèle Lamont, and Mario Luis Small, eds., *The Annals of the American Academy of Political and Social Science* 629 (May 2010).

14   **The structure of human memory:** E. R. Kandel, *In Search of Memory: The Emergence of a New Science of Mind* (New York: W. W. Norton, 2007).

1. FOCUSING AND TUNNELING

19   *Do you have an idea for your story yet?*: MOOD—Calvin and Hobbes—Full Story. Retrieved from http://web.mit.edu/manoli/mood/www/calvin-full.html.

19   **all the reviewers raved about:** *Dirtcandy.* Retrieved from http://www.dirtcandynyc.com/?p=731.

20   **"The Crispy Tofu that's on the menu":** *Dirtcandy.* Retrieved from http://www.dirtcandynyc.com/?p=2508. One might think that Amanda Cohen had put this dish on her menu simply to capitalize on her *Iron Chef* celebrity: people come in wanting to taste the dish from the show. But she had the dish on her menu well before the show even aired. This was more than a marketing gimmick.

20   **months and years of prior experience and hard work:** The relationship between creativity and time pressure is significantly more complicated than this story implies. In many cases time pressure can inhibit creativity. Here's an intuition that has worked for us. When the task requires fanning out—the generation of new ideas—time pressure is an impediment. When the task requires fanning in—synthesizing a large set of ideas into one (as in Cohen's case)—time pressure can be helpful. A very nice article that reviews these ideas and their original extensive research is Teresa M. Amabile, Constance N. Hadley, and Steven J. Kramer, "Creativity Under the Gun," *Harvard Business Review* (August 1, 2002).

21   **has made a living out of studying them:** Though there has been follow-up work, the original article on this topic remains a good first read: Connie J. Gersick, "Time and Transition in Work Teams: Toward a New Model of Group Development," *Academy of Management Journal* 31, no. 1 (1988): 9–41. In this original research, she

sat through every group meeting of eight groups. Though we simplify and talk about one meeting, the process she studied takes place over several meetings. Ruth Wageman, Colin M. Fisher, and J. Richard Hackman, in "Leading Teams When the Time Is Right" (*Organizational Dynamics* 38, no. 3 [2009] 192–203), discuss how these insights can be used by leaders. At the midpoint transition, the group will be particularly primed for a change, one that leaders can use.

22   **undergraduates were paid to proofread three essays:** D. Ariely and K. Wertenbroch, "Procrastination, Deadlines, and Performance: Self-Control by Precommitment," *Psychological Science* 13, no. 3 (2002): 219–24. An earlier study found that college students were more likely to return an optional worksheet for pay when they had only one week to complete it compared to when they had three weeks; A. Tversky and E. Shafir, "Choice under Conflict: The Dynamics of Deferred Decision," *Psychological Science* 3, no. 6 (1992): 358–61. Economists have theorized about the power of deadlines using a different framework—hyperbolic discounting—our tendency to disproportionately weigh the present over the future. See Shane Frederick, George Loewenstein, and Ted O'Donoghue, "Time Discounting: A Critical Review," *Journal of Economic Literature* (2002) for an overview. Intermediate deadlines make us more effective, in this view, by translating distant future rewards into immediate present ones.

23   **A study by the psychologist Jaime Kurtz:** J. L. Kurtz, "Looking to the Future to Appreciate the Present: The Benefits of Perceived Temporal Scarcity," *Psychological Science* 19, no. 12 (2008): 1238–41. doi:10.1111/j.1467-9280.2008.02231.x.

23   **some customers are mailed a coupon:** J. J. Inman and L. McAlister, "Do Coupon Expiration Dates Affect Consumer Behavior?" *Journal of Marketing Research* (1994): 423–28; A. Krishna and Z. J. Zhang, "Short or Long-Duration Coupons: The Effect of the Expiration Date on the Profitability of Coupon Promotions," *Management Science* 45, no. 8 (1999): 1041–56.

23   **salespeople work hardest:** An example of a paper documenting this effect is Paul Oyer, "Fiscal Year Ends and Nonlinear Incentive Contracts: The Effect on Business Seasonality," *The Quarterly Journal of Economics* 113, no. 1 (1998): 149–85. His interpretation is less psychological than ours—attributing it to substitution of effort over time.

23   **as payday got closer:** S. Kaur, M. Kremer, and S. Mullainathan, "Self-Control and the Development of Work Arrangements," *American Economic Review Papers and Proceedings* (2010).

23   **"An Englishman's mind works best":** M. Hastings, *Finest Years: Churchill as Warlord, 1940–45* (London: HarperPress, 2009).

24   **a video game based on Angry Birds:** Here we describe a set of studies briefly. Details of these, including sample sizes and more careful statistical tests, can be found in Shah, Mullainathan, and Shafir, "Some Consequences of Having Too Little," *Science* 338, no. 6107 (November 2012): 682–85.

26   **the blueberry rich did not earn anywhere near twice as much:** It is also not the case that the blueberry rich simply got bored or did not want to spend as much time with the task. If that were the case, they could have played fewer rounds overall and stopped early.

27   **Just as we cannot effectively tickle ourselves:** Evidence on self-tickling ranges from experiments where self-tickling happens through control of an independent object to fMRI data. A wonderful review is in Sarah-Jayne Blakemore, Daniel Wolpert, and Chris Frith, "Why Can't You Tickle Yourself?" *Neuroreport* 11, no. 11 (2000): R11–R16. The prevailing view is that self-produced movement can be predicted and its effects can be attenuated. We know of no such careful empirical work on imagined deadlines or time pressure. The renegotiation problem is often discussed. An imagined deadline does not feel pressing because in the back of one's mind is the knowledge that you can always renegotiate it with yourself.

27   **At 10 p.m. on April 23, 2005:** *State Fire Marshal's Office Firefighter Fatality Investigation*, no. 05-307-04, Texas Department of Insurance, Austin, Texas. We thank Jessica Gross for helpful research on this case, and Dr. Burton Clark for helpful correspondence.

28   **vehicle accidents as the second leading cause of firefighter deaths:** P. R. LeBlanc and R. F. Fahy, *Full Report: Firefighter Fatalities in the United States—2004* (Quincy, Mass.: National Fire Protection Association, 2005).

28   **between 20 and 25 percent of firefighter fatalities:** Firefighter fatality retrospective study, April 2002. (Prepared for the Federal Emergency Management Agency, United States Fire Service, National Fire Data Center, by TriData Corporation, Arlington, Virginia).

28   **had graduated from a safety class the year before:** C. Lumry (January 21, 2010). *Amarillo Firefighter Fatality—COFT | Council On Firefighter Training.* Retrieved from http://www.coft-oklahoma.org /news-updates/m.blog/21/amarillo-firefighter-fatality.

28   **"I don't know of a firefighter":** C. Dickinson, *Chief's Corner* (February 27, 2007), retrieved from http://www.saratogacofire.com/ seatbelt.htm.

29   **the narrowing of the visual field:** L. J. Williams, "Tunnel Vision Induced by a Foveal Load Manipulation," *Human Factors* 27, no. 2 (1985): 221–27. By *tunneling* vision, researchers refer to something quite concrete that they have studied for years, sometimes at the level of the actual eye. People are made to focus on a target that's in front of the fovea, the center of the eye's retina. Then, items are presented at the parafoveal level, surrounding the fovea, where visual acuity is lower. And they measure people's ability to detect those items at the periphery while they perform various tasks at the center. And what they find is quite remarkable. They keep all the visual information intact and slightly alter people's task. For example, all subjects see the same *A*, and some have to decide whether it's the letter *A* (easy) whereas others have to decide whether it's a vowel (harder). And what they find is that although the visual experience is identical, those who have to think harder about the foveal *A* are less good at detecting items at the periphery. As they focus more on the task, they tunnel and lose peripheral vision. While this is at the level of the physical eye, *tunneling* also refers to the cognitive equivalent of this visual experience. It is a single-mindedness that misses much of what's peripheral.

29   **"To photograph is to frame":** Susan Sontag, *Regarding the Pain of Others* (New York: Farrar, Straus and Giroux, 2002), 46.

31   *not* **to give you "milk" and "snow":** N. J. Slamecka, "The Question of Associative Growth in the Learning of Categorized Material," *Journal of Verbal Learning and Verbal Behavior* 11, no. 3 (1972): 324–32. Another study asked people to name states in the United States and found that "helping" them by giving them some state names only decreased the total number recalled. See Raymond Nickerson, "Retrieval Inhibition from Part-Set Cuing: A Persisting Enigma in Memory Research," *Memory and Cognition* 12, no. 6 (November 1984): 531–52.

31   **subjects were asked to write down a personal goal:** J. Y. Shah, R.

Friedman, and A. W. Kruglanski, "Forgetting All Else: On the Antecedents and Consequences of Goal Shielding," *Journal of Personality and Social Psychology* 83, no. 6 (2002): 1261.

31   **Psychologists call this *goal inhibition*:** C. M. MacLeod, "The Concept of Inhibition in Cognition," in *Inhibition in Cognition*, ed. David S. Gorfein and Colin M. Macleod (Washington, D.C.: American Psychological Association, 2007), 3–23.

34   **Subjects had to retrieve from memory:** The illustration here shows only a few items in shades of gray. The actual experiment differed from this in two ways. First, subjects faced many more items. Second, the items were in different colors and these colors also had to be recalled.

34   **They earned less even though they had more total guesses:** These results are from an unpublished experiment. Subjects earned 7 percent less when given one and three guesses than when given one guess in both cases ($N = 33$, $p < .05$).

35   *I took a speed-reading course:* Woody Allen—Biography, IMDb, http://www.imdb.com/name/nm0000095/bio.

35   *So you want to save an extra $10,000:* B. Arends, "How to Save $10,000 by Next Thanksgiving," *Wall Street Journal*, November 20, 2011. Retrieved from http://online.wsj.com/article/SB100014 24052970204323904577040101565437734.html.

36   **from health insurance to crop insurance:** A brief discussion and a list of examples can be found in Michael J. McCord, Barbara Magnoni, and Emily Zimmerman, "A Microinsurance Puzzle: How Do Demand Factors Link to Client Value?" *MILK Brief*, no. 7. Available at http://www.microinsurancecentre.org/milk-project /milk-docs/doc_details/835-milk-brief-7-a-microinsurance-puzzle -how-do-demand-factors-link-to-client-value.html.

36   **more than 90 percent of farmers:** X. Giné, R. Townsend, and J. Vickery, "Patterns of Rainfall Insurance Participation in Rural India," *The World Bank Economic Review* 22, no. 3 (2008): 539–66.

36   **The same is true of health insurance:** A. Aizer, "Low Take-Up in Medicaid: Does Outreach Matter and for Whom?" *The American Economic Review* 93, no. 2 (2003): 238–41.

36   **worse than driving at above legal alcohol levels:** D. L. Strayer, F. A. Drews, and D. J. Crouch, "A Comparison of the Cell Phone Driver and the Drunk Driver," *Human Factors* 48, no. 2 (2006): 381–91. Also, D. Redelmeier and R. Tibshirani, "Association Between

Cellular-Telephone Calls and Motor Vehicle Collisions," *New England Journal of Medicine* 336, no. 7 (1997), 453–58. Note also that a recent large-scale naturalistic study surprisingly found little effect of cell phone use on crash probabilities. See Saurabh Bhargava and Vikram Pathania, "Driving Under the (Cellular) Influence" (2008), available at SSRN 1129978. This latter study, which avoids some of the problems that typically plague field-based studies of driving risk, is intriguing, yet it contradicts a large body of other data and will need to await follow-up investigation.

36   **eating while driving can be as big a danger:** There are no experiments we know of on eating while driving. The best data we have are from the "100-car study" in which one hundred cars were fitted with monitoring devices and tracked for twelve to thirteen months, resulting in 43,000 hours and over two million vehicle miles worth of data. They found that eating while driving increased the odds of a crash or near crash by 57 percent. Talking on a cell phone increased the risk by 29 percent. Dialing the cell phone, however, increases the risk by 279 percent, illustrating a key finding of the study that visual distraction is still extremely deadly. See Sheila G. Klauer et al., "The Impact of Driver Inattention on Near-Crash/Crash Risk: An Analysis Using the 100-Car Naturalistic Driving Study Data," no. HS-810 594 (2006).

36   **41 percent of Americans:** See Paul Taylor and C. Funk, "Americans and Their Cars: Is the Romance on the Skids?" (2006), available on the Pew Research Center website.

36   **people consume more calories when they are distracted:** B. Boon, W. Stroebe, H. Schut, and R. Ijntema, "Ironic Processes in the Eating Behaviour of Restrained Eaters," *British Journal of Health Psychology* 7, no. 1 (2002): 1–10.

37   *In lean times, many small businesses:* "Recession-Proof Your Business," *About.com Small Business: Canada*, retrieved October 22, 2012, from http://sbinfocanada.about.com/od/management /a/recessionproof.htm.

38   **the person himself regrets it:** The idea that we are at conflict with ourselves—that we do something that we ourselves do not want us to do—has a rich history. Most often it is viewed as a consequence of self-control problems. See, e.g., T. C. Schelling, "Self-

Command in Practice, in Policy and in a Theory of Rational Choice," *American Economic Review* 74 (1984): 1–11.

2. THE BANDWIDTH TAX

41   **the single umbrella term** *bandwidth*: Bandwidth, or computational capacity, has been studied under various guises, including several measures of intelligence, reasoning ability, short-term memory capacity, working-memory capacity, fluid intelligence, cognitive control, executive control, control of attention, conflict monitoring, and so forth. For professional researchers, some of these capture relevant distinctions, which are largely beyond our current scope. (Some researchers, for example, have posited that working-memory capacity is the prime component underlying many other measures; see, e.g., R. W. Engle, "Working Memory Capacity as Executive Attention," *Current Directions in Psychological Science* 11 (2002): 19–23.)

42   **the conditions of a school in New Haven:** A. L. Bronzaft, "The Effect of a Noise Abatement Program on Reading Ability," *Journal of Environmental Psychology* 1, no. 3 (1981): 215–22; A. L. Bronzaft and D. P. McCarthy, "The Effect of Elevated Train Noise on Reading Ability," *Environment and Behavior* 7, no. 4 (1975): 517–28. doi:10.1177/001391657500700406.

42   **the powerful effects of even slight distraction:** A major focus in cognitive psychology has been the role of distraction in cognitive performance, particularly as it interacts with attention and cognitive load. Even supposedly minor distractions have been shown to have profound effects, often far beyond what intuition would suggest. Experimental studies of the effects of distraction have ranged from response time experiments to the use of simulators and to field studies and have looked at tasks as diverse as visual, auditory, and pain perception, driving, surgery, work performance, and educational attainment.

44   **Behavioral and neuroimaging studies:** Several studies by Lavie and colleagues have documented increased attentional capture by salient distractors during high memory load. In one study, for example, two unrelated tasks—visual attention and working memory—were combined. Increased load in the working memory

task was predicted to lower people's ability to avoid visual distractors. Imagine participating in this rather unusual experiment. You stare at a computer monitor and see a sequence of digits, say, 0, 3, 1, 2, 4, which you need to memorize. Then, you see famous names appear on the screen, which you are asked to classify as pop stars or politicians. The names are accompanied by faces, which you are asked to ignore. Then, at some point a digit appears, say, a 2, and your task is to report the digit that follows in the sequence you memorized (in this case, 4.) To make this more interesting, there are two variations. First, the load manipulation: under high memory load, the sequence of digits to memorize was different on each trial, whereas under low memory load, the digits were in a fixed order: 0, 1, 2, 3, 4. Clearly, you'd need to rehearse the fixed order sequence hardly at all, whereas the novel sequences would need to be actively rehearsed. In addition, the faces to be ignored changed: in the low distraction condition, the faces and names were "congruent"; Bill Clinton's face appeared with his name, and so did Mick Jagger's. But in the high distraction condition, these were incongruent: Clinton's face appeared with Jagger's name, and vice versa. This turns out to be quite distracting! And it turns out to be a lot more distracting when your working memory is loaded. The impact of the incongruent faces was much greater when people were under high- as opposed to low-memory load. See N. Lavie, "Distracted and Confused?: Selective Attention under Load," *Trends in Cognitive Sciences* 9, no. 2 (2005): 75–82.

44   **push a button when you see a red dot on the screen:** R. M. Piech, M. T. Pastorino, and D. H. Zald, "All I Saw Was the Cake: Hunger Effects on Attentional Capture by Visual Food Cues," *Appetite* 54, no. 3 (2010): 579. The notion that certain mental or physical events can capture attention has been an enduring topic in the study of attention owing to the importance of understanding how goal-directed and stimulus-driven processes interact in perception and cognition.

45   **we gave subjects word searches:** This is from unpublished work with Christopher Bryan; C. J. Bryan, S. Mullainathan, and E. Shafir, "Tempting Food, Cognitive Load and Impaired Decision-Making," invited talk at the United States Department of Agriculture, Economic Research Service, Washington, D.C., April 2010.

46   **The *DONUT* was the problem:** 389 subjects participated in the study. The difference in time taken by dieters after seeing food words versus neutral words was highly significant (p = .003). As well, there was a significant interaction between the difference in times taken for neutral versus food words by dieters versus nondieters (p = .047). Subjects were given modest incentives to find as many words as they could.

47   **Much like a central processor:** Cognitive and neuroscience researchers have focused on the mechanisms and brain structures by which executive or cognitive control guides behavior. See, for example, G. J. DiGirolamo, "Executive Attention: Conflict, Target Detection, and Cognitive Control," in *The Attentive Brain*, ed. Raja Parasuraman (Cambridge, Mass.: MIT Press, 1998), 401–23.

48   **Raven's Progressive Matrices test:** J. Raven et al., *Manual for Raven's Progressive Matrices and Vocabulary Scales*, research supplement no. 3, 2nd/3rd edition (Oxford: Oxford Psychologists Press/San Antonio, Tex.: The Psychological Corporation, 1990 /2000): A compendium of international and North American normative and validity studies together with a review of the use of the RPM in neuropsychological assessment.

48   **It is a common component of IQ tests:** J. Raven, "The Raven's Progressive Matrices: Change and Stability over Culture and Time," *Cognitive Psychology* 41, no. 1 (2000): 1–48.

49   **Those who have familiarity with tests and test taking:** J. Raven, Ibid. It is worth noting that researchers have argued that gains from education can explain only a small fraction of gains in IQ scores; see, e.g., J. R. Flynn, "Massive IQ Gains in 14 Nations: What IQ Tests Really Measure," *Psychological Bulletin* 101 (1987): 171–91. A forceful case for environmental and cultural influences on IQ is Richard Nisbett's *Intelligence and How to Get It: Why Schools and Cultures Count* (New York: W. W. Norton, 2010).

49   **people in a New Jersey mall:** These experiments are summarized along with details on sample sizes and p-values in Anandi Mani, Sendhil Mullainathan, Eldar Shafir, and Jiaying Zhao, "Poverty Impedes Cognitive Function" (working paper, 2012).

50   **unable to come up with $2,000 in thirty days:** A. Lusardi, D. J. Schneider, and P. Tufano, *Financially Fragile Households: Evidence*

and Implications (National Bureau of Economic Research, Working Paper No. 17072, May 2011).

51 **the effects were equally big:** For those interested in the magnitude, the effect size ranged between Cohen's *d* of 0.88 and 0.94. Cohen's *d* can be calculated as the difference between means divided by the pooled standard deviation.

51 **a benchmark from a study on sleep:** L. Linde and M. Bergströme, "The Effect of One Night without Sleep on Problem-Solving and Immediate Recall," *Psychological Research* 54, no. 2 (1992): 127–36. In general, a large body of research has shown the detrimental effects of lack of sleep on a variety of cognitive processes, from attention and memory to planning and decision making. A compendium of the latest research is in Gerard A. Kerkhof and Hans Van Dongen, *Human Sleep and Cognition: Basic Research* 185 (Amsterdam: Elsevier Science, 2010).

52 **about five IQ points:** "What Is a Genius IQ Score?" *About.com Psychology*, retrieved October 23, 2012, from http://psychology .about.com/od/psychologicaltesting/f/genius-iq-score.htm.

52 **Walter Mischel and his colleagues:** W. Mischel, E. B. Ebbesen, and A. Raskoff Zeiss, "Cognitive and Attentional Mechanisms in Delay of Gratification," *Journal of Personality and Social Psychology* 21, no. 2 (1972): 204. In follow-up studies years later, Mischel and colleagues found a remarkable predictability of cognitive and social competencies in their now grown subjects, which has enriched researchers' thinking about the role of individual versus situational determinants of behavior; W. Mischel, Y. Shoda, and P. K. Peake, "The Nature of Adolescent Competencies Predicted by Preschool Delay of Gratification," *Journal of Personality and Social Psychology* 54, no. 4 (April 1988): 687–96.

53 **"the intimate contest for self-command":** Thomas C. Schelling, *Choice and Consequence* (Boston: Harvard University Press, 1985).

53 **personality, fatigue, and attention:** Roy Baumeister, Kathleen Vohs, Mark Muraven, and their collaborators have conducted numerous studies documenting what they call ego depletion, and the maintenance and reduction of executive and self-control. For a recent statement and review of the literature, see R. F. Baumeister and J. Tierney, *Willpower: Rediscovering the Greatest Human Strength* (New York: Penguin Press, 2011).

53   **The children who were most successful in resisting:** Mischel, Ebbesen, and Raskoff Zeiss, "Cognitive and Attentional Mechanisms."

53   **"Once you realize that willpower":** J. Lehrer, "DON'T!" *New Yorker*, May 18, 2009.

54   **a memory task:** B. Shiv and A. Fedorikhin, "Heart and Mind in Conflict: The Interplay of Affect and Cognition in Consumer Decision Making," *Journal of Consumer Research* 26, no. 3 (1999): 278–92. doi:10.1086/209563.

54   **a chicken foot cooked in a Chinese style:** W. von Hippel and K. Gonsalkorale, "'That Is Bloody Revolting!': Inhibitory Control of Thoughts Better Left Unsaid," *Psychological Science* 16, no. 7 (2005): 497–500. doi:10.1111/j.0956-7976.2005.01563.x.

57   **As we expected:** The details of this study can also be found in Mani, Mullainathan, Shafir, and Zhao, "Poverty Impedes Cognitive Function."

58   **It is hard for the same reason:** The standard Stroop task asks subjects to name the font colors of strings of letters. So *XKYD* may be written in a blue font and subjects must say "Blue." The challenge of Stroop is that some of the strings themselves spell out a color. So for example *RED* may be written in a blue font, posing a challenge. A very nice summary of Stroop is found in Colin M. MacLeod, "Half a Century of Research on the Stroop Effect: An Integrative Review," *Psychological Bulletin* 109, no. 2 (March 1991): 163–203. An oft-repeated anecdote is that the Stroop test was used to detect Soviet spies. Seeing *синий* written in a red font poses no problem for most of us. But spies—due to their hidden fluency in Russian—would stumble on naming the red font because this is the Russian word for "blue."

58   **On the executive control task:** Details in Mani, Mullainathan, Shafir, and Zhao, "Poverty Impedes Cognitive Function."

59   **Worse nutrition and simple hunger:** See, for example, K. Alaimo, C. M. Olson, and E. A. Frongillo Jr., "Food Insufficiency and American School-Aged Children's Cognitive, Academic, and Psychosocial Development," *Pediatrics* 108, no. 1 (2001): 44–53.

60   **There are other minor quibbles:** One problem is that postharvest subjects were taking these tests a second time. Improved performance postharvest could be due just to experience with the test. To control for this, we held back one hundred randomly selected

farmers and had them take the test for the first time postharvest. Since they were randomly selected, we compared them to preharvest farmers and found a similar effect, suggesting our effects are not due to experience with the tests. We also surveyed a sample of farmers who were postharvest but who, due to delay in payments, were still poor. These postharvest farmers behaved similarly to the preharvest farmers, suggesting the mechanics of harvest do not drive our results.

60   *About that time, it occurred to me*: N. Kusz, "The Fat Lady Sings," in *The Bitch in the House: 26 Women Tell the Truth About Sex, Solitude, Work, Motherhood, and Marriage* (New York: William Morrow, 2002).

60   **because they are partly preoccupied with food**: D. Borchmann, *Fasting, Restrained Eating, and Cognitive Performance—A Literature Review from 1998 to 2006.*

61   **from a simple lack of calories**: One study found that giving dieters a chocolate bar—and thereby calories—actually worsened cognitive performance. This was attributed to the fact that they were now more preoccupied with food ("What will I need to give up for this chocolate bar?"). N. Jones and P. J. Rogers, "Preoccupation, Food, and Failure: An Investigation of Cognitive Performance Deficits in Dieters," *International Journal of Eating Disorders* 33, no. 2 (March 2003): 185–92.

61   **a *dichotic listening task***: J. T. Cacioppo, J. M. Ernst, M. H. Burleson, M. K. McClintock, W. B. Malarkey, L. C. Hawkley, R. B. Kowalewski et al., "Lonely Traits and Concomitant Physiological Processes: The MacArthur Social Neuroscience Studies," *International Journal of Psychophysiology* 35, no. 2 (2000): 143–54.

61   **verbal information presented to the right ear is easier**: Ibid.

62   **now the lonely did significantly less well**: For an overview of all these studies, see John T. Cacioppo and William Patrick, *Loneliness: Human Nature and the Need for Social Connection* (New York: W. W. Norton, 2009).

62   **either socially well adjusted or else very lonely**: R. F. Baumeister, J. M. Twenge, and C. K. Nuss, "Effects of Social Exclusion on Cognitive Processes: Anticipated Aloneness Reduces Intelligent Thought," *Journal of Personality and Social Psychology* 83, no. 4 (2002): 817.

62   **they ate roughly twice as many:** R. F. Baumeister, C. N. DeWall, N. J. Ciarocco, and J. M. Twenge, "Social Exclusion Impairs Self-Regulation," *Journal of Personality and Social Psychology* 88, no. 4 (2005): 589.

62   **a substantially higher consumption of fatty foods:** W. Lauder, K. Mummery, M. Jones, and C. Caperchione, "A Comparison of Health Behaviours in Lonely and Non-Lonely Populations," *Psychology, Health and Medicine* 11, no. 2 (2006): 233–45. doi:10.1080/13548500500266607.

62   **do worse on the heart–flower task:** The details of this study can also be found in Mani, Mullainathan, Shafir, and Zhao, "Poverty Impedes Cognitive Function."

63   **considerable progress in the understanding of stress:** L. E. Bourne and R. A. Yaroush, "Stress and Cognition: A Cognitive Psychological Perspective," unpublished manuscript, NASA grant NAG2-1561 (2003), retrieved from http://humansystems.arc.nasa.gov/eas/download/non_EAS/Stress_and_Cognition.pdf. See also Bruce McEwen's *The End of Stress as We Know It* (New York: Joseph Henry Press/Dana Press, 2002).

63   **the biochemistry of the generalized stress response:** A wonderful summary of this area of research can be found in Robert M. Sapolsky, *Why Zebras Don't Get Ulcers* (New York: Henry Holt, 1994).

64   **stress *heightens* working memory:** S. Vijayraghavan, M. Wang, S. G. Birnbaum, G. V. Williams, and A. F. T. Arnsten, "Inverted-U Dopamine D1 Receptor Actions on Prefrontal Neurons Engaged in Working Memory," *Nature Neuroscience* 10, no. 3 (2007): 376–84. doi:10.1038/nn1846.

64   **executive control might improve during periods of stress:** G. Robert and J. Hockey, "Compensatory Control in the Regulation of Human Performance under Stress and High Workload: A Cognitive-Energetical Framework," *Biological Psychology* 45, no. 1 (1997): 73–93.

3. PACKING AND SLACK

70   *The cost of one modern heavy bomber is this:* Dwight D. Eisenhower, *The Chance for Peace* (U.S. Government Printing Office, April 16, 1953).

72   **a survey of commuters:** Just over one hundred commuters were interviewed; p < .05.

72   **The poor reported trade-off thinking almost twice as often as the better off:** Interesting related results can be found here as well: Stephen Spiller, "Opportunity Cost Consideration," *Journal of Consumer Research* (forthcoming).

73   **both the rich and the poor reported trade-offs:** 274 subjects in Tamil Nadu were surveyed in 2009. Income here was proxied for by comparing rural and urban respondents—there was a sixfold difference between them in income. The difference for the blender was significant at p < .01. The difference for the TV was neither economically nor statistically significant (58.6 percent vs. 60.8 percent).

74   **"don't have to; [they] make enough money":** K. Van Ittersum, J. Pennings, and B. Wansink, "Trying Harder and Doing Worse: How Grocery Shoppers Track In-Store Spending," *Journal of Marketing* (2010), retrieved from http://papers.ssrn.com/sol3/papers.cfm?abstract_id=1546461.

74   **A Dutch study:** G. Antonides, I. Manon de Groot, and W. Fred van Raaij, "Mental Budgeting and the Management of Household Finance," *Journal of Economic Psychology* 32, no. 4 (2011): 546–55. doi:10.1016/j.joep.2011.04.001.

74   **leaving 10 percent aside as "fun money":** Simpler saving: "The 60% Solution," *MSNMoney*, retrieved October 24, 2012, from http://money.msn.com/how-to-budget/a-simpler-way-to-save-the-60-percent-solution-jenkins.aspx?page=0.

75   **This mindset is a feature of abundance:** For an alternative treatment of anticipated time slack, see G. Zauberman and J. G. Lynch, "Resource Slack and Propensity to Discount Delayed Investments of Time Versus Money," *Journal of Experimental Psychology: General* 134, no. 1 (2005): 23–37.

75   **No man-made structure:** J. M. Graham, *The Hive and the Honey Bee* (Hamilton, Ill.: Dadant & Sons, 1992).

75   **a 10 percent tolerance:** The reader fascinated by plywood tolerances can dig into various plywood tolerances in *Plywood Standards*, Voluntary Product Standard PS 1-09, National Institute of Standards and Technology, U.S. Department of Commerce, available at http://gsi.nist.gov/global/docs/vps/PS-1-09.pdf.

75   **mud dauber wasps are also nest builders:** H. J. Brockmann, "Diversity in the Nesting Behavior of Mud-Daubers (Trypoxylon

politum Say; Sphecidae)," *Florida Entomologist* 63, no. 1 (1980): 53–64.

77   **When the rich take a pause:** This rationale for slack is reminiscent of Herbert Simon's argument that people do not maximize: they satisfice, doing well enough to get by. See Herbert A. Simon, "Rational Choice and the Structure of the Environment," *Psychological Review* 63, no. 2 (1956): 129. In his view people lacked the cognitive resources to optimize. If we were to use his language, we would say that scarcity allows less satisfing behavior. While this captures some elements of slack, the impact of scarcity is more automatic and less controllable than this description implies. As we will see, the uncontrollability plays a central role in understanding scarcity.

77   *A house is just a pile of stuff:* George Carlin, *Brain Droppings* (New York: Hyperion, 1997), 37.

77   *cabinet castaways:* A terrific discussion of cabinet castaways can be found in Brian Wansink, S. Adam Brasel, and Stephen Amjad, "The Mystery of the Cabinet Castaway: Why We Buy Products We Never Use," *Journal of Family and Consumer Science* 92, no. 1 (2000): 104–8. One reason we end up with so many castaways is what economists might call "option value." When we buy we do not know if we will use the item but value the option of having it around just in case. The psychology can be more complex than this simple narrative. Under scarcity, we would argue, one would think more carefully—indeed, focus—on the odds of eventual use, carefully evaluating the option value, rather than opting for the nonchalant "just in case" scenario.

77   **over $12 billion is spent annually on self-storage:** *SSA | 2012 SSA Fact Sheet*, retrieved from http://www.selfstorage.org/ssa/Content /NavigationMenu/AboutSSA/FactSheet/default.htm.

77   **"every American could stand":** Ibid.

78   *"Human laziness has always been a big friend":* J. Mooallem, "The Self-Storage Self," *New York Times*, September 6, 2009, retrieved from http://www.nytimes.com/2009/09/06/magazine /06self-storage-t.html.

79   **hypothetical decision we presented to a group of university students:** D. A. Redelmeier and E. Shafir, "Medical Decision Making in Situations That Offer Multiple Alternatives," *JAMA—Journal of the American Medical Association* 273, no. 4 (1995): 302–5.

80   free *not* to choose: M. Friedman and R. Friedman, *Free to Choose: A Personal Statement* (Orlando, Fla.: Mariner Books, 1990).

81   estimate the time required to finish their senior theses: R. Buehler, D. Griffin, and M. Ross, "Exploring the 'Planning Fallacy': Why People Underestimate Their Task Completion Times," *Journal of Personality and Social Psychology* 67, no. 3 (1994): 366.

81   end up in "time trouble": M. Sigman, "Response Time Distributions in Rapid Chess: A Large-Scale Decision-Making Experiment," *Frontiers in Neuroscience* 4 (2010). doi:10.3389/fnins.2010.00060.

82   the *temptation tax* is regressive: A. Banerjee and S. Mullainathan, *The Shape of Temptation: Implications for the Economic Lives of the Poor* (Working Paper No. w15973, National Bureau of Economic Research, 2010).

83   **Psychological biases often persist despite more extreme consequences:** People will behave differently if the stakes are high, was an early argument against the relevance of psychological findings for social phenomena. In the last two decades, research has shown that people's psychological biases affect decisions as consequential as their retirement or their health and mortality.

85   **needing to navigate a world that is computationally more complex:** The notion of computational complexity here can be understood by contrasting linear programming to integer programming. In linear programming, items can be infinitely subdivided—the logical extension of granularity. In integer programming, items must be packed in fixed units—the logical extension of bulkiness. Computer scientists have shown in a precise mathematical sense that integer programming is inherently harder than linear programming. A detailed introduction to these ideas can be found in Alexander Schrijver, *Theory of Linear and Integer Programming* (West Sussex, England: John Wiley & Sons, 1998).

86   **As Henry David Thoreau observed:** Thoreau himself took a different lesson from this observation. He advocated not for increasing your wealth but for moderating your desires. In our language, there are two ways to get slack. Either you get a bigger suitcase or you reduce the number of things you wish to pack into it.

86   **"A man is rich in proportion":** Henry David Thoreau, *Walden* (Yale University Press, 2006), 87.

4. EXPERTISE

87   **40 rupees (80 cents):** In this book we will simply use the nominal
exchange rates to describe the value of foreign currency (rupees in
this case) in dollars. This is perfectly valid for some uses, such as
how much Alex should value the rupees. But in some cases this
can be misleading because exchange rates do not account for price
differences between countries. For example, a rupee goes further
in India because many things are also cheaper there. In trying to
assess income differences across countries, most economists adjust
not only for exchange rates but also for *purchasing power parity*—a
measure of price differences. Since this book is not intended to be
a careful cross-country comparison of incomes, for ease of reading we simply use nominal exchange rates. But the reader should
keep this distinction in mind.

89   *Imagine you have spent the day shopping:* This is a slightly
updated (for inflation) version of Tversky and Kahneman's famous
"jacket-calculator" problem; A. Tversky and D. Kahneman, "The
Framing of Decisions and the Psychology of Choice," *Science* 211,
no. 4481 (1981): 453–58. See also R. Thaler, "Mental Accounting
Matters," *Journal of Behavioral Decision Making* 12 (1999):
183–206.

89   **one can change the value of an hour:** Ofer H. Azar, "Relative
Thinking Theory," *The Journal of Socio-Economics* 36, no. 1
(2007): 1–14.

90   **college students, MBAs, professional gamblers, and executives of
all stripes:** Some studies have found similar effects using incentives. In one study, people were asked to solve algebra questions
and were paid 6¢ for each correct answer. Some were given a base
show-up fee of $1, some $3, and some $10. The 6¢ per correct
answer looked big for the $1 group and small for the $10 group.
And indeed the $1 group worked harder and answered more
questions when their reward for their effort "looked larger." Some
researchers with a sense of humor went to the 2003 North
American Summer Meetings of the Econometric Society and
obtained similar data with professional economists. Turns out
that economists are no more skilled at rational decision making
than the rest of us.

90   **a version of the laptop/DVD question:** The proportions of those
        advising to opt for the savings in the $100 and $1,000 conditions
        differed significantly for the high-income participants (Princeton
        Junction) but not for the low-income participants (Trenton); this
        study had N = 123. C. C. Hall, *Decisions Under Poverty: A Behav-*
        ioral Perspective on the Decision Making of the Poor (PhD diss.,
        Princeton University, 2008).

91   **The slight increase may be due to the feeling:** It is unlikely that
        these results are not merely due to "ceiling" effects, by there being
        less room for the poor to increase their willingness to go. While
        they are higher than for the well off, they are still well below 100
        percent in their willingness to travel.

92   **a blindfolded subject held in one hand:** H. E. Ross, "Weber Then
        and Now," *Perception* 24, no. 6 (1995): 599.

92   **people use more detergent when the cap is larger:** G. Trotta,
        "Some Laundry-Detergent Caps Can Lead to Overdosing," June
        5, 2009, retrieved from http://news.consumerreports.org/home
        /2009/06/laundry-detergent-overdosing-caps-procter-and-gamble
        -method-sun-era-tide-cheer-all-consumer-reports-.html.

93   **to replicate intervals of six, twelve, eighteen, and twenty-four sec-**
        onds: S. Grondin and P. R. Killeen, "Tracking Time with Song and
        Count: Different Weber Functions for Musicians and Nonmusi-
        cians," *Attention, Perception, and Psychophysics* 71, no. 7 (2009):
        1649–54.

93   **less likely to be affected by bottle height:** B. Wansink and K. Van
        Ittersum, "Bottoms Up! The Influence of Elongation on Pouring
        and Consumption Volume," *Journal of Consumer Research* 30,
        no. 3 (2003): 455–63.

93   **shoppers exiting a supermarket:** I. M. Rosa-Díaz, "Price Knowl-
        edge: Effects of Consumers' Attitudes Towards Prices, Demo-
        graphics, and Socio-cultural Characteristics," *Journal of Product*
        and Brand Management 13, no. 6 (2004): 406–28. doi:10.1108
        /10610420410560307.

93   **commuters in Boston:** The difference in proportion of correct
        answers between the high- and low-income respondents was sta-
        tistically significant, p < .05, N = 104.

94   **rich and poor smokers respond:** Jacob Goldin and Tatiana
        Homonoff, "Smoke Gets in Your Eyes: Cigarette Tax Salience and

Regressivity," *American Economic Journal: Economic Policy* 5, no. 1 (February 2013): 302–36.

94   **they are better at deciphering that the total price:** If all this paints a picture of the poor giving more attention because the stakes are higher, that is part of the point. The interesting implication here, though, is how this greater attentiveness changes the decision process, how it changes the "biases" that have been documented for a broad class of people.

94   **25 percent of brands:** J. K. Binkley and J. Bejnarowicz, "Consumer Price Awareness in Food Shopping: The Case of Quantity Surcharges," *Journal of Retailing* 79, no. 1 (2003): 27–35. doi: 10.1016/S0022-4359(03)00005-8.

94   **"sneaky consumer product trick":** "Sold Short? Are You Getting Less Than You Think? Let Us Count the Ways," (*Consumer Reports*) February 2000, 24–26.

94   **supermarkets in low-income neighborhoods:** Ibid.

96   **"You would say, 'I like vacations in the Bahamas'":** Dan Ariely articulates the challenge of trade-off thinking here: http://bigthink .com/ideas/17458.

98   **purchased a cognac truffle for $3:** Shane Frederick, Nathan Novemsky, Jing Wang, Ravi Dhar, and Stephen Nowlis, "Opportunity Cost of Neglect," *Journal of Consumer Research* 36, no. 4 (2009): 553–61.

99   **The checker-shadow illusion:** There is a large array of demonstrations of the context dependence of perception. Ted Adelson's checker-shadow illusion is one of our favorites. It is reproduced with permission. To experience this and other such illusions you can go to http://web.mit.edu/persci/people/adelson/checker-shadow_illusion.html. For a more detailed discussion of the cognitive mechanisms underlying illusions such as these, see Edward H. Adelson, "Lightness Perception and Lightness Illusions," *The New Cognitive Neurosciences* (1999): 339.

100   *Imagine you are lying on the beach on a hot day:* This is based on Richard Thaler, "Mental Accounting and Consumer Choice," *Marketing Science* 4, no. 3 (1985): 199–214. Data collected with Anuj Shah in 2012. The well off showed a significant difference between frames, whereas the poor did not; $p < .01$ (N = 148).

101   **when gasoline prices go up:** J. Hastings and J. M. Shapiro, *Mental*

Accounting and Consumer Choice: Evidence from Commodity Price Shocks (Cambridge, Mass.: National Bureau of Economic Research, Working Paper No. 18248, 2012).

101   **The poor should be less prone to show this effect:** Data collected with Anuj Shah in 2012 support this prediction. We presented participants with versions of the tax-rebate versus the stock value scenarios. The well off showed a different proneness to spend under the two frames, whereas the poor did not; p < .05 (N = 141).

102   *You purchase a small season ticket package:* Data collected with Anuj Shah in 2012. The rich were more likely to choose the historical cost and the poor the replacement cost; p < .05 in both cases (N = 98).

102   **$0 because the ticket is already paid for:** E. Shafir and R. H. Thaler, "Invest Now, Drink Later, Spend Never: On the Mental Accounting of Delayed Consumption," *Journal of Economic Psychology* 27 (2006): 694–712.

103   **Paul Ferraro and Laura Taylor:** Paul J. Ferraro and Laura O. Taylor, "Do Economists Recognize an Opportunity Cost When They See One? A Dismal Performance from the Dismal Science" (2005).

103   **"I have a hard time believing that this is possible":** This is from the blog *Marginal Revolution.* http://marginalrevolution.com/marginalrevolution/2005/09/opportunity_cos.html.

5. BORROWING AND MYOPIA

105   *There is nothing in the prospect:* J. A. Riis, *How the Other Half Lives* (Boston, Mass.: Bedford/St. Martin's, 2010).

105   *Once a student in the Head Start child development program:* The Center for Responsible Lending's description of Sandra Harris's story can be found here: http://www.responsiblelending.org/payday-lending/tools-resources/victims-2.html.

107   **more than 23,000 payday lender branches:** M. Fellowes and M. Mabanta, *Banking on Wealth: America's New Retail Banking Infrastructure and Its Wealth-Building Potential* (Washington, D.C.: Brookings Institution, 2008).

107   **more than all the McDonald's:** McDonald's restaurants statistics—countries compared—NationMaster, retrieved from http://www.nationmaster.com/graph/foo_mcd_res-food-mcdonalds-restaurants.

107   **and Starbucks:** Loxcel Starbucks Store Map FAQ, retrieved from
        http://loxcel.com/sbux-faq.html.

107   **$3.5 billion in fees each year:** Fast Facts, retrieved October 24,
        2012, from http://www.responsiblelending.org/payday-lending/
        tools-resources/fast-facts.html. Repeat business is so common in this
        industry that 98 percent of loan volume goes to repeat borrowers.

107   **18 percent of the poorest families:** A wonderful discussion of
        these issues can be found in Michael Barr, *No Slack* (Washington,
        D.C.: Brookings Institution Press, 2002).

107   **nearly 5 percent of the annual income of the poor:** K. Edin and L.
        Lein, *Making Ends Meet: How Single Mothers Survive Welfare
        and Low-Wage Work* (New York: Russell Sage Foundation Publi-
        cations, 1997). For a captivating update on the economic lives of
        the American poor, see Sarah Halpern-Meekin, Kathryn Edin,
        Laura Tach, and Jennifer Sykes, *It's Not Like I'm Poor: How
        Working Families Make Ends Meet in a Post-Welfare World*
        (Berkeley: University of California Press, forthcoming).

108   **informal moneylenders who charge rates every bit as extreme:** See
        Abhijit Banerjee, "Contracting Constraints, Credit Markets, and
        Economic Development," in *Advances in Economics and Econo-
        metrics: Theory and Application,* Eighth World Congress of the
        Econometric Society, vol. 3, ed. Mathias Dewatripont, Lars Han-
        sen, and S. Turnovsky (Cambridge: Cambridge University Press,
        2004), 1–46.

110   **loans are particularly attractive:** The other common reason cited
        for excessive borrowing is myopia of some form. What is interest-
        ing in this narrative is that myopia here—tunneling—is not a
        generalized personal trait. Everyone tunnels when faced with scar-
        city. And recall that the same force that generates tunneling also
        generates the focus dividend. Unlike myopia, tunneling has posi-
        tive consequences as well.

112   **Princeton undergraduates to play *Family Feud* in a controlled
        setting:** These studies can be found in Anuj Shah, Sendhil Mul-
        lainathan, and Eldar Shafir, "Some Consequences of Having Too
        Little," *Science* 338 (2013): 682–85.

114   *present bias:* A nice overview of present bias and other models of
        time discounting can be found in Shane Frederick and George
        Loewenstein, "Time Discounting and Time Preference: A Critical
        Review," *Journal of Economic Literature* (2002).

115   *Because machine uptime was important*: R. E. Bohn and R. Jai-kumar, *Firefighting by Knowledge Workers* (Information Storage Industry Center, Graduate School of International Relations and Pacific Studies, University of California, 2000), retrieved from http://isic.ucsd.edu/pdf/firefighting.pdf.

117   **Steven Covey finds it helpful to classify tasks:** S. R. Covey, *The Seven Habits of Highly Effective People* (New York: Free Press, 2004).

119   **approximately one in four rural bridges:** *Bridges—Report Card for America's Infrastructure*, retrieved from http://www.infra-structurereportcard.org/fact-sheet/bridges.

119   **scarcity makes this problem a whole lot worse:** There are many studies of the planning fallacy. Good reviews are: Roger Buehler, Dale Griffin, and Michael Ross, "Inside the Planning Fallacy: The Causes and Consequences of Optimistic Time Predictions," in *Heuristics and Biases: The Psychology of Intuitive Judgment*, ed. Thomas Gilovich, Dale Griffin, and Daniel Kahneman (Cambridge: Cambridge University Press, 2002), 250–70; D. Lovallo and D. Kahneman, "Delusions of Success," *Harvard Business Review* (2003): 1–8. While there is no explicit study of the impact of scarcity, it follows naturally that the planning fallacy would prove more pronounced among those who are especially tunneling, as occurs under scarcity.

6. THE SCARCITY TRAP

123   *Everywhere is walking distance*: Quote from Steven Wright. In W. Way, *Oxymorons and Other Contradictions* (Bloomington, Ind.: AuthorHouse, 2005).

123   **A typical vendor buys about 1,000 rupees:** These data draw from Dean Karlan and Sendhil Mullainathan, "Debt Traps" (working paper, 2012).

123   **a little over $2:** In this book when we report dollar equivalents, we simply convert using prevailing exchange rates. Yet many experts feel this can paint a misleading impression because people in different countries also face different prices. So the vendor, for example, will also have lower prices for food and other items. As a result, her income in nominal dollar terms does not adequately

reflect her purchasing power. Economists have suggested using purchasing power parity instead of nominal exchange rates. In the case of India, this would result in an income that is roughly 2.5 times higher for the vendor.

126   **An initial scarcity is compounded by behaviors that magnify it:** Economists and especially development economists have focused on what they call *poverty traps*—the notion that those who begin poor will stay poor. A commonly discussed mechanism is a lucrative investment opportunity that requires a fixed amount of capital. The rich have enough capital to make the investment while the poor will find it hard to save up enough money to do so. Other mechanisms discussed include aspirations and myopia. Relevant references can be found in Debraj Ray, "Development Economics," *The New Palgrave Dictionary of Economics,* ed. Lawrence Blume and Steven Durlauf (2007).

127   **jewel loans at 13 percent annual interest:** This work can be found in Michael Faye and Sendhil Mullainathan, "Demand and Use of Credit in Rural India: An Experimental Analysis" (working paper, Harvard University, 2008).

129   **about ten distinct financial instruments on average:** Daryl Collins, Jonathan Morduch, Stuart Rutherford, and Orlanda Ruthven, *Portfolios of the Poor: How the World's Poor Live on $2 a Day* (Princeton, N.J.: Princeton University Press, 2010).

129   **they work very few hours those days:** Though time use data in developing countries can be hard to come by, a very nice set of studies is found in Quentin Wodon and Mark Blackden, *Gender, Time Use, and Poverty in Sub-Saharan Africa* (Washington, D.C.: World Bank Press, 2006).

132   **little evidence to show that willpower capacity increases with use:** M. Muraven and R. F. Baumeister, "Self-Regulation and Depletion of Limited Resources: Does Self-Control Resemble a Muscle?" *Psychological Bulletin* 126, no. 2 (2000): 247–59. doi:10.1037//0033-2909.126.2.247.

132   **in a room with some highly tempting snacks:** K. D. Vohs and T. F. Heatherton, "Self-Regulatory Failure: A Resource-Depletion Approach," *Psychological Science* 11, no. 3 (2000): 249–54.

136   **not able to come by $2 every day:** D. Collins et al., *Portfolios of the Poor.*

136   *[Automotive] repairs themselves are unexpected expenses*: New Amsterdam Consulting, "Stability First Pilot Test: Pre-Test Interviews Narrative Report" (March 2012).

138   **$2,000 in thirty days**: A. Lusardi, D. J. Schneider, and P. Tufano, *Financially Fragile Households: Evidence and Implications* (National Bureau of Economic Research, 2011), retrieved from http://www.nber.org/papers/w17072.

140   **the lonely overfocus**: A nice description of many such experiments can be found in John T. Cacioppo and William Patrick, *Loneliness: Human Nature, and the Need for Social Connection* (New York: W. W. Norton, 2009).

141   **2,750 free throws in a row**: J. Friedman, "How Did Tom Amberry Set the World Free Throw Record?" *Sports Illustrated*, October 17, 1994, retrieved from http://sportsillustrated.cnn.com/vault/article/magazine/MAG1005796/index.htm.

141   **only 40 percent of his free throws**: Bruce Bowen, Basketball-Reference.com, retrieved October 31, 2012, from http://www.basketball-reference.com/players/b/bowenbr01.html.

142   **they are *better* at doing them automatically**: S. L. Beilock, A. R. McConnell et al., "Stereotype Threat and Sport: Can Athletic Performance Be Threatened?" *Journal of Sport and Exercise Psychology* 26, no. 4 (2004): 597–609.

142   **an inverted U-curve**: R. M. Yerkes and J. D. Dodson, "The Relation of Strength of Stimulus to Rapidity of Habit-Formation," *Journal of Comparative Neurology and Psychology* 18, no. 5 (1908): 459–82.

143   **an ironic process**: Daniel M. Wegner, David J. Schneider, Samuel R. Carter, and Teri L. White, "Paradoxical Effects of Thought Suppression," *Journal of Personality and Social Psychology* 53, no. 1 (1987): 5–13; D. M. Wegner, *White Bears and Other Unwanted Thoughts: Suppression, Obsession, and the Psychology of Mental Control* (New York: Viking, 1989).

7. POVERTY

147   *Before you criticize someone*: J. Carr and L. Greeves, *Only Joking: What's So Funny About Making People Laugh?* (New York: Gotham Books, 2006).

147   **22,000 children die each day:** *Levels and Trends in Child Mortality* (Washington, D.C.: The UN Inter-Agency Group for Child Mortality Estimation [IGME], 2010).

147   **Nearly one billion people are so illiterate:** http://www.globalissues.org/article/26/poverty-facts-and-stats.

147   **Half the children in the world:** The World Bank uses a poverty rate of $2.50 a day. This focuses on "absolute" poverty. By this measure, no U.S. children would be in poverty. These and other facts on global poverty can be found at Anup Shah, "Poverty Facts and Stats," *Global Issues* 26 (2008). For an incisive and insightful examination of poverty around the world, see Abhijit Banerjee and Esther Duflo, *Poor Economics: A Radical Rethinking of the Way to Fight Global Poverty* (New York: PublicAffairs, 2011).

147   **Nearly 50 percent of all children in the United States:** see Mark R. Rank and Thomas A. Hirschl, "Estimating the Risk of Food Stamp Use and Impoverishment during Childhood," *Archives of Pediatrics and Adolescent Medicine* 163, no. 11 (2009): 994.

147   **About 15 percent of American households:** See Alisha Coleman-Jensen et al., "Household Food Security in the United States in 2010," *USDA-ERS Economic Research Report* 125 (2011).

148   **carbon monoxide, a deadly pollutant:** B. Ritz and F. Yu, "The Effect of Ambient Carbon Monoxide on Low Birth Weight Among Children Born in Southern California Between 1989 and 1993," *Environmental Health Perspectives* 107, no. 1 (1999): 17.

148   **The ingredients of poverty create circumstances that are particularly hostile:** For another original and highly engaging perspective on some ingredients behind poverty and its persistence, see Charles Karelis, *The Persistence of Poverty: Why the Economics of the Well-Off Can't Help the Poor* (New Haven: Yale University Press, 2009).

150   **285 million people worldwide:** International Diabetes Federation, *Atlas.* http://www.diabetesatlas.org/content/some-285-million-peopleworldwide-will-live-diabetes-2010.

151   **take their medication only 50 to 75 percent of the time:** This wide range of estimates is because adherence rates depend on the population under study. How adherence is measured—such as self-reports, drug refill rates, electronic monitoring—also affects the measure. As a starting point, see Eduardo Sabaté, ed., *Adherence to Long-Term Therapies: Evidence for Action* (Geneva: World

Health Organization, 2003). This book also contains adherence data for a wide variety of diseases.

152   **more than 28 percent of total yield:** December 15, 2009. The benefits of weeding for any one farmer may be hard to generalize from these studies, which rely on model plots or on cross-sectional data. A careful randomized control trial of the benefits to farmers of weeding would be particularly useful in this area. For the current estimates in Africa, see L. P. Gianessi et al., "Solving Africa's Weed Problem: Increasing Crop Production and Improving the Lives of Women," *Proceedings of "Agriculture: Africa's 'engine for growth'—Plant Science and Biotechnology Hold the Key," Rothamsted Research, Harpenden, UK, October 12–14, 2009* (Association of Applied Biologists, 2009).

152   **up to 50 percent of total rice output:** See D. E. Johnson, "Weed Management in Small Holder Rice Production in the Tropics," *Natural Resources Institute, University of Greenwich Ghatham, Kent, UK* 11 (1996), retrieved from http://ipmworld.umn.edu/chapters /johnson.htm.

152   **harsher with their kids:** J. Lexmond, L. Bazalgette, and J. Margo, *The Home Front* (London: Demos, 2011).

152   **They are more likely to take out their own anger on the child:** An early study is J. Garbarino, "A Preliminary Study of Some Ecological Correlates of Child Abuse: The Impact of Socioeconomic Stress on Mothers," *Child Development* (1976): 178–85. A more recent study using larger data is in Christina Paxson and Jane Waldfogel, "Work, Welfare, and Child Maltreatment," *Journal of Labor Economics* 20, no. 3 (July 2002): 435–74.

153   **they fail to engage with their children in substantive ways:** J. S. Lee and N. K. Bowen, "Parent Involvement, Cultural Capital, and the Achievement Gap Among Elementary School Children," *American Educational Research Journal* 43, no. 2 (2006): 193–218.

153   **they will have the kid watch television rather than read to her:** A. T. Clarke and B. Kurtz-Costes, "Television Viewing, Educational Quality of the Home Environment, and School Readiness," *Journal of Educational Research* (1997): 279–85.

153   **The poor in the United States are more obese:** A. Drewnowski and S. E. Specter, "Poverty and Obesity: The Role of Energy Den-

sity and Energy Costs," *The American Journal of Clinical Nutrition* 79, no. 1 (2004): 6–16.

153   **the poor are less likely to send their children to school:** R. Tabberer, "Childhood Poverty and School Attainment, Causal Effect and Impact on Lifetime Inequality," in *Persistent Poverty and Lifetime Inequality: The Evidence—Proceedings from a Workshop Held at HM Treasury, Chaired by Professor John Hills, Director of the ESRC Research Centre for Analysis of Social Exclusion* (1998).

153   **The poor are less likely to get their children vaccinated:** N. Adler, J. Stewart, S. Cohen, M. Cullen, A. D. Roux, W. Dow, and D. Williams, "Reaching for a Healthier Life: Facts on Socioeconomic Status and Health in the U.S.," *The John D. and Catherine T. MacArthur Foundation Research Network on Socioeconomic Status and Health* 43 (2007).

153   **least likely to wash their hands:** The correlation between income and hand washing or water treatment has been observed in many places. In Peru, one study looked at behavior of mothers or others taking care of children. It found that only 46 percent of caregivers washed their hands after using the toilet. Even within the data, there was a strong correlation with income: 56.5 percent of people in the top income quartile washed their hands after using the toilet whereas only 34 percent of the bottom quartile did. They reported similar differences for hand washing after cleaning children's bottoms or prior to feeding children. See Sebastian Galiani and Alexandra Orsola-Vidal, "Scaling Up Handwashing Behavior," Global Scaling Up Handwashing Project, Water and Sanitation Program (Washington, D.C., 2010).

153   **less likely to eat properly or engage in prenatal care:** Adler et al., "Reaching for a Healthier Life."

154   **a video of a young girl, Hannah, taking a test:** John M. Darley and Paget H. Gross, "A Hypothesis-Confirming Bias in Labeling Effects," *Journal of Personality and Social Psychology* 44, no. 1 (1983): 20–33.

155   **air traffic controllers:** R. L. Repetti, "Short-Term and Long-Term Processes Linking Job Stressors to Father–Child Interaction," *Social Development* 3, no. 1 (2006): 1–15.

157   **most likely to be acting out:** L. A. Gennetian, G. Duncan, V. Knox,

W. Vargas, E. Clark-Kauffman, and A. S. London, "How Welfare Policies Affect Adolescents' School Outcomes: A Synthesis of Evidence from Experimental Studies," *Journal of Research on Adolescence* 14, no. 4 (2004): 399–423.

159   **smokers with financial stress:** M. Siahpush, H. H. Yong, R. Borland, J. L. Reid, and D. Hammond, "Smokers with Financial Stress Are More Likely to Want to Quit but Less Likely to Try or Succeed: Findings from the International Tobacco Control (ITC) Four Country Survey," *Addiction* 104, no. 8 (2009): 1382–90.

159   **rates of extreme obesity and diabetes dropped:** Jens Ludwig, et al. "Neighborhoods, Obesity, and Diabetes—A Randomized Social Experiment," *New England Journal of Medicine* 365, no. 16 (2011): 1509–19.

159   **thirty-eight good sleepers were instructed to go to sleep:** R. T. Gross and T. D. Borkovec, "Effects of a Cognitive Intrusion Manipulation on the Sleep-Onset Latency of Good Sleepers," *Behavior Therapy* 13, no. 1 (1982): 112–16.

160   **more likely to be worriers:** F. N. Watts, K. Coyle, and M. P. East, "The Contribution of Worry to Insomnia," *British Journal of Clinical Psychology* 33 no. 2 (2011): 211–20.

160   **they sleep less well and get fewer hours:** J. T. Cacioppo, L. C. Hawkley, G. G. Berntson, J. M. Ernst, A. C. Gibbs, R. Stickgold, and J. A. Hobson, "Do Lonely Days Invade the Nights? Potential Social Modulation of Sleep Efficiency," *Psychological Science* 13, no. 4 (2002): 384–87.

160   **lower-quality sleep:** N. P. Patel, M. A. Grandner, D. Xie, C. C. Branas, and N. Gooneratne, "Sleep Disparity in the Population: Poor Sleep Quality Is Strongly Associated with Poverty and Ethnicity," *BMC Public Health* 10 (2010): 475–75.

160   **can lead soldiers to fire on their own troops:** G. Belenky, T. J. Balkin, D. P. Redmond, H. C. Sing, M. L. Thomas, D. R. Thorne, and N. J. Wesensten, "Sustaining Performance During Continuous Operations: The U.S. Army's Sleep Management System," in *Managing Fatigue in Transportation. Proceedings of the 3rd Fatigue in Transportation Conference* (1998).

160   **The oil tanker *Exxon Valdez*:** See Alaska Oil Spill Commission, *Spill: The Wreck of the Exxon Valdez*, vol. 3 (State of Alaska, 1990). An approachable discussion of the sleep literature as a

whole can be found in William C. Dement and Christopher Vaughan, *The Promise of Sleep: A Pioneer in Sleep Medicine Explores the Vital Connection Between Health, Happiness, and a Good Night's Sleep* (New York: Dell, 1999).

160   **comparable to going without sleep for two nights in a row:** See Hans PA van Dongen et al., "The Cumulative Cost of Additional Wakefulness: Dose-Response Effects on Neurobehavioral Functions and Sleep Physiology from Chronic Sleep Restriction and Total Sleep Deprivation," *SLEEP* 26, no. 2 (2003): 117–29. A nice overview of the literature on chronic sleep deprivation can be found in D. F. Dinges, N. L. Rogers, and M. D. Baynard, "Chronic Sleep Deprivation," *Principles and Practice of Sleep Medicine* 4 (2005): 67–76.

160   **when income rises, so, too, does cognitive capacity:** A growing literature has in fact argued that early childhood experience can affect brain development. See, most recently for example, Clancy Blair et al., "Salivary Cortisol Mediates Effects of Poverty and Parenting on Executive Functions in Early Childhood," *Childhood Development* 82, no. 6 (November/December 2011): 1970–84. Our results suggest that in addition to these kinds of effects, there is still a very large direct effect of poverty on cognitive function even in later life.

8. IMPROVING THE LIVES OF THE POOR

167   **the recurrence of "wheels-up" crashes:** A. Chapanis, "Psychology and the Instrument Panel," *Scientific American* 188 (1953): 74–82.

168   **Low-income training programs in the United States:** A nice collection of papers on training programs in the United States illustrates these challenges: Burt S. Barnow and Christopher T. King, eds., *Improving the Odds: Increasing the Effectiveness of Publicly Funded Training* (Washington, D.C.: Urban Institute Press, 2000).

168   **loans are used to pay off other debts:** Two recent impact evaluations of microfinance illustrate the potential problems quantitatively: Dean Karlan and Jonathan Zinman, "Microcredit in Theory and Practice: Using Randomized Credit Scoring for Impact Evaluation," *Science* 332, no. 6035 (2011): 1278–84;

Abhijit Banerjee et al., "The Miracle of Microfinance? Evidence from a Randomized Evaluation" (MIT working paper, 2010).

171   **do not undo hard work:** Some of this argument can be made without resort to the psychology of scarcity. Much of policy design makes the presumption of rationality. Simply allowing for people to have natural psychological limitations already can improve policy making. This view has recently been wonderfully articulated by Richard H. Thaler and Cass R. Sunstein, *Nudge: Improving Decisions about Health, Wealth, and Happiness* (New Haven, Conn.: Yale University Press, 2008). See also Eldar Shafir, ed., *The Behavioral Foundations of Public Policy* (Princeton, N.J.: Princeton University Press, 2012). We have previously used this logic to argue that we can better understand poverty just by understanding that the poor can have the same psychological quirks that affect everyone else: Marianne Bertrand, Sendhil Mullainathan, and Eldar Shafir, "A Behavioral-Economics View of Poverty," *American Economic Review* (2004): 419–23. By compromising bandwidth, scarcity magnifies and expands on these arguments. Psychologically insightful policy is particularly important in the context of poverty.

172   **for a total of five years over her lifetime:** D. Ellwood and R. Haskins, *A Look Back at Welfare Reform, IPRNews* (Winter 2008), retrieved from http://www.ipr.northwestern.edu/publications/newsletter/iprn0801/dppl.html.

172   **one study in rural Rajasthan, India:** A. Cappelen, O. Mæstad, and B. Tungodden, "Demand for Childhood Vaccination—Insights from Behavioral Economics," in *Forum for Development Studies* 37, no. 3 (November 2010): 349–64.

173   **depends on the good behaviors she exhibits:** L. B. Rawlings and G. M. Rubio, "Evaluating the Impact of Conditional Cash Transfer Programs," *The World Bank Research Observer* 20, no. 1 (2005): 29–55.

174   **a microfinance institution in the Dominican Republic called ADOPEM:** A. Drexler, G. Fischer, and A. Schoar, *Keeping It Simple: Financial Literacy and Rules of Thumb* (London: Centre for Economic Policy Research, 2010).

178   **the high demand for loans that averaged less than $10:** See *Emergency Hand Loan: A Product Design Case Study*, Financial Access

Initiative, ideas42 and IFC. Discussion and document at http://www.financialaccess.org/blog/2011/05/product-design-poor-emergency-hand-loan.

179   **One cash transfer program in Malawi:** S. Baird, J. De Hoop, and B. Ozler, "Income Shocks and Adolescent Mental Health," *World Bank Policy Research Working Paper Series*, no. 5644 (2011).

180   **bound to return to it again and again:** The return rates to welfare programs in the United States have been studied extensively. For example, see J. Cao, "Welfare Recipiency and Welfare Recidivism: An Analysis of the NLSY Data," *Institute for Research on Poverty Discussion Papers* 1081–96, University of Wisconsin Institute for Research on Poverty (March 1996).

180   **from low-income to higher-income neighborhoods:** The program, Moving to Opportunity, had positive effects on well-being but none on economic self-sufficiency. See J. Ludwig, G. J. Duncan, L. A. Gennetian, L. F. Katz, R. Kessler, J. R. Kling, and L. San-bomatsu, "Neighborhood Effects on the Long-Term Well-Being of Low-Income Adults," *Science* 337 (September 21, 2012): 1505–10, online edition.

180   **unlikely to change the fundamental logic of poverty:** A synthesis of the existing studies of the impact of microfinance can be found here: M. Duvendack, R. Palmer-Jones, J. G. Copestake, L. Hooper, Y. Loke, and N. Rao, "What Is the Evidence of the Impact of Microfinance on the Well-Being of Poor People?" (London: EPPI-Centre, Social Science Research Unit, Institute of Education, University of London, 2011).

9. MANAGING SCARCITY IN ORGANIZATIONS

183   **St. John's Regional Health Center:** The discussion of St. John's draws heavily from S. Crute, "Case Study: Flow Management at St. John's Regional Health Center," *Quality Matters* (2005). See also "Improving Surgical Flow at St. John's Regional Health Center: A Leap of Faith," Institute for Healthcare Improvement. Last modified: 07/13/2011. Posted at http://www.ihi.org/knowledge/Pages/ImprovementStories/ImprovingSurgicalFlowatStJohnsRegionalHealthCenterSpringfieldMOALeapofFaith.aspx. This case and others are well discussed in E. Litvak, M. C. Long, B. Prenney,

K. K. Fuda, O. Levtzion-Korach, and P. McGlinchey, "Improving Patient Flow and Throughput in California Hospitals Operating Room Services," Boston University Program for Management of Variability in Health Care Delivery. Guidance document prepared for the California Healthcare Foundation (CHCF), 2007.

185   **further improvement followed:** St. John's is not some exceptional case. See Mark van Houdenhoven et al., "Improving Operating Room Efficiency by Applying Bin-Packing and Portfolio Techniques to Surgical Case Scheduling," *Anesthesia and Analgesia* 105, no. 3 (2007): 707–14, for a careful analytical example. A review of the literature on better hospital bed scheduling can be found in Brecht Cardoen, Erik Demeulemeester, and Jeroen Beliën, "Operating Room Planning and Scheduling: A Literature Review," *European Journal of Operational Research* 201, no. 3 (2010): 921–32.

186   **Many systems require slack:** John Gribbin, *Deep Simplicity: Bringing Order to Chaos and Complexity* (New York: Random House, 2005).

187   **use their time "more efficiently":** Tom DeMarco has a fascinating discussion of the importance of slack for organizations. "It's possible to make an organization more efficient without making it better. That's what happens when you drive out slack. It's also possible to make an organization a little less efficient and improve it enormously. In order to do that, you need to reintroduce enough slack to allow the organization to breathe, to reinvent itself, and to make necessary change." See Tom DeMarco, *Slack: Getting Past Burnout, Busywork, and the Myth of Total Efficiency* (New York: Broadway, 2002).

188   **a perception that many corporations were "bloated":** A great discussion of leveraged buyouts is in Steven N. Kaplan and Per Stromberg, "Leveraged Buyouts and Private Equity," *Journal of Economic Perspectives* 23, no. 1 (Winter 2009): 121–46.

188   **leveraged buyouts did improve corporate performance:** F. R. Lichtenberg and D. Siegel, "The Effects of Leveraged Buyouts on Productivity and Related Aspects of Firm Behavior," *Journal of Financial Economics* 27, no. 1 (1990): 165–94.

189   **left at the brink of bankruptcy:** The possibility that leveraged buyouts leave firms in danger when there are economic shocks has been widely discussed. See, for example, Krishna G. Palepu, "Con-

sequences of Leveraged Buyouts," *Journal of Financial Economics* 27, no. 1 (1990): 247–62.

189   **NASA launched the Mars Orbiter:** See Arthur G. Stephenson et al., "Mars Climate Orbiter Mishap Investigation Board Phase I Report, 44 pp.," NASA, Washington, D.C. (1999). A readable discussion is here: James Oberg, "Why the Mars Probe Went Off Course," *IEEE Spectrum* 36, no. 12 (1999): 34–39.

192   **firefighting organizations have several features in common:** We owe our understanding of firefighting and several of the examples to Roger E. Bohn and Ramchandran Jaikumar, *Firefighting by Knowledge Workers* (Information Storage Industry Center, Graduate School of International Relations and Pacific Studies, University of California, 2000).

192   **"If you look at our resource allocation on traditional projects":** N. P. Repenning, "Reducing Cycle Time at Ford Electronics, Part II: Improving Product Development," case study available from the author (1996).

193   **28,000 *known* bugs:** This number is cited in Bohn and Jaikumar, *Firefighting by Knowledge Workers*. It is actually part of a larger controversy about whether or not Microsoft shipped with 61,000 known bugs. See the terrific discussion at *Gripes about Windows 2000*, retrieved from http://www.computergripes.com /Windows2000.html#28000bugs.

193   **stay perpetually behind:** A recent study illustrated how judges can also spread themselves too thin and end up juggling too many cases. See Decio Coviello, Andrea Ichino, and Nicola Persico, "Don't Spread Yourself Too Thin: The Impact of Task Juggling on Workers' Speed of Job Completion" (National Bureau of Economic Research Working Paper No. 16502, 2010).

194   *The truly efficient laborer:* Henry David Thoreau quotes. See H. D. Thoreau, *A Week on the Concord and Merrimac Rivers* (Princeton; N.J.: Princeton University Press, 2004).

195   **Ten states now ban the use of handheld cell phones while driving:** *State Cell Phone Use and Texting While Driving Laws* (November 2012), retrieved from http://www.ghsa.org/html/stateinfo/laws /cellphone_laws.html.

195   **drivers holding a cell phone:** Cell Phone Accident Statistics and Texting While Driving Facts, edgarsnyder.com, retrieved November

2, 2012, from http://www.edgarsnyder.com/car-accident/cell
-phone/cell-phone-statistics.html.

195   **so are drivers using a headset:** J. Wilson, M. Fang, S. Wiggins, and
P. Cooper, "Collision and Violation Involvement of Drivers Who
Use Cellular Telephones," *Traffic Injury Prevention* 4, no. 1 (2003):
45–52.

195   **missed twice as many traffic signals:** D. L. Strayer, F. A. Drews, and
D. J. Crouch, "A Comparison of the Cell Phone Driver and the
Drunk Driver," *Human Factors* 48, no. 2 (2006): 381–91. Follow-
up studies have used high-fidelity driving simulators to compare
the performance of drivers on the phone (no hands) with drivers
who were intoxicated and concluded that the increased risk of
distraction by phone is comparable to that found for driving with
a blood alcohol level above the legal limit.

195   ***When Henry Ford famously adopted a 40-hour workweek:*** A nice
discussion is in E. Robinson, "Why Crunch Mode Doesn't Work:
6 Lessons," *IGDA* (2005), retrieved February 17, 2009. Another
readable article is Sara Robinson, "Bring Back the 40-Hour Work
Week," *Slate*, March 14, 2012. Both have a clear position they are
pushing, namely, shorter workweeks, and present their cases
extremely well.

196   **"where a work schedule of 60 or more hours per week":** Robinson, "Why Crunch Mode Doesn't Work."

196   **a software developer notes:** See "Scrum & Overtime?" posted on
the blog *Agile Game Development,* June 9, 2008.

196   **the number of patients per medical service worker:** Diwas S. Kc
and Christian Terwiesch, "Impact of Workload on Service Time
and Patient Safety: An Econometric Analysis of Hospital Operations," *Management Science* 55, no. 9 (2009): 1486–98.

196   ***At the end of each interview:*** Seonaidh McDonald, "Innovation,
Organisational Learning and Models of Slack," *Proceedings of
the 5th Organizational Learning and Knowledge Conference*
(Lancaster University, 2003).

197   **when workers sleep less:** D. T. Wagner, C. M. Barnes, V. K. Lim,
and D. L. Ferris, "Lost Sleep and Cyberloafing: Evidence from the
Laboratory and a Daylight Saving Time Quasi-Experiment," *Journal of Applied Psychology* 97, no. 5 (2012): 1068.

197   **20 percent more time cyberloafing:** Ibid.

197   *When we met him a year ago*: "Manage Your Energy, Not Your Time," *Harvard Business Review*, retrieved November 3, 2012, from http://hbr.org/2007/10/manage-your-energy-not-your-time/ar/1.

198   a pilot "energy management" program: Ibid.

198   look away from the screen every twenty minutes or so: This is the so called 20-20-20 rule. See, for example, http://www.mayoclinic.com/health/eyestrain/DS01084/DSECTION=prevention.

198   "stretched to their limits and beyond with no margin": J. De Graaf, D. Wann, and T. H. Naylor, *Affluenza: The All-Consuming Epidemic* (San Francisco, Calif.: Berrett-Koehler, 2005).

199   Hiroaki ("Rocky") Aoki: See http://www.rockyhaoki.com/biography.html for a brief biography.

201   ten cents more in profit per dollar of revenue: This discussion is based on the wonderful HBS case study on Benihana's business model: W. Earl Sasser and J. Klug, *Benihana of Tokyo* (Boston: Harvard Business School, 1972). See also Ernst Ricardo and Glen M. Schmidt, "Benihana: A New Look at an Old Classic," *Operations Management Review* 1 (2005): 5–28.

201   Sheryl Kimes: S. E. Kimes, "Restaurant Revenue Management Implementation at Chevys Arrowhead," *Cornell Hotel and Restaurant Administration Quarterly* 45, no. 1 (2004): 52–67.

202   "Nobody goes there anymore; it's too crowded": Y. Berra, *The Yogi Book* (New York: Workman Publishing, 1997).

10. SCARCITY IN EVERYDAY LIFE

207   Bolivia, Peru, and the Philippines: D. Karlan, M. McConnell, S. Mullainathan, and J. Zinman, *Getting to the Top of Mind: How Reminders Increase Saving* (National Bureau of Economic Research, Working Paper No. w16205, 2010).

208   "impulse savings": "Impulse Savings," ideas42 case study.

208   the Massachusetts Registry of Motor Vehicles: *Snopes.com*: "Massachusetts License Renewal" (November 4, 2008), retrieved from http://www.snopes.com/politics/traffic/massrenewal.asp.

210   researchers changed the consequences of neglecting the form: J. J. Choi, D. Laibson, B. C. Madrian, and A. Metrick, "For Better or for Worse: Default Effects and 401(k) Savings Behavior," in

Perspectives on the Economics of Aging, ed. D. A. Wise (Chicago: University of Chicago Press, 2004), 81–126.

211   **Keep the Change:** http://www.bankofamerica.com/promos/jump/ktc_coinjar/.

211   **not by trying to curb their impulses to spend:** Bank of America's Keep the Change program: "Keep Your Savings Elsewhere," *BloggingStocks*, retrieved November 1, 2012, from http://www.blog gingstocks.com/2007/04/23/bank-of-americas-keep-the-change -program-keep-your-savings-e/.

213   **"cooling off periods":** L. E. Willis, "Against Financial Literacy Education" (2008), retrieved from http://works.bepress.com/lau ren_willis/1/.

214   **Save More Tomorrow:** R. H. Thaler and S. Benartzi, "Save More Tomorrow™: Using Behavioral Economics to Increase Employee Saving," *Journal of Political Economy* 112, no. S1 (2004): S164–87.

216   **a study of payday loans:** M. Bertrand and A. Morse, "Information Disclosure, Cognitive Biases, and Payday Borrowing," *The Journal of Finance* 66, no. 6 (2011): 1865–93.

217   **God's gift of time:** R. Levine, *A Geography of Time: The Temporal Misadventures of a Social Psychologist, or How Every Culture Keeps Time Just a Little Bit Differently* (New York: Basic Books, 1997).

218   **"Perceived rule complexity":** J. Mata, P. M. Todd, and S. Lippke, "When Weight Management Lasts: Lower Perceived Rule Complexity Increases Adherence," *Appetite* 54, no. 1 (2010): 37–43. doi:10.1016/j.appet.2009.09.004.

219   **maize farmers in Kenya:** E. Duflo, M. Kremer, and J. Robinson, *Nudging Farmers to Use Fertilizer: Theory and Experimental Evidence from Kenya* (No. w15131, National Bureau of Economic Research, 2009).

219   **researchers created a simple and clever intervention:** Ibid.

219   **cash and bandwidth rich:** The researchers interpret this in the context of a hyperbolic discounting model, as a solution to our generic challenge of delaying gratification. Our data on bandwidth increasing around harvest suggest that more might be going on here, that the very act of making the decisions at the time when farmers have greatest bandwidth could also improve the quality of decisions.

220   **low-income high school graduates:** K. Haycock, "Promise Abandoned: How Policy Choices and Institutional Practices Restrict College Opportunities" (Washington, D.C.: Education Trust, 2006).

221   **They divided eligible high school graduates:** E. P. Bettinger, B. T. Long, P. Oreopoulos, and L. Sanbonmatsu, *The Role of Simplification and Information in College Decisions: Results from the H&R Block FAFSA Experiment.* National Bureau of Economic Research, (2009), retrieved from http://www.nber.org/papers/w15361.

223   **allowed to choose their own binding deadlines:** D. Ariely and K. Wertenbroch, "Procrastination, Deadlines, and Performance: Self-Control by Precommitment," *Psychological Science* 13, no. 3 (2002): 219–24.

224   **underappreciate the likelihood of many low-probability events:** C. F. Camerer and H. Kunreuther, "Decision Processes for Low Probability Events: Policy Implications," *Journal of Policy Analysis and Management* 8, no. 4 (1989): 565–92.

CONCLUSION

227   *As our island of knowledge grows:* John A. Wheeler, as quoted in J. Horgan, "The New Challenges," *Scientific American* 267, no. 6 (1992): 10.

231   **improve productivity by offering the right financial products and creating bandwidth:** This idea is being explored by a nonprofit (which we helped found) called ideas42, which uses behavioral insights to create products and policies. The interested reader is invited to visit www.ideas42.com.

231   **GlowCaps:** *Vitality-About GlowCaps.* Retrieved from http://www.vitality.net/glowcaps.html.

ACKNOWLEDGMENTS

This book did not suffer from scarcity of help and good advice. Wonderful collaborators helped shape our ideas and ran crucial studies: Chris Bryan, Lisa Gennetian, Anandi Mani, and Jiaying Zhao. Anuj Shah took the project on with particular force, and was wonderfully insightful and instrumental throughout. We also had extraordinary research assistants: Annie Liang and Shannon White tirelessly and creatively found relevant studies and illustrations. Jessica Gross found some early material, and Lily Jampol and Ani Momjian helped run some studies. They all asked incisive and enthusiastic questions, as did Izzy Gainsburg and David Mackenzie, who joined late yet provided invaluable help and attention. The wonderful folks at ideas42 provided encouragement and inspiration. Katinka Matson helped us see that in the mix of many ideas there was a book worth writing.

The emerging drafts benefited from the wisdom of good friends, colleagues, and loved ones. We especially thank Bindu Ananth, Samura Atallah, Amber Batata, Emily Breza, Andy Conway, Katherine Edin,

Alissa Fishbane, Lawrence Katz, Michael Lewis, Lori Lieberman, Jens Ludwig, Anastasia Mann, Frank Schilbach, Antoinette Schoar, Heather Schofield, Josh Schwartzstein, Sharoni Shafir, Andrei Shleifer, Richard Thaler, Laura Trucco, Nick Turk-Browne, and Eric Wanner. The research for this book was generously supported by the Kellogg Foundation, the National Science Foundation, the Canadian Institute for Advanced Research, and the National Institute on Aging, as well as our home institutions, Harvard and Princeton. Students in the classes we taught as the book was taking shape—two at Princeton and two at Harvard—were an excellent early audience, attentive, receptive, and critical. Several other audiences tolerated our not-quite-ready-for-primetime talks and gave terrific feedback. Through it all, Paul Golob was a dream editor, patient and wise.

We have in the last few years consumed more than our fair share of emotional support. For that we are particularly grateful to Amber Batata, Sailu Challapalli, Alissa Fishbane, Srikanth Kadiyala, Anastasia Mann, Jim, Jackie, and Ali Mann, Miri and Sharoni Shafir, and Sophie and Mia Mann-Shafir. And we apologize for the missed phone calls, the missed vacations, the missing bandwidth, and generally for going missing. We'll blame scarcity for all that.

Collaborations are a famously tricky business. No matter how in synch you are, there will be occasional disagreements and frustration. And yet, at the end of this long road, each of us knows we could not have found a more perfect partner and better friend for the journey. We can only hope all this comes through in the book.

Any shortcomings should not be attributed to all the wonderful people who helped us—we both agree they are the other one's fault.

INDEX

Page numbers in *italics* refer to illustrations.

ABOUT THE AUTHORS

SENDHIL MULLAINATHAN, a professor of economics at Harvard University, is a recipient of a MacArthur Foundation "genius grant" and conducts research in behavioral economics and development economics. He lives in Cambridge, Massachusetts.

ELDAR SHAFIR is the William Stewart Tod Professor of Psychology and Public Affairs at Princeton University. He conducts research in cognitive science, judgment and decision making, and behavioral economics. He lives in Princeton, New Jersey.

Mullainathan and Shafir are co-founders of ideas42, a nonprofit that designs behavioral economics solutions to social problems.